WITHDRAWN

About Island Press

Island Press is the only nonprofit organization in the United States whose principal purpose is the publication of books on environmental issues and natural resource management. We provide solutions-oriented information to professionals, public officials, business and community leaders, and concerned citizens who are shaping responses to environmental problems.

In 1994, Island Press celebrated its tenth anniversary as the leading provider of timely and practical books that take a multidisciplinary approach to critical environmental concerns. Our growing list of titles reflects our commitment to bringing the best of an expanding body of literature to the environmental community throughout North America and the world.

Support for Island Press is provided by The Geraldine R. Dodge Foundation, The Energy Foundation, The Ford Foundation, The George Gund Foundation, William and Flora Hewlett Foundation, The James Irvine Foundation, The John D. and Catherine T. MacArthur Foundation, The Andrew W. Mellon Foundation, The Pew Charitable Trusts, The Rockefeller Brothers Fund, The Tides Foundation, Turner Foundation, Inc., The Rockefeller Philanthropic Collaborative, Inc., and individual donors.

WILDLIFE POLICIES

IN THE U.S. NATIONAL PARKS

333.954
W646w

WILDLIFE POLICIES

IN THE U.S. NATIONAL PARKS

Frederic H. Wagner
Ronald Foresta
R. Bruce Gill
Dale R. McCullough
Michael R. Pelton
William F. Porter
Hal Salwasser

Consultation on
law and policy
by Joseph L. Sax

ISLAND PRESS

Washington, D.C. • Covelo, California

Copyright © 1995 by Island Press

All rights reserved under International and Pan-American Copyright Conventions. No part of this book may be reproduced in any form or by any means without permission in writing from the publisher: Island Press, 1718 Connecticut Avenue, N.W., Suite 300, Washington, DC 20009.

ISLAND PRESS is a trademark of The Center for Resource Economics.

Library of Congress Cataloging-in-Publication Data

Wildlife policies in the U.S. national parks / Frederic H. Wagner...
[et al.]; consultation on law and policy by Joseph L. Sax.
    p.   cm.
    Includes bibliographical references (p.   ) and index.
    ISBN 1-55963-404-9 (cloth).—ISBN 1-55963-405-7 (paper)
    1. Wildlife management—Government policy—United States.
2. Natural parks and reserves—United States—Management.
3. Nature conservation—Government policy—United States. 4. United
States. National Park Service. I. Wagner, Frederic H. II. Sax,
Joseph L. III. Title: Wildlife policies in the United States
national parks.
SK361.W53   1995
333.95'4'0973—dc20   94-47917
                                                               CIP

Printed on recycled, acid-free paper ♲

Manufactured in the United States of America
10   9   8   7   6   5   4   3   2   1

Contents

CA1Apr1596

4-5-96 mLS 26.57

ALLEGHENY COLLEGE LIBRARY

1

Professional Review of a Great System

History and Structure of the U.S. National Park System

Since the establishment of Yellowstone National Park, the world's first national park, by act of Congress in 1872, the American National Park System (the System) has grown into an assemblage of more than 360 units. These units comprise "some 20" (Mackintosh 1991) types of areas, including (among others) national parks, monuments, seashores, preserves, recreation areas, wild and scenic rivers, historic sites, and battlefields. They occur in almost every state and are distributed from Alaska to Guam, Hawaii, and American Samoa on the west; and from Maine to Puerto Rico and the Virgin Islands on the east. In total, they represent a magnificent and invaluable collection of remnants and relics of natural and cultural wonders of the nation, and of its pre- and post-Columbian history, a collective museum of incalculable educational, cultural, scenic, and scientific value. Some are classified among the natural wonders of the world.

National Park Service (NPS) historian Richard Sellars (1989) comments that "scenic preservation was the major factor at the beginning of the national park system." Caughley and Sinclair (1994:268) contrast the "philosophical springs" from which the African and American national parks flowed, the former to preserve great wildlife resources and the latter to protect spectacular scenery. Indeed many of the major American parks and monuments (e.g., Grand Canyon, Hawaii Volcanoes, Yosemite, Glacier Bay) were established primarily to protect and make available to the American public scenic and geologic wonders.

But Caughley and Sinclair's dichotomy no longer holds for today's System. Many of the American areas were established primarily to conserve unique and spectacular biotas: coral reefs, wading-bird populations, desert vegetation, forests. In fact, elements of this concern go back as far as the passage of the National Parks Organic Act, which, in 1916, stipulated that:

> The fundamental purpose of said parks is to conserve the scenery and the natural and historic objects and the wildlife therein and to provide for the enjoyment of the same in such manner and by such means as will leave them unimpaired for the enjoyment of future generations.

The first monograph in the NPS series, *Fauna of the National Parks of the United States* (Wright et al. 1933), set forth a "Suggested National-Park Policy for the Vertebrates."

Moreover, despite the variety of purposes for the areas, 250 of them have "significant" natural resources (Michael Ruggiero, personal communication, February 24, 1992). Many of those established to preserve cultural features develop wildlife problems that impinge on their primary purposes. On some recreation areas, NPS officials manage biological resources according to the same policies set for parks (Freemuth 1991). And in a Park Service symposium in Denver on March 18, 1990, John Dennis, chief of the Science Branch of the NPS Wildlife and Vegetation Division, commented that all NPS units are encouraged to preserve their native biotas. Thus the status and management of biological resources are major policy issues in the System, ranging from preservation of the biota to problems of controlling plants and animals that, for whatever reasons, are detrimental to units of the System.

The System is administered by the National Park Service, which employs over 12,000 permanent personnel (Risser et al. 1992) and perhaps twice as many on a temporary or seasonal basis. Its central administrative office in Washington, D.C., is presided over by a director and a deputy director, both political appointees. The Service has had 14 directors in its 88-year history, seven of whom had prior NPS experience (Mackintosh 1991). Four of the remaining seven had had some professional administrative experience in the natural-resources field. Average term in office of six of the first seven directors was approximately 10 years (Arthur Demaray, who served only eight months in 1951, was not included in this average). But the six directors between 1973 and 1993 averaged only 3.7 years.

The director and deputy are assisted by five associate directors who supervise programs that essentially have staff functions: Natural Resources, Cultural Resources, Park Operations, Budget and Administration, and Planning and Development. The associate director for Natural Resources administers four divisions: Wildlife and Vegetation, Water Resources, Air Quality, and Geographic Information Systems (M. Ruggiero, personal communication, February 24, 1992). Park Operations is subdivided into five functions: Resource Management, Interpretation, Law Enforcement, Maintenance, and Administration.

As this is written in mid-1994, NPS is divided into ten regions, with the agency's line authority flowing from the director to the deputy director to regional directors to park superintendents. However, consideration is being given to reorganizing the agency by condensing the ten regions into seven field directorates, each with a field director. The line authority would then flow from the deputy director to the field directors to the superintendents. Consideration is also being given to combining the Natural Resources and Cultural Resources divisions and abolishing one associate directorship.

A Review of System Wildlife Policies

This book is the product of a five-year review of management policies for biological resources in the System, with special attention to the wildlife. The wildlife profession has long maintained concern for the welfare of wildlife resources in the System. Concern developed over the impacts of a rising elk population on the Yellowstone biota as far back as the 1920s with the work of M. P. Skinner (1928) and NPS biologist William Rush (1932); similar concerns expanded to a number of western parks in the early 1930s with the work of George M. Wright. This independently wealthy park naturalist decided that the biological resources of the System were so important that he began a program at his own expense to survey the fauna of the national parks. By the 1940s, wildlife research was under way in a number of parks (cf. Ratcliffe and Sumner 1945, Aldous and Krefting 1946, Kittams 1959).

Following something of a lull during World War II, professional concerns continued. In an undated position paper in late 1961 or 1962, six wildlife professors at (then) Montana State University (Missoula) and two employees of the U.S. Fish and Wildlife Service based on the M.S.U. campus endorsed Yellowstone's reduction of its elk herd. Leslie Pengelly, one of the paper's authors, would later be elected president of The Wildlife Society (TWS), the professional organization of wildlife scientists and managers. The paper was sent to NPS director Conrad L. Wirth. On March 2, then–TWS president E. L. Cheatum (1962) wrote one of the authors complimenting him on the report, which he considered "highly professional" and "ethically proper."

On December 3, 1962, the new TWS president, Wendell G. Swank, sent to all Society members a position paper (Anon. 1962a) entitled "Statement Regarding Control of Excess Wildlife Populations within National Parks." The paper left the door open for public hunting in national parks if carefully considered and controlled, something the Montana State University document recommended against. But the statement's major concern was with proper management of wildlife populations, and it approved population reduction by NPS employees if needed.

In 1961, Secretary of Interior Stewart L. Udall appointed an advisory board on wildlife management. Comprised of four eminent wildlife professionals and University of Michigan plant ecologist Stanley A. Cain, the board was chaired by A. S. Leopold, who also served as president of TWS. One of its charges was to review wildlife management in the national parks. The board's report, "Wildlife Management in the National Parks" (A. S. Leopold et al. 1963) was submitted to Secretary Udall on March 4, 1963; Chairman Leopold also presented it to the wildlife profession on the same date before the 28th North American Wildlife and Natural Resources Conference in Detroit.

During the 1970s, NPS director Gary Everhardt called on the services of a national parks advisory board, of which A. S. Leopold was a member. Durward L. Allen, former chief of research for the U.S. Fish and Wildlife Service and also a TWS president, was a member of the board's council. Allen and Leopold (1977) submitted a 15-page memorandum to Director Everhardt on the NPS Natural Science Program. In 1981, the council, now chaired by Allen, reported to Secretary of Interior James G. Watt on "a review and recommendations on animal problems and related management needs in units of the National Park System" (Erickson et al. 1981).

In 1988 TWS president James G. Teer, concerned about the condition of wildlife resources in a number of national parks, authorized formation of the TWS Ad Hoc Committee on National Park Policies and Strategies. In a letter to F. H. Wagner, whom he appointed as chair, Teer (1988) charged:

> The committee . . . to examine and evaluate policies and strategies that are being used in management of lands and

life under jurisdiction of the National Park Service. Of course, results of policies and management strategies are expressed in the conditions of national parks ecosystems and the life in it. Interaction of elk with vegetation in the North Range of Yellowstone National Park is but one example of these policies. Goats in Olympic National Park is another, and feral pigs in Great Smoky Mountain National Park is still another. While you will certainly consider these situations in your evaluations, the challenge is to evaluate their causes. Biological problems are often the result of political decisions that direct policy.

The study continued through 1992, and first and second drafts of the committee report were finished on January 2 and May 1 of 1993. Then–TWS president Hal Salwasser appointed a council subcommittee to review the report and make recommendations.

The subcommittee conducted its own review and also sought reactions from two outside reviewers. The lengthy, excellent comments from both of these sources were incorporated into a third draft, which was then submitted to the council subcommittee on September 7, 1993. We extend our appreciation for the many helpful suggestions provided by subcommittee members Len H. Carpenter, Thomas H. Franklin, Nova Silvy, and especially Chairman James M. Peek for his detailed comments. And we are equally appreciative of comments from external reviewers Duncan T. Patten and David R. Stevens. While the great majority of the comments were incorporated in Draft 3, they should not be held responsible for errors of fact or interpretation, or necessarily for the philosophical positions of this work.

The review subcommittee recommended acceptance of Draft 3 to the council at its September 1993 meeting. During a subsequent November telephone poll, council members voted acceptance subject to unspecified editorial treatment of the final version and approved release if marked a draft. But thereafter fundamental differences arose between the authors and the council over the length, content, and general message of the report; and the council reversed its decision to allow release of a draft. On December 13, 1993, the committee withdrew the report from submission to the council and elected to publish it independently. This book is the final version of that effort, its substance essentially that of Draft 3 with only minor modification, and its authors the members of the former Ad Hoc Committee.

Philosophy of This Review

We have adopted a central philosophy for this review that we believe is consistent with the emerging protocols for setting public policies on natural resources. Our basic premise is that national parks are a public resource established to satisfy societal values. The National Park Service is the professional organization charged both with ensuring, through its management programs, that the resource fulfills the public's values and with protecting the resource so that its values endure in perpetuity.

Policies are prescriptions for management programs designed to guide the agency in making good on its dual charge. A vital component in the entire process is the goals set for both the National Park System and the individual parks. Goals serve the pivotal roles of addressing and serving the public values, as well as being focal points toward which policies and management are directed.

Since goals are established to satisfy public values, setting them should be a public process. There is no reason why the personal values of a small group of professionals, or indeed an entire profession, should weigh disproportionately in goal establishment. For this reason, we do not in this work advocate wildlife-management goals and policies for the System and individual parks, although we all have personal values that we attach to this treasure. Hence, this review differs from previous reviews which did so advocate.

Because goals serve as beacons toward which policies strive, policies, and the management they prescribe, are best analyzed, perhaps only appropriately analyzed, in the context of how effectively they fulfill public values and achieve public goals. This analytic approach is the central theme of this review.

In our view the unique role that the wildlife profession, and indeed all professions, can fill is a dual one. First, it can evaluate and render scientific judgments on the technical consequences of contemplated, alternative goal and policy options, without value-based advocacy of preferences among them. Second, it can critique how well current policies and programs are reaching those goals that are in place. In our opinion, the professions have an ethical obligation to be self-critical. As Aldo Leopold once commented, "A profession is a group of people who demand higher standards of themselves than do their clients." No one has the level of specialized knowledge with which to make insightful judgments of performance quality that the professional insiders have. Only they can ensure true quality control. Hence they do the public, the resources, and their professions a service by self-evaluation.

For the above reasons, this book proceeds in the following sequence:

Chapter 2 reviews, but does not advocate among, the public values that have been attached to the System's natural resources through its history, and the goals and policies established to satisfy those values. President Teer's original charge was to evaluate policies relating to "lands and life" in the System. Although the assignment was from The Wildlife Society, and central concern has been with "wildlife" policies, we have come to use the term *wildlife* as synonymous with essentially the entire fauna. And since the fauna functions in, and is dependent upon, entire ecosystems for its survival, much of this book addresses entire ecological or natural resources.

Chapter 3 evaluates the condition of ecological or natural resources in the System to determine whether public values and goals are being met.

Chapters 4, 5, and 6 examine how well Park Service policies and practices are achieving ecological- or natural-resources goals.

Chapter 7 discusses the need for more explicit goals at the park level, procedures for goal setting, different management protocols that can be used to achieve goals, and alternative administrative structures by which science can best serve goal setting, policy formation, and management in the System.

Study Procedures

In a very real sense, this study has spanned two to three decades, during which we all, to varying degrees and in various ways, have been involved with, studied, and in most cases written about policies and wildlife management in the National Park System. Several have served as actual consultants to the National Park Service. Much of what follows draws on that experience. As a formal committee effort, this study occupied approximately five years, as discussed earlier.

We began the study in the context of five objectives:

1. Articulate a set of possible wildlife purposes or goals of national parks. There was general agreement that the study

should not be prescriptive, but rather that we consider a range of possible purposes among which we would not advocate.

2. Review existing wildlife-management policies in a sample of national parks, and assess how well the policies are serving alternative park purposes and goals. This was again intended as a nonadvocating analysis. Originally, we agreed to concentrate on a sample of ten units in the NPS system; but other units were studied outside the committee's tenure. For example, McCullough had previously served on a National Research Council study of bear management in Yellowstone, as consultant to NPS on Death Valley, and as a member of an advisory board for Glacier Bay; Pelton had conducted research on Great Smoky for a number of years prior to the committee's appointment.

Beyond these, a number of us have had experiences of varying duration and intensity with a broader range of parks: Foresta and Sax in the course of their policy studies, Porter with a number of eastern parks both doing research and serving as a consultant to NPS, Wagner supervising a five-year graduate study in Yellowstone.

3. Analyze how wildlife policies are formed and what forces shape those policies.

4. Review NPS research programs and the effectiveness with which they are serving park policies.

5. Evaluate alternative policies from the vantage point of how well they would address park purposes.

We synthesized material from personal interviews; published and unpublished literature, reports, documents, theses and dissertations; and our collective experience with a large number of parks, monuments, and other units in the System.

We interviewed and corresponded with individuals in the Washington NPS offices of the Division of Natural Resources and the Office of Policy Development; regional chief scientists; a number of park superintendents; numerous park scientists, resource-management personnel, and temporary or seasonal employees; leaders of cooperative park study units; and former NPS employees. Several of us were contacted voluntarily by a number of NPS employees who wanted to volunteer their views of the organization.

In addition, we contacted between 50 and 60 university faculty and graduate students who were either conducting, or had conducted, research in the parks. Also interviewed were numerous personnel in other federal land-managing agencies, especially those with lands adjacent to parks, and a number of employees of state departments of fish and game. National Park System issues were discussed with a number of individuals in nongovernment organizations, especially conservation groups, which are particularly supportive of the System and NPS. And we conferred with a number of the members of animal-welfare organizations.

We have provided attribution for all of our sources except in certain cases where individuals asked to remain anonymous. Most of these were NPS employees who were deeply concerned for the welfare of their agency and the System, but who felt somewhat at risk for their positions. Some were university faculty members who were receiving NPS research funds and did not wish to risk continued support.

2

Natural-Resources Values, Goals, and Policies of the System

From Values to Management

The major purpose of this chapter is to elucidate natural-resources policies for the System. We have adopted the working definition of public policies as orders, statements of intent, and/or plans charging a governmental organization to achieve public purposes or goals through management programs.

But as we argued in Chapter 1, public policies are appropriately evaluated from the standpoint of how well goals are achieved; and in turn, goals are expressions of social values. Thus we see the causal sequence progressing from social values to management programs established to satisfy them:

Social → Management → Public → Management
Values → Goals → Policy → Programs

The ultimate purpose of public service is to satisfy those values, and how well that is achieved depends on (1) how well the goals reflect the values, (2) how explicitly policies address the goals, (3) how clearly policies set forth appropriate management programs, and (4) how effectively management programs carry out policy directives.

This chapter reviews the values that the American people have attached to the National Park System, the goals that have been set to satisfy those values, and the policies that have been put in place to achieve the goals. We have attempted to be nonprescriptive in the review.

Natural-Resources Values

The National Park System has value to the American people both in its entirety and at the level of the various units, which, obviously, have different resources and therefore different values. Thus, goals need to be set not only for the System but also for each unit. Our concern at this point in our discussion is with the former.

The many renewable natural-resources values of the parks can be generalized into four categories: recreational, educational, scientific, and environmental. These are very close to the values expressed by a 1963 National Academy of Sciences/National Research Council study of research in the System (Ackerman et al. 1963). The committee's report (hereinafter referred to as the Robbins report, after the committee's chair) commented that "the national parks of the United States represent one of the most valuable heritages of this country." It concluded "that the preeminent objectives and purposes of the national parks are with due consideration for the enjoyment by their owners, the people of the United States, of the aesthetic, spiritual, inspirational, educational, and scientific values which are inherent in natural wonders, and nature's creatures."

Recreational Values

In an era of burgeoning human populations, and profound alteration of the earth's ecosystems to extract commodities, national parks provide a small, total area in which such alteration has been minimal. Coupled with the spectacular scenery of a Grand Canyon, Yosemite, Teton, Sequoia, Glacier Bay, or Haleakala, these natural areas, along with the nation's wilderness areas, provide the American citizenry with a range of aesthetic and emotional experiences that cannot be had anywhere else in the country. We are collectively calling these experiences *recreation.*

Sax (1980) identifies a broad range of recreational experiences that people from different socio-economic settings need and seek. At one extreme, these include such activities as racing motorcycles across the desert and automobile touring of park roads to see wildlife, vegetation, and spectacular geological features. He cautions against elitism by the "preservationists" in passing judgment on these uses unless they reach a point of degrading or destroying the resources, as occurs in the carnival atmosphere of Yosemite

(Reinhardt 1989). Sax comments that "the inexperienced, urbanized visitor is precisely the one who needs the most attention and on whom the most imagination needs to be expended" (p. 81).

At the other extreme, Sax (1980) includes emotional and spiritual values, including Maslowian self-actualization achieved by hiking and contemplation away from other humans and their artifacts. Rolston (1990) extols the values of "naturalness" and "wildness" in national parks, with minimal human intervention, that can lead to an environmental ethic. Nash (1973:249) speaks of the evidence that a wilderness experience "is an important ingredient in the mental health of people hard-pressed by an expanding civilization" and that such experiences promote humility and restraint in a society heavily committed to competition and dominance. In a passionate lament over what he sees as decline in the System, Frome (1992) contends that the units should be outdoor museums of natural history, field museums of human history, laboratories of science, and sources of art, literature, and spiritual inspiration.

Clearly there is an entire range of aesthetic and emotional values that tens of millions of Americans attach to the national parks and avail themselves of each year.

Educational Values

Aldo Leopold (1949) acknowledged all of these values, but further included education as one aspect of recreation, which he considered the most important: "To promote perception is the only truly creative part of recreational engineering" (p. 173). The parks have incalculable educational value for informing the public about the nature of the preindustrial world and the undeveloped natural resources out of which the nation's wealth was developed. Leopold called wilderness "the raw material out of which man has hammered the artifact called civilization" (p. 188). Once gone, these aspects of the nation's heritage can never again be learned first-hand.

Just seeing the coral reefs in Biscayne Bay, the wading-bird rookeries in Everglades, the forests in Redwood and Olympic, and the desert vegetation in Joshua Tree and Organ Pipe is a tremendously broadening experience for all citizens, especially born-and-reared urbanites. When these experiences of amazement and awe are deepened with the interpretive message of ecological function, it not only vastly enriches the emotional experiences but also goes a long way toward enlightening the citizenry to the need for effective, national environmental policies.

Scientific Values

The allusion in the Robbins report to scientific value is an example of one of the newer values of the National Park System that has emerged in its later years. As minimally altered ecosystems, the parks are now considered to have immense scientific value. The contemporary science of ecology is committed to developing an understanding of the structure and function of whole ecosystems in order to manage the globe for sustainable natural-resources use and environmental protection. Ecologists generally agree on the need for having systems minimally disturbed by industrial man to serve as reference points (Wagner and Kay 1993).

Ecosystems exist along a continuum from little or no human disturbance to complete human alteration. A thorough understanding of how they respond to different intensities of human perturbation, what constitutes ecosystem sustainability, and how profoundly altered systems can be restored is facilitated by a knowledge of ecosystem structure and function along the entire continuum, including the minimally disturbed end. As Aldo Leopold (1941) commented on wilderness, and could as well have been referring to national parks, "A science of land health needs, first of all, a base-datum of normality, a picture of how healthy land maintains itself as an organism. . . . The most perfect norm is wilderness."

Big Bend National Park provides an excellent example of the important role that the parks could serve in contributing to an ecological knowledge base for sound natural-resources management. What is now classified as the northern extension of the Chihuahuan Desert in west Texas and southern New Mexico was once, according to vegetation descriptions in early land surveys, "desert grassland" or southern Great Plains at the time of first European contact. Vegetation change during the past 400 years is attributed to heavy livestock grazing, which removed the grasses. The result was not only conversion of grassland to the present creosotebush (*Larrea tridentata*) and mesquite (*Prosopis juliflora*) desert, but release of the soil to wind and water erosion (Gardner 1951, York and Dick-Peddie 1968, Schlesinger et al. 1990). In some areas the loss of several inches of topsoil exposed gravelly desert pavement, in others an accumulation of soil around shrub islands. The changes are considered essentially irreversible in a time scale relevant to human generation time.

This example and others in North America, Africa, and Australia have become the basis in range ecology and management for what is sometimes termed the nonequilibrium paradigm, or perhaps more appropriately the multiple-equilibrium paradigm. This new paradigm holds that, under a heavy burden of environmental pressures, notably grazing, an ecosystem can be moved out of one state into a new domain of conditions from which it will not return merely by removing ungulate grazing, and in some cases under any regime of human intervention (Westoby 1979/80, Ellis and Swift 1988, Friedel 1991, Laycock 1991).

The lower, nonmontane elevations in the Big Bend Park region are extremely arid, creosotebush desert, essentially a type specimen of what is now classified in the United States as Chihuahuan Desert. At the time the park was formed four decades ago, its vegetation was indistinguishable from that on the surrounding private ranches. But after four decades of protection from livestock use, vegetation over major areas of the park has recovered to a luxuriant grassland.

The question that now arises is whether the ecological conditions at Big Bend are unique and permit a response from grazing relief when many other arid areas do not, or whether the multiple-equilibrium paradigm is not as well established as contemporary range ecology would have it. A well-designed and integrated ecosystem research program initiated at the formation of the park could have answered this question. There have been a number of research projects carried out in Big Bend during its history as a park; but much of this work has been done in recent years, and the studies have typically investigated individual species or processes without integration into a total-ecosystem design. Hence, according to Superintendent Robert Arnberger, the research to date cannot answer the question at hand (personal communication, February 24, 1992). Clearly, ecosystem research in the park could have provided valuable input into an important issue of natural-resources policy and management.

Environmental/Preservational Values

More than 120 species of threatened or endangered (T and E) plants and animals are known or suspected to occur in the National Park System. Because they are areas in which there are no competing commodity uses of the land, and therefore can be protected and manipulated to provide optimum conditions for precariously poised species, parks play an important role in preserving T and E species from extinction. Indeed, an attractive NPS brochure (Anon. n.d.) states that "The National Park Service role is to provide undisturbed habitat in the U.S., where all species, including endangered ones, can continue to exist subject only to the forces of nature."

While proposed legislation to preserve biological diversity has not yet found its way successfully through Congress, it is clear that biodiversity is a high national value. The National Forest Management Act of 1976 charges the U.S.D.A. Forest Service with managing the national forests for "biodiversity of plant and animal communities." State Department policies for Third World development programs carry the proviso that proposed projects must be sensitive to the effects on biodiversity in host countries. This issue is a high priority on the contemporary ecological agenda (Lubchenco et al. 1991).

In a symposium on Ecosystem Management for Parks and Wilderness, Salwasser (1988) proposed inclusion of national parks in a network of various kinds of conservation areas for protecting biological diversity. A 1988 workshop on protecting biological diversity in national parks, with the Park Service as one of three sponsors, recommended policy and/or legislation establishing protection and restoration of biological diversity as a priority of the National Park Service (Dottavio et al. 1990). And more recently (February 24–26, 1992), a joint workshop between NPS officials and academic ecologists to explore application of the Ecological Society of America's Sustainable Biosphere Initiative (Lubchenco et al. 1991) explored the role of national parks in contributing to, and providing a research setting for, biological diversity (Risser and Lubchenco 1992).

General System Goals for Natural Resources

Given these values, what are the goals for natural resources in the System, and how well do values and goals agree? There should be a close correspondence between values and goals: goals should be set to satisfy public values.

A recent NPS document, "Planning for the Future: A Strategic Plan for Improving the Natural Resource Program of the National Park Service" (Fox and Coffey 1993), lists four goals that "will direct the actions of the natural resource program": improving "natural resource management and research," providing a scientific foundation for management, strengthening the utility of data in planning and management, and enhancing an understanding of management and research. These are primarily operational goals

ALLEGHENY COLLEGE LIBRARY

and not the substantive natural-resources goals to which the System strives in order to satisfy the four social values mentioned earlier. Hence we explore further to elucidate the goals implied by the agency's history.

The pivotal function of goals that we stressed in Chapter 1 is only beginning to be recognized in natural-resources management. W. F. Porter and H. B. Underwood (Porter 1991, Underwood and Porter 1991) have been among recent U.S. advocates, as has R. J. Underwood (1989) in Australia. Lacking realization of this key function for goals, early NPS natural-resources goal statements tended to be general, indefinite, and implicit. Yet their general intent can be inferred from the sequence of statements that have come out over the years in a succession of documents and legislation.

One such intent is the preservation of "intact" or "healthy" ecosystems in some degree similar to the pre-Columbian state and minimally altered by postindustrial humans. As we commented in Chapter 1, despite Sellars' (1989) point that the major early NPS agenda was to preserve scenery, the natural-ecosystem thread began with the Yellowstone Act ("preservation, from injury or spoliation, of all timber, mineral deposits, natural curiosities . . . and their retention in their natural condition"). It continued with the Organic Act ("conserve . . . the natural and historic objects and the wildlife therein . . . by such means as will leave them unimpaired for the enjoyment of future generations").

Subsequent documents continued this early legislative intent. The first publication of the *Fauna of the National Parks* series (Wright et al. 1933) asserted "That one function of the national parks shall be to preserve the flora and fauna in the primitive state." This was followed 30 years later by the Leopold Committee's "vignettes of primitive America" and by the 1963 Robbins report allusion to "ecosystems," with its charge that "Every method should be made to preserve these areas . . . because of their scientific value as outdoor natural laboratories." And today, the Park Service's current policy manual, *Management Policies* (Anon. 1988a), reflects this theme with its policy of "providing the American people with . . . natural environments evolving through natural processes minimally influenced by human actions."

Hence, this goal of preserving intact ecosystems appears well established, and is, in fact, the central goal of natural-resources management in the System. It addresses all four of the values attached to the System that were discussed earlier, and clearly addresses the scientific and environmental/preservational values. Satisfying the educational value also implies preservation of ecosystems in some semblance of pre-European condition to portray the natural environments out of which the nation's postindustrial culture evolved. And it addresses that end of Sax's recreation scale, which seeks the spiritual experiences derived from communing with wilderness settings largely unsullied by the actions of postindustrial humans.

The total-ecosystem goal may not address the casual-observer end of Sax's scale, which finds value in easy visibility of nearby, large numbers of animals. The dense populations of some species that provide such visual opportunities can be inimical to the goal of healthy ecosystems.

The goal of preserving one or more T and E species may involve management protocols different from preservation of whole ecosystems. Park ecosystems may need to be altered significantly in order to favor species in trouble; and substantial intervention may also be needed for conserving biodiversity, including landscape modification. A mix of late, middle, and early seral stages may require active and continued management to perpetuate that aspect of landscape diversity (A. S. Leopold et al. 1963). But there is now a substantial record, including legislation in the case of T and E species, that attests to the values that the American public attaches to preservation of such species and maintenance of biodiversity. And NPS policy documents recognize these values by establishing System goals to satisfy them.

In historic and cultural parks, the goals may be to preserve landscapes similar to those that prevailed at the time of the historic events being commemorated. Although such goals may require significant landscape alteration, they clearly address cultural values different from those attached to natural ecosystems. But where compatible with the goals of historic and cultural parks, it may be appropriate to encourage and manage for T and E species.

In total, the National Park System has a set of goals that clearly address the values of the American public. We now examine System policies to assess the degree to which they prescribe management programs appropriate to achieving the goals.

NPS Natural-Resources Policies

Public policies are set at a number of governmental levels that are subject to varying kinds and combinations of pressures. Elucidating this complexity is a major challenge for policy analysis.

The Versions of Public Policy

At the highest policy-setting levels, Congress enacts laws and presidents issue executive orders. These orders and laws are characteristically general and generic, and executive branch agencies must particularize them in order to carry out their mandates of translating high-level policies into action programs. Consequently, the intent of Congress or the president, as it is delegated down the administrative levels to the operational ones, is interpreted and inferred into ever more specific versions (policies).

Policy setting and implementation at each of these levels are shaped by varying complexes of political, economic, and bureaucratic influences. Yaffee (1982) described the bureaucratic impediments to aggressive implementation of the Endangered Species Act within the agencies charged with carrying out the legislative intent. Rose (1992) observed that implementation of the act has been more politicized than its passage.

Policy setting for the National Park System is similarly tiered. At the highest level, numerous national monuments have been established by executive order; and Congress has passed the National Park Service Act of 1916 (the Organic Act) and the enabling legislation establishing each park. (Other acts of Congress that have influenced System policy will be discussed later in this chapter.) These high-level mandates are then elaborated into System policies by the Department of Interior and National Park Service, and given further specificity at the individual park level by planning procedures in the units of the System. Freemuth's (1991) penetrating analyses disclose the kinds of pressures exerted on the tiers and how System policies shift with changing political tides in ways that may not coincide with the original intent of Congress.

Interpretations of policy, and policies themselves, also change over time as public values and tastes change and as new knowledge accrues. It is a continuing challenge to public agencies to determine whether newly proposed goals and policies fit within the intent of policy mandates issued at a much earlier time. This is clearly the case with national parks, for which the Organic Act was passed more than three-quarters of a century ago and to which the public today attaches a number of new values.

Throughout the remainder of this chapter, the tiers of natural-resources policy in the System will be elaborated in a historical context. The purposes are to evaluate the congruence between the policies of the tiers and to examine the change in policies over time.

Early Congressional Action and Intent

The act establishing Yellowstone in 1872, the formal beginning of what is now the System, authorized the park as "a pleasuring ground for the benefit and enjoyment of people in order to protect for all times this outstanding natural area." Mackintosh (1991:11) quotes from the act, which charges the Secretary of Interior to "provide for the preservation, from injury or spoliation, of all timber, mineral deposits, natural curiosities, or wonders within said park, and their retention in their natural condition."

The 1916 Organic Act stipulated that "The fundamental purpose of said parks is to conserve the scenery and the natural and historic objects and the wildlife therein and to provide for the enjoyment of the same in such a manner and by such means as will leave them unimpaired for the enjoyment of future generations." Mackintosh (1991:19) quotes a May 13, 1918, letter from Secretary of Interior Franklin K. Lane to the first NPS director, Stephen T. Mather, impressing upon Mather that "Every activity of the Service is subordinate to the duties imposed upon it to faithfully preserve the parks for posterity in essentially their natural state."

The most thoroughgoing assessment of early Congressional intent is currently being conducted by NPS historian Richard W. Sellars (1989, 1992, 1993a, personal communication). He emphasizes several aspects of early intent:

> [Early advocates of an Organic Act] promoted the parks as ... the country's premier scenic areas, which should be vigorously developed to improve the people's mental health and physical well-being and help the national economy. [This] gained strong support from the tourism industry, especially the railroads and the fledgling automobile associations [1992]. Scenic preservation was the major factor at the beginning of the national park system [1989]. [The concern for leaving the areas] unimpaired [referred to] the parks' scenery.

Concern for preserving images and scenery, what Sellars terms "facade management," resulted in landscape architecture being the most influential profession in the NPS in the early years and, to a considerable degree, up to the present. Frederick L. Olmsted Jr., a landscape architect, was one of the strong proponents of the Organic Act. Several of the directors have been LAs, as are some of the current regional directors. The Landscape Engineering

Division was established in 1919, only three years after passage of the Organic Act; and according to Sellars the NPS is the world's largest employer of LAs. Sellars (1993b) cites a 1951 report stating that in the mid-1930s NPS employed as many as 400 LAs at one time while supporting only 27 biologists.

This emphasis on scenery experience and tourism, essentially put in place by Director Mather, was the major, if not sole, force driving the System not only during the first half century after passage of the Organic Act but also up to the present (Sellars 1993b). Sellars encapsulates the System's history as "120 years of recreational tourism management." Indeed, NPS senior scientist Theodore Sudia in the Washington office has emphasized on two occasions (personal communication, March 16, 1989; Sudia 1989) that the major purpose of the National Park Service is tourism. For this reason, according to Sudia, the Park Service operates on a wholly different plane from the Fish and Wildlife Service, Forest Service, and the Bureau of Land Management. Resource management is the major purpose of these agencies; for NPS it is a virtual sideline. Sellars' and Sudia's comments are in full accord with the NPS budget figures. In fiscal 1993–1994, only 8 percent of the agency's $1.1 billion budget was allocated to natural-resources management (Michael Coffey, personal communication, August 22, 1994).

Sellars (1992) further emphasizes that the Organic Act and many of the enabling acts allowed a considerable amount of consumptive use: leases for the development of tourist accommodations; destruction of native animal and plant life (predators, and trees killed by insects); livestock grazing in all parks but Yellowstone; and in its first four years before it was rescinded, a provision for establishing rights of way for powerlines, pipelines, canals, and ditches, along with water plants, dams, and reservoirs. Sellars concludes that these provisions "slanted the Organic Act toward multiple use of the parks' natural resources."

Further detracting from the image of the parks as a collection of areas providing refuge for pristine, unspoiled nature is the fact that many units of the System have been established with the proviso that the uses in practice at the time of park formation be allowed to continue. The Robbins report (Ackerman et al. 1963) mentioned mining in Organ Pipe, Death Valley, and McKinley; hunting in McKinley; grazing in "various" parks; TV relay stations in Shenandoah and Death Valley; and Air Force missile testing at White Sands National Monument.

Sellars (1992) emphasized that:

> [Early Service officials] made no sustained effort to comprehend the parks in a scientific sense—for example, to understand native populations of flora and fauna and how they interact with their natural environment. [And despite] a strong preservation mandate, the founders had little concern for strict biological preservation as it is known today. [Rather,] the National Park Service founders . . . propelled park management along a course destined to collide with later environmental thinking.

Rockwood (1988) comments in a similar vein: "Places such as Yellowstone were created to preserve the awesome manifestations of nature, not to retain the whole of the natural environment of the area in its pristine state . . . at the time Yellowstone was created and the National Park Service was established the concept of an 'ecosystem' did not exist."

In sum, the original natural-resources intent of Congress was the preservation of a system of spectacular scenery to provide for the recreational and aesthetic desires of the public. It thus addressed only two of the four general values, outlined earlier, which society assigns to the System today. The public's early desires and associated NPS goals involved much less understanding of the nature and complexity of the System's resources and of the management programs we now know are needed to meet contemporary values.

The Beginnings of Science and Nature-Preservation Policies

R. G. Wright (1992a) traces the early evolution of NPS concern for wildlife and the realization that proper management in the parks requires a knowledge base. William Rush was the only NPS research scientist in the years following passage of the Organic Act, and was assigned in 1928 to study large mammals in Yellowstone. But as discussed in Chapter 1, a key early event occurred in 1929 (Sellars 1993c), when G. M. Wright, a wealthy park naturalist, began a program at his own expense to survey the fauna of the national parks. Wright hired two other biologists, and by 1932 the surveys had achieved sufficient recognition to prompt Congress to appropriate funding for the continuation and formalization of Wright's activities into a Wildlife Division within the NPS Branch of Research and Education.

Needing a publication outlet for his work, Wright initiated a series entitled *Fauna of the National Parks of the United States,* with the first number published in 1933. This publication (Wright et al. 1933) could well have been the origin of many of the policies that guide the System today. The correlation is so strong that in Table 2.1, we reproduce passages from a section entitled. "Suggested National-Park Policy for the Vertebrates" (pp. 147–148).

The policies Wright et al. proposed might have instituted a new emphasis in NPS on science-based management of biological resources. But Wright was killed in an automobile accident in 1936, and the energy and leadership he had brought to the new directions died with him. The Wildlife Division gradually lost influence and was transferred out of NPS to the Bureau of Biological Survey (later the Fish and Wildlife Service) in 1939, and the NPS Branch of Research and Education was abolished (R. G. Wright 1992a:18). Heavy emphasis on recreation management continued and expanded during the New Deal era to the virtual exclusion of any interest in science-based resource management (Sellars 1993a).

World War II distracted attention and resources that could have been directed to a major program of science and biological management; and there was little impetus in the 1950s. The dawn of the environmental movement provided the setting and stimulus in which these directions could finally grow and challenge the existing heavy preponderance of emphasis on scenery and tourism management (Sellars 1989).

Sellars (1989) considers the appointment by Interior Secretary Udall of an Advisory Board on Wildlife Management, and its subsequent report (A. S. Leopold et al. 1963), to be one of the key events in the new directions of NPS. The Leopold report was, in Sellars' (1989) judgment, "the most influential statement on park management since the 1916 Act establishing the National Park Service."

Indeed the Leopold report is widely cited and often given credit for stimulating contemporary NPS policies. But the report is frequently cited selectively, and even misinterpreted and misquoted. The origins of certain policies, at times attributed to the Leopold report, appear to lie elsewhere. Hence this much-discussed and written-about document needs to be visited one more time.

A key point on which the analysis must turn is the word *natural,* a term that is highly influential in current NPS policies. There are

TABLE 2-1

Selected Passages from No. 1 of the Series **Fauna of the National Parks of the United States** *(Wright et al. 1933)*

Suggested National-Park Policy for the Vertebrates

Every tenet covering the vertebrate life in particular must be governed by the same creed which underlies administration of wild life in general throughout the national parks system, namely:

That one function of the national parks shall be to preserve the flora and fauna in the primitive state and, at the same time, to provide the people with maximum opportunity for the observation thereof.

In the present state of knowledge, and until further investigations make revision advisable, it is believed that the following policies will best serve this dual objective as applied to the vertebrate land fauna.

Relative to areas and boundaries—

1. That each park shall contain within itself the year-round habitats of all species belonging to the native resident fauna.

2. That each park shall include sufficient areas in all these required habitats to maintain at least the minimum population of each species necessary to insure its perpetuation.

3. That park boundaries shall be drafted to follow natural faunal barriers, the limiting faunal zone, where possible.

4. That a complete report upon a new park project shall include a survey of the fauna as a critical factor in determining area and boundaries.

Relative to management—

5. That no management measure or other interference with biotic relationships shall be undertaken prior to a properly conducted investigation.

6. That every species shall be left to carry on its struggle for existence unaided, as being to its greatest ultimate good, unless there is real cause to believe that it will perish if unassisted.

7. That, where artificial feeding, control of natural enemies, or other protective measures are necessary to save a species that is unable to cope with civilization's influences, every effort shall be made to place that species on a self-sustaining basis once more; whence these arti-

continues

TABLE 2-1

Continued

Suggested National-Park Policy for the Vertebrates

ficial aids, which themselves have unfortunate consequences, will no longer be needed.

8. That the rare predators shall be considered special charges of the national parks in proportion that they are persecuted everywhere else.

9. That no native predator shall be destroyed on account of its normal utilization of any other park animal, excepting if that animal is in immediate danger of extermination, and then only if the predator is not itself a vanishing form.

10. That species predatory upon fish shall be allowed to continue in normal numbers and to share normally in the benefits of fish culture.

11. That the numbers of native ungulates occupying a deteriorated range shall not be permitted to exceed its reduced carrying capacity and, preferably, shall be kept below the carrying capacity at every step until the range can be brought back to original productiveness.

12. That any native species which has been exterminated from the park area shall be brought back if this can be done, but if said species has become extinct no related form shall be considered as a candidate for reintroduction in its place.

13. That any exotic species which has already become established in a park shall be either eliminated or held to a minimum provided complete eradication is not feasible.

14. That the threatening invasion of the parks by other exotics shall be anticipated; and to this end, since it is more than a local problem, encouragement shall be given for national and State cooperation in the creation of a board which will regulate the transplanting of all wild species.

Relative to relations between animals and visitors—

15. That presentation of the animal life of the parks to the public shall be a wholly natural one.

16. That no animal shall be encouraged to become dependent upon man for its support.

continues

TABLE 2-1

Continued

Suggested National-Park Policy for the Vertebrates

17. That problems of injury to the persons of visitors or to their property or to the special interests of man in the park shall be solved by methods other than those involving the killing of the animals or interfering with their normal relationships, where this is at all practicable.

Relative to faunal investigations—

18. That a complete faunal investigation, including the four steps of determining the primitive faunal picture, tracing the history of human influences, making a thorough zoological survey and formulating a wild-life administrative plan, shall be made in each park at the earliest possible date.

19. That the local park museum in each case shall be repository for a complete study skin collection of the area and for accumulated evidence attesting to original wild-life conditions.

20. That each park shall develop within the ranger department a personnel of one or more men trained in the handling of wild-life problems, and who will be assisted by the field staff appointed to carry out the faunal program of the Service.

---

two related, but nevertheless distinct, implicit uses with which the term is commonly linked to the Leopold report and NPS policy.

The first use of *natural* is that of an adjective describing the character of the ecosystems being managed in the parks. Although there are inconsistencies in the contemporary uses of the word (Wagner and Kay 1993), as a first approximation it commonly implies ecosystems not significantly altered by human actions. Some version of this connotation is clearly intended in the Leopold report, best articulated in the most widely quoted passage of the document:

> As a primary goal, we would recommend that the biotic associations within each park be maintained, or where necessary re-created, as nearly as possible in the condition that prevailed when the area was first visited by the white man. A national park should represent a vignette of primitive America.

The reference to "biotic associations" is also given credit for focusing attention on the management of whole park ecosystems.

Indeed, this thinking can be found in two passages from the current NPS policy document *Management Policies* (Anon. 1988a):

1. "The natural resource policies of the National Park Service are
   aimed at providing the American people with the opportunity
   to enjoy and benefit from natural environments evolving
   through natural processes minimally influenced by human
   actions" (p. 4:1).

2. "The National Park Service will seek to perpetuate the native
   animal life (mammals, birds, reptiles, fish, insects, worms,
   crustaceans, etc.) as part of the natural ecosystems of parks"
   (p. 4:5).

Leopold's report, with its elegant prose, may well have strengthened attention to these characteristics of park ecosystems and pro-
pelled them into explicit acceptance in NPS policy. Its publication
in the hospitable climate of the Environmental Era certainly made
it timely. But the sense of "naturalness" as a park condition had
been present in the System for nearly a century. The earlier quotation from the Yellowstone Act refers to retention of the natural
wonders "in their natural condition." The quote from Secretary
Lane's letter following passage of the Organic Act instructs
Director Mather to "preserve the parks . . . in essentially their natural state." And the passages from Wright's *Fauna* Series No. 1
(Table 2-1), actually completed in 1932, advocate a policy "to preserve the flora and fauna in a primitive state," so that "the presentation of animal life of the parks to the public shall be a natural
one."

It is with the second implicit use of the word *natural* that we consider the Leopold report to be widely misread and its influence on
policy misinterpreted. In this context, the word is taken as a
description of the management measures used to achieve the "natural" state in the park ecosystems. Numerous, contemporary
authors have taken it to mean, in essence, as little advertent
human management action as possible, and preferably none. In
particular it implies to them no anthropogenic controls on animal
populations. Wright (1988) refers to this approach as "natural regulation," a reliance in the management of ungulates "on natural
processes to regulate herd size."

Many observers have inferred this connotation in the Leopold
report, use it as a basis for justifying the current NPS policy of non-

intrusive management, and credit the report with influencing that policy:

Natural regulation was given professional credibility with the publication of the report of the Special Advisory board on Wildlife Management. (Wright 1988)

[T]he Park Service has adopted a resource management philosophy based upon the 1963 Leopold Report, which recommended that "a national park should represent a vignette of primitive America," or a place where natural biological processes prevail without human intervention. (Keiter 1989)

The Leopold report was precedent setting in that it recommended management and research directed at whole park ecosystems, with attention paid to all biological components. Controls on populations were to be by natural means. (Risser et al. 1992)

But the Leopold report articulated a very different message: a firm recommendation for positive and active management. In addition to the vignette passage, the report does state that "Above all other policies, the maintenance of naturalness should prevail"—this in relation to closing down such recreation facilities as golf courses, ski lifts, and marinas. And it acknowledges that "The traditional, simple formula of protection may be exactly what is needed to maintain . . . climax associations." But:

Reluctance to undertake biotic management can never lead to a realistic presentation of primitive America, much of which supported successional communities that were maintained by fires, floods, hurricanes, and other natural forces. . . . The major policy change which we would recommend to the National Park Service is that it recognize the enormous complexity of ecological communities and the diversity of management procedures required to preserve them. . . . Management may at times call for the use of the tractor, chainsaw, rifle, or flame-thrower. . . . [T]he controlled use of fire is the most "natural" and much the cheapest and easiest to apply. . . . Other situations may call for the use of the bulldozer, the disc harrow, or the spring-tooth harrow. . . . In the absence of the great [buffalo] herds, wallows can be simulated.

And on the matter of animal population control:

> Good park management requires that ungulate popula-
> tions be reduced to the level that the range will carry.
> ... [C]ontrol through natural predators should be encour-
> aged ... although predation alone can seldom be relied
> upon [trapping and removal are acceptable but have lim-
> ited utility]. ... [P]ublic hunting outside the park bound-
> aries ... is by far the best method ... [but w]here other
> methods of control are inapplicable or impractical, excess
> park ungulates must be removed by killing. ... [S]uch
> shooting [to] be conducted ... under the sole jurisdiction
> of the National Park Service. ... [C]ontrol of animal pop-
> ulations in the national parks would appear to us to be an
> integral part of park management. ... Protection alone,
> which has been the core of Park Service wildlife policy, is
> not adequate to achieve this goal.

In total, the Leopold report urged, as goals for national parks, the
science-based preservation and restoration of ecological systems in
the conditions that prevailed at the time of European contact and
the development of a strong science program in NPS. Preservation
and restoration were to be accomplished through a program of
active and diverse management that was to include animal control
through shooting by NPS personnel if necessary and likely. Four
years later, at Senate hearings in Wyoming on elk control in
Yellowstone, convened by that state's Senator Gale McGee, Leopold
was no less positive on the issue (U.S. Senate 1967):

> Your elk herd is headed for extinction, and so also are
> many other forms of wildlife that are affected adversely by
> the elks [sic] overbrowsing of the grass ranges. ... [T]he
> reduction and control of elk numbers is obviously the key-
> stone to maintenance of the habitat. ... I have no reason
> whatsoever to alter my views that this is the manner in
> which that herd has to be regulated. ... Again, we recom-
> mend that direct control continue! And I have not changed
> my mind on this. ... [T]his is one tool that will be in use a
> hundred years from now. (pp. 19–20)

This interpretation of the Leopold report as a charge for active
management was also drawn by a study of NPS policies commis-
sioned by the National Parks and Conservation Association in the
1980s. The Gordon Commission report (Bishop et al. 1989) concluded: "The [Leopold] report's philosophy is crucial, yet has been

widely misunderstood; the Leopold report never suggested that a Park Service commitment to 'natural regulation' justified a laissez faire approach." And Craighead (1991:32) commented:

[The Leopold report] did not advocate a "hands-off" management policy, but rather urged active management of park resources using the most advanced techniques. . . . This [NPS] policy of "naturalism" rests on a misinterpretation of the committee's advice to maintain or re-create "the primitive conditions" of pre-park times.

In fact, rather than being a management turning point, the Leopold report was to a considerable degree a reaffirmation of the existing NPS general policy to engage in active natural-resources management in the parks. Park management had been controlling fires, forest-insect outbreaks, and predators, and had been feeding ungulates. As the emphasis on natural conditions in the parks grew, these measures were phased out; but harbingers of such changes were already evident in Wright's *Fauna* Series No. 1 (cf. Table 2-1). Park management now changed to controlled burning, control of exotics, and the habitat management urged by Leopold.

The parks had been very much in the business of ungulate herd control, something *Fauna 1* had advocated 30 years earlier. As R. G. Wright (1988) comments: "many western parks had active programs to regulate the numbers of ungulates—primarily Rocky Mountain elk and mule deer—in order to keep their numbers at some desired level of carrying capacity." A two-page mimeographed document issued in Yellowstone Park that appeared the year before the Leopold report (Anon. 1962b), entitled "Long Range Management Plan for Northern Yellowstone Wildlife and Range," stated:

Opportunities for public enjoyment of all forms of wildlife and plant life within Yellowstone National Park require that all wildlife populations be maintained at a point compatible with a rejuvenation of the vegetative cover of the northern range, so that there will be a restoration of many decimated plant forms, especially deciduous shrubs and trees. . . . Maintain the Northern Yellowstone elk herd at 5,000 for a period sufficient to determine response of vegetation. . . . [T]here is full realization that shooting by rangers in the Park will be done as necessary to hold the Northern Yellowstone herd at the approximate 5,000 level.

After the Leopold report was forwarded to Secretary Udall on

March 4, 1963, he sent a memorandum on May 2, 1963, to NPS Director Wirth, stating: "The report of the Advisory Board on Wildlife Management of the National Parks . . . has been reviewed. . . . You should, accordingly, take such steps as appropriate to incorporate the philosophy and the basic findings into the administration of the National Park System."

Four years later, at the March 11, 1967, Senate hearings in Wyoming, then-Director Hartzog stated: "direct control is an integral part of wildlife management in national parks, and may always be essential just as it is this year" (U.S. Senate 1967:17). And on September 22 of the same year, the director sent a memorandum to "All Field Offices" on the subject "Implementation of the Leopold Committee Report, 'Wildlife Management in the National Parks.'" Its concern was with the NPS manpower needs for controlling the populations of both native ungulates and feral animals ("such as goats, pigs, and burros") and the appropriate procedures for disposing of carcasses. "To insure the orderly implementation of this program, each superintendent carrying on a wildlife management program in which direct reduction of animals is required shall submit a plan of the proposed reduction to this office, not less than 90 days in advance of undertaking the reduction."

In 1968, NPS issued the first comprehensive policy manuals. Secretary Udall had in the early 1960s authorized a study of "the long-range objectives, organization, and management" of the NPS (Anon. 1968:76). On the basis of this study, he concluded that the purposes, appropriate policies, and management programs for natural areas, historical areas, and recreation areas were sufficiently different that they required separate policy manuals. The one for natural areas (Anon. 1968), entitled *Compilation of the Administrative Policies for the National Parks and National Monuments of Scientific Significance (Natural Area Category)*, was issued in August 1968.

In addition to being the policy document for natural areas as of that date, it contained 12 appendices that included correspondence, study reports, presidential proclamations, and excerpts from legislation spanning the period 1918 to 1968, all of which were relevant to the management policies of natural areas. Significantly, the appendices included Secretary Udall's May 2, 1963, memorandum conveying the Leopold report to NPS Director Wirth, the Leopold report itself, and Director Hartzog's September 22, 1967, memorandum to the NPS field offices authorizing implementation of the Leopold report.

The 1968 policy document itself bears the distinct influence of the Leopold report. The first paragraphs of the "Resource Management Policy" section state:

> In earlier times, the establishment of a park and the protection of its forests and wildlife from careless disturbance were sufficient to insure its preservation as a natural area. . . . This condition prevails no more, for the parks are fast becoming *islands* of primitive America, increasingly influenced by resource use practices around their borders, and by the impact of increasing millions of visitors. . . . Passive protection is not enough. Active management of the natural environment, plus a sensitive application of discipline in park planning, use, and development, are requirements for today.

The section "Fish and Wildlife Management Policy" states:

> [P]rotection, though it is important, is not in itself a substitute for adequate habitat. . . . Wildlife populations will be controlled when necessary to maintain the health of the species, the native environment and scenic landscape and to safeguard public health and safety. Ungulate populations will be maintained at the level that the range will carry in good health and without impairment to the soil, the vegetation, or to habitats of the several species in an area. . . . Insofar as possible, control through natural predation will be encouraged. Public hunting outside of the area is recognized as the next most desirable means of controlling wildlife populations. . . . Other control measures, as necessary, shall be undertaken as follows: (1) Live-trapping in the areas for transplanting elsewhere; (2) research specimens for National Park Service and cooperating scientists; and (3) direct reduction by National Park Service personnel.

As a further indication of the linkage between the Leopold report and the 1968 *Administrative Policies* document, the reproduction of the NPS director's September 22, 1967, memorandum to the field offices authorizing implementation of the report had the parenthetical insert "For full text of policies see *Fish and Wildlife Management Policy* section." The reference was to the section cited above.

In sum, the influence of the Leopold report was three-fold:

1. It strengthened NPS policy resolve to manage biological resources in the parks by focusing attention on preserving samples of ecosystems in the conditions that prevailed at the time of European contact (vignettes of primitive America). The extent to which that preservation became an explicit goal of park management alongside tourism is no doubt part of the directional change in NPS policy that Sellars infers.

2. The strong emphasis on an active-management program strengthened that aspect of operational policy. Clearly it was incorporated into the 1968 natural-area policy manual virtually carte blanche.

3. It made a firm case for a sound, scientific basis for park management and recommended a strong research program in NPS. While this recommendation, along with 11 similar ones over the years, has not been significantly followed (Risser et al. 1992), it undoubtedly was part of the collective force that elicited the strong 1992 National Research Council criticism of NPS for failing to do so.

One influence widely attributed to the Leopold report is that it is a philosophical basis for natural-regulation management. However, the evidence does not support the view that the report was a nodal event stimulating change in this form of NPS animal-control policies. The impetus for the natural-regulation management policies lies elsewhere, as we will discuss.

A second important study of the NPS was also released in 1963. Secretary Udall had asked the National Academy of Sciences (NAS) in April 1962 for assistance in planning and organizing an expanded program in natural-history research. A ten-person committee, chaired by William J. Robbins, submitted a 171-page report, which was forwarded to the secretary by NAS president Frederick Seitz on August 1. Although the document, generally called the Robbins report (Ackerman et al. 1963), concentrated on research issues, it nonetheless reached a number of conclusions similar to those of the Leopold report:

1. The importance of research to illuminate management measures.

2. The purpose of national parks should be the preservation of nature, the maintenance of natural conditions, and the avoidance of artificiality.

3. "Management of natural parks is unavoidable."

4. "Each park should be regarded as a system of interrelated plants, animals, and habitat (an ecosystem) in which evolutionary processes will occur under such human control and guidance as seems necessary to preserve its unique features." But to "attempt to maintain them in any fixed condition, past, present, or future, would not only be futile but contrary to nature."

5. The NPS should define the objectives and purposes of each park.

6. "Every method should be made to preserve these areas ... because of their scientific value as outdoor natural laboratories ... a nature's biological bank."

While the Robbins report is not cited as often as Leopold's, it is well known in the NPS. And the similarity of the two messages must certainly have strengthened the influence of those aspects that were eventually carried into present policies.

Contemporary Natural-Resources Policies

The following acts of Congress have been major legislative influences driving policy in those units of the System that have significant responsibility for managing natural resources:

1. The Congressional enabling acts, which established specific units of the System, and the Antiquities Act of 1906, which authorized the president to establish national monuments.

2. The National Park Service Act of 1916, which established NPS.

3. The Wilderness Act of 1964, which applies to national parks as it does to other forms of public land. Its emphasis on "naturalness" (e.g., banning the use of mechanized equipment) and prohibition against commercial uses strengthen NPS policies in those areas of parks that are designated wilderness.

4. The National Environmental Policy Act of 1969, which requires public agencies to prepare environmental impact statements (EIS) on proposed activities that are likely to affect the environment. The influence of NEPA on NPS is exemplified by the recent preparation of an EIS on wolf "reintroduction" into Yellowstone.

5. The General Authorities Act of 1970, which advises NPS that "each area within the national park system shall be administered in accordance with the provisions of any statute made specifically applicable to that area" and to systemwide authorities.

6. The Endangered Species Act of 1973, which prohibits public agencies from engaging in activities that could affect the survival of populations of listed species, including damage to their habitat.

7. The so-called Redwood Act of 1978, which amended the General Authorities Act of 1970, notified NPS that its management programs "shall not be exercised in derogation of the values and purposes for which these various areas have been established."

Policies are also set at the top administrative levels within NPS. The major compendium of current System policies, "the basic servicewide policy document of the National Park Service," is the 1988 *Management Policies* (Anon. 1988a). Secretary Udall's 1968 decision to separate policies for natural, historic, and recreation areas into separate manuals was reversed and all are now treated in this single volume.

The document begins on a seemingly contradictory note by stating that "the Congress . . . [is] the principal body for making national park . . . preservation policy through the property clause" (p. ix). But it then goes on to declare the following:

All policy will be articulated in writing, approved by an NPS official authorized to issue the policy. Servicewide policy will be articulated by the Director of the National Park Service. . . . Park-specific instructions, procedures, directives, and other guidance supplementary to and in conformance with applicable NPS policies . . . may be set by superintendents within formal delegations of authority. . . . Servicewide policy may be waived only by the Secretary, the Assistant Secretary, or the Director. (p. ix)

In fact these statements are in accord with our earlier comment that public policy is made at numerous levels of government. NPS policy is made at the levels of Congress, the director of NPS ("servicewide policy"), and for individual parks at the superintendent level. Moreover, the passages in the manual's foreword make it clear that servicewide policy must conform to federal law, and park-specific policy must conform to servicewide policy unless the latter is waived by the three top administrators.

Key language from the sections of *Management Policies* relevant to natural resources is now quoted or paraphrased below.

1. Introduction

It is NPS policy to treat potential impairments in the same manner as known impairments. When there is thought to be potential for resource impairment, actions shall be based on strategies that retain the resource in an unimpaired condition until such time as doubts are resolved. For example, if a development might impair a park resource, the development will be postponed or reconfigured until it can be established whether "might" is "will" or "will not," within reasonable limits of certainty. Absent that assurance, the action will not be taken. (p. 1:4)

[This policy clearly follows from the charge in the Organic Act that the parks shall be left unimpaired for the enjoyment of future generations.]

2. Park System Planning

[Park planning involves at least three major steps. The first is preparation of a statement for management, reviewed every two years by the superintendent and regional director. This document assesses park purposes, natural resources, and identifies management issues. The second step is preparation of a general management plan (GMP), which outlines a management concept for each unit. In conformance with NEPA, each GMP is accompanied by an environmental assessment or an EIS, depending on the anticipated effects of the proposed management. Each GMP includes, as a third step, one or more "implementation plans." Resource management plans (RMPs), of interest to us here, are one such.]

[The planning process at all stages calls for provision of public input.] Opportunities for public participation may include public workshops and meetings, informal work sessions on particular issues, and public review and comment on draft documents.

4. Natural-Resource Management

The natural-resource policies of the National Park Service are aimed at providing the American people with the opportunity to enjoy and benefit from natural environments evolving through natural processes minimally influenced by human actions. . . . Natural resources will be managed with a concern for fundamental ecological processes as well as for individual species and features. Managers and resource specialists will not attempt solely to preserve individual species (except threatened or endangered species) or individual natural processes; rather, they will try to maintain all the components and processes of naturally evolving park ecosystems, including the natural abundance, diversity, and ecological integrity of the plants and animals. (p. 4:1)

The National Park Service [recognizing the prevalence of change] will not seek to preserve natural systems in natural zones as though frozen at a given point in time. (p 4:2)

Interference with natural processes in park natural zones will be allowed only (1) when directed by the Congress, (2) in some emergencies when human life and property are at stake, or (3) to restore native ecosystem functioning that has been disrupted by past or ongoing human activities. . . . The extent and degree of management actions taken to protect or restore park ecosystems or their components will be determined in light of management objectives and prevailing scientific theory and methodologies. (p. 4:2)

A program of natural and social science research will be conducted to support NPS staff carrying out the mission of the National Park Service by providing an accurate scientific basis for planning, development, and management decisions. . . . Park research needs will be documented in each park's resource management plan. (pp. 4:2–4:3)

[The NPS will assemble baseline inventories on its natural resources and monitor them over time to detect or predict changes. (p. 4:4)]

The National Park Service will seek to perpetuate the native animal life . . . as part of the natural ecosystems of parks. Management emphasis will be on minimizing human impacts on natural animal population dynamics.

... Any species that have moved onto park lands directly or indirectly as the result of human activities are not considered native. (p. 4:5)

Individual animals within a population may be removed only when ... control of specific animal populations is required for park ecosystem maintenance. ... Unnatural concentrations of native species caused by human activities may be controlled if the activities causing the concentrations cannot be controlled. (p. 4:6)

Animal populations or individuals will be controlled in natural, cultural, and development zones when they present a direct threat to visitor safety and health, and in cultural and development zones when necessary to protect property and landscaped areas. ... Natural processes will be relied on to control populations of native species to the greatest extent possible. ... Other management measures that may be used as necessary separately or together include live trapping for transplanting elsewhere, gathering of research specimens for NPS and cooperating scientists, public hunting on lands outside the park, habitat management, predator establishment, sterilization, and destruction by NPS personnel or their authorized agents. In controlling wildlife populations, highest priority will be given to encouraging public hunting outside the parks and live trapping within parks for transplanting elsewhere. (p. 4:6)

In natural, cultural, and park development zones, fisheries management will seek to preserve or restore natural aquatic habitats and the natural abundance of native aquatic species, including fish, together with the associated terrestrial habitats and species. (p. 4:8)

Terrain and plants may be manipulated where necessary to restore natural conditions on lands altered by human activities. (p. 4:9)

Consistent with the purposes of the Endangered Species Act, the National Park Service will identify and promote the conservation of all federally listed, threatened, endangered, or candidate species within park boundaries and their critical habitats. ... Active management programs will be conducted as necessary to perpetuate the natural distribution and abundance of threatened or endangered species and the ecosystems on which they depend. (p. 4:11)

[Exotic plants and animals which threaten park resources will be managed] up to and including eradication. (p. 4:12)

As these passages indicate, the 1988 policies substantially amplify the 1968 policies. In essence, they reiterate the Leopold report and 1968 enjoiners for active management, but are generally muted through the cautionary concerns for "naturalness." Hence the policies have evolved from the Leopold report in this and two other respects:

First, the Leopold charge for preserving "vignettes of primitive America" has been widely taken as a recommendation to freeze park ecosystems in their 1492 state. Because ecosystems are constantly changing naturally over time, this charge is looked on as prescribing management that is contrary to nature, technically difficult, and, in most cases, impossible. There is nothing sacred about the state of the systems at one point in time ("snapshots"). As we mentioned earlier, this point (captured in the passage from page 4:2) had already been made in the Robbins report.

Second, closely related to the first point is a new emphasis on preserving natural processes. To preserve the components (e.g., plant and animal species) *in toto*, and in the abundance and distribution in which they occurred in 1492, would be tantamount to freezing the systems in their states as of that date. Shifting emphasis on preserving the processes of the systems allows for natural change in the components and eliminates any constraint to freeze them according to some point in time.

This evolution from the 1968 policies began well ahead of the 1988 document's publication. The 1978 *Management Policies* (Anon. 1978) contained verbatim several of the passages quoted above, although Chapter IV ("Natural-Resource Management") was not as detailed as the 1988 section in discussing biological resource management (Anon. 1988a: pp. 4:5–4:14). Moreover, the 1978 document begins in the second paragraph of the first page of Chapter IV with the following unequivocal statement:

Management of park lands possessing significant natural features and values is concerned with ecological processes and impact of people upon these processes and resources. The concept of perpetuation of a total natural environment or ecosystem, as compared with the protection of individual features or species, is a distinguishing aspect of the Service's management of natural lands.

In 1991, NPS published a massive (677 pp.) document entitled *Natural Resources Management Guideline NPS-77* (Anon. 1991a). It gives a first impression of being a management manual but is in essence a detailed elaboration, clarification, and definition of the policy issues set forth in the 1988 *Management Policies*. Chapter 2 ("Natural-Resources Management") contains the sections "Vegetation Management," "Native Animal Management," "Freshwater Resources Management," "Marine Resources Management," "Geological Resources Management," "Soil Resources Management," "Cave Management," "Paleontological Resources Management," "Air Resources Management," "Protection of Aesthetic Values," "Fire Management," "Integrated Pest Management," "Endangered, Threatened, and Rare Species Management," "Exotic Species Management," "Hazardous Waste Management," and "Public Health and Safety." Chapters that follow discuss resource uses, planning, and program administration and management. In total, *NPS-77* is an enormous compendium to provide systemwide guidance for an extensive program of natural-resources management.

By its title, and the detailed discussions of when and under what circumstances active management should be engaged in, *NPS-77* reaffirms a policy and program of active park management. As such, it culminates three decades since the Leopold report and six decades since Wright's *Fauna 1* of policy intent authorizing active management. Since *NPS-77* and the 1988 *Management Policies* are the most recent policy statements, active management remains the current, systemwide policy intent.

In our judgment, the contemporary policies the System adopts are appropriate for achieving its goals. They clearly show the influence of George Wright and his coworkers, the Leopold Committee, and Robbins' National Academy study. Those sources and current policies are sensitive to the public values and goals we summarized earlier, and appear to us to be sufficient basis for agency management programs designed to satisfy those values.

Correspondence between System and Park-Level Policies

Accounts vary within NPS as to where policy is made in the System and how effectively the Washington office influences park operations. In general, Washington personnel maintain that policy is developed in the national office (senior scientist Ted Sudia, personal communication, March 16, 1989; policy chief Carol Aten, personal communication, July 17, 1992). And the 1988 *Management*

Policies states that "Servicewide policy will be articulated by the Director."

But Rockwood (1988:64) concludes from his interviews with NPS personnel that the regional and Washington offices are not in close touch with the problems in the parks: "The parks act as autonomous sub-units within the Park Service, with the parks having primary responsibility to identify and respond to the issues which face them." He paraphrases a former superintendent (1988:65): "the regional and Washington offices are there out of bureaucratic necessity and they should not be actively involved in the management of the parks." Rockwood terms this relationship between Washington and the parks "loose coupling . . . to study policy regarding management of the grizzly bear in Yellowstone National Park the park itself has to be the focal point of study. . . . Yellowstone operates as a semi-autonomous sub-unit of the National Park Service" (pp. 65–66).

Whether or not we term the procedures under which the parks operate *policy*, they nonetheless have the essence of policy, according to our definition at the beginning of this chapter. Indeed, as we will discuss below, some of the policies that originate at the park level eventually move up to become System policies.

For these reasons, it is of interest to examine the correspondence between System and park-level management policies. If natural-resources goals are not being met, it is then desirable to examine whether System policies are inappropriate; or whether it is park-level policies, different from those at the System level, that are failing the natural-resources goals.

Probably the most generally agreed-upon System policy—dating back 60 years to recommendations in *Fauna 1* (cf. Table 2-1)—is the control, and where possible elimination, of exotics. Numerous parks are acting on this policy. Feral burros have been virtually or fully eliminated from Grand Canyon National Park and from Death Valley and Bandelier National Monuments. Feral goats have been eradicated from Channel Islands National Park and, along with feral pigs, have been largely removed and fenced out of the higher elevations of the Hawaiian parks. Efforts have been made to eradicate European rabbits from Haleakala. European boar control has been attempted in Great Smoky Mountains National Park for some years, but with mixed success and not yet full eradication.

Part of the NPS policy on exotics is the position that species native to a region but not originally occurring in a park, and which appear in the park through direct or indirect human action, are to be considered nonnative and eliminated like feral domestics or exotic species. In compliance with this provision, Olympic National Park contends that mountain goats did not occur in the park until individuals spread into it from human introductions in the region in the 1920s. Although the park has not yet succeeded in eliminating a population that had grown to 1,200 animals, it has made significant reductions. In the same vein, Rocky Mountain National Park has systematically eliminated individual mountain goats that have immigrated from populations established elsewhere in the Rockies by introductions.

Exotic plant control is more problematic but is engaged in where there is some hope of achieving a result. The possibility of tamarisk control along the Rio Grande stretches of Big Bend National Park has been given some attention.

Some effort has been applied to reintroduction of extirpated species. Current preparation of an environmental impact statement on wolf "reintroduction" into Yellowstone is a step toward what some observers believe is almost certain reestablishment. Interior Secretary Bruce Babbitt has approved reestablishment. Consideration is being given to introduction of the endangered Mexican bolson tortoise in Big Bend, where a closely related species occurred in Pleistocene times (Risser and Lubchenco 1992). NPS also is pondering whether it should reintroduce wolves onto Isle Royale if the present, dangerously low and diseased population should go extinct. Rocky Mountain has moved actively to reestablish peregrine falcons (Hess 1993), as well as river otter, greenback cutthroat trout, Colorado River cutthroat trout, and bighorn sheep (D. R. Stevens, personal communication, July 7, 1993).

A number of parks engage in prescribed burning to achieve various vegetation goals. Sequoia-Kings Canyon burns sequoia-forest understory vegetation to simulate prehistoric lightning and Native American fire effects that perpetuated the seral, sequoia-forest type. Wind Cave National Park burns its grasslands to preserve prairie conditions. Everglades burns pine-woodlands understory to maintain a seral condition favoring red-cockaded woodpeckers, an endangered species. To the contrary, Yellowstone does not engage in controlled burning on its northern range despite the fact that Houston (1982) documented a 20- to 25-year fire frequency prior to park formation in 1872.

It is in the avoidance of native-animal population control that current park management departs most conspicuously from formal System policy. A recent workshop on ecological research in NPS attended by 27 participants, half NPS personnel and half academic persons, reported that in "many" parks, "animal populations, par-

ticularly ungulates, have reached unprecedented populations"
(Risser and Lubchenco 1992). These are affecting natural, historic,
and recreation areas in ways that are contrary to their goals.

The avoidance of native-animal control is commonly taken as
part of, or tantamount to, "natural-regulation" management, and
the simultaneous origin of both has been traced to Yellowstone.
Wright (1992a:78–79) describes the circumstances surrounding the
1967 cessation of elk control in Yellowstone; and Kay (1990a) and
Chadde and Kay (1991) trace the origins of the natural-regulation
"policy" to publication by park biologists. Indeed, one of the documents announcing the new management protocol, and issued by
the park, was entitled "Administrative Policy for the Management
of Ungulates" (Anon. 1967b). That document appeared a year
before NPS released its *Administrative Policies* for natural areas
(Anon. 1968), which, as cited above, firmly advocated population
control "as necessary."

Wright (1992a:78–79) comments that "The decision [to stop
ungulate control in Yellowstone] was soon applied to other parks,
and there has essentially been no ungulate control in the parks
since then." The statement is a bit too sweeping: Wright mentions
in an end note that some deer have been shot in Great Smoky
Mountains National Park; and Wind Cave National Park has
culled bison, elk, and prairie dogs for a number of years. Moreover,
in recent years, park rangers have shot bison outside of the
Yellowstone northern boundary to supplement the sport-hunting
kill in order to reduce the herd and address the brucellosis problem. But certainly, animal control is not generally practiced today.
Noncontrol has become de facto System policy.

In summary, there is a general tendency in the NPS to back away
from, or at least be ambivalent over, the active management advocated by the Leopold Committee and current policy documents. We
do not suggest that it is universal. In this chapter we have given
numerous examples, and will give more in later chapters, of active
resource management being practiced. But attitudes within the
Service are clearly mixed.

Several instances illustrate this point. Kay (1990a:22) points out
differences of opinion within Yellowstone personnel. He cites a letter by resource-management specialist Consolo (1989) to TWS
president Teer challenging Teer's comment that the park's management policy is a "no management policy." Yet Yellowstone
biologist Meagher (1974) had previously written that "bison management in Yellowstone National Park may be termed 'no management.'" The Gordon Commission, in the quotation cited earlier,

referred to NPS management as "laissez faire," as did Keiter (1989). And the recent NRC report *Science and the National Parks* (Risser et al. 1992) comments in two places (pp. 20 and 39) to the effect that "We see an evolution in NPS attitudes regarding human interference with the natural functioning of park ecosystems—a trend toward less interference."

To a considerable degree the ambivalence turns on the continuing ambiguity and implications of the concept of "naturalness." In our early discussions with Washington NPS officials at the beginning of our study, they asked us to ponder the propriety of advertent management for T and E species when such management would intrude on the naturalness of parks—this despite the fact that the 1988 *Management Policies* explicitly prescribes such management and that some is already under way (e.g., prescribed burning in Everglades for red-cockaded woodpeckers). The same question was raised in connection with management for biodiversity. At the 1992 Albuquerque workshop on ecological research in NPS, seven management dilemmas facing different parks were presented by NPS personnel. A one-page brief, distributed with each presentation, emphasized at some length the concerns over whether contemplated management measures would encroach on the Service's policy commitment to the preservation of naturalness. The published report of the workshop (Risser and Lubchenco 1992) only summarized five of the case histories, and with considerably less attention to the naturalness issue.

The hesitancy over advertent management also stems in part from the concerns over past management failures in the parks. Predator control, ungulate feeding, and introduction of exotic fish appeared to be valid practices in the early years of NPS, when wildlife ecology and management were not yet even in their infancy. Can we assume that our knowledge today is sufficient to prevent us from making similar mistakes? Washington NPS officials also raised this question with us in our early discussions.

3

Wildlife "Problems" in the Parks

Introduction

Whether or not wildlife resources in parks come to be considered problems depends on whether or not their numbers and actions coincide with the goals intended for them (Porter 1991). In this chapter, we are using the word "problem" in this sense.

A 1986 servicewide NPS survey (Anon. 1988b) summarized (1) the types of resources; (2) their condition graded as good, fair, poor, or unknown; (3) the threats to the resources graded as severe, moderate, and low; and (4) the major issues involving the resources in terms of demanding substantial funding and/or requiring more attention to reduce the threats.

Roughly two-thirds of the units in the System contain natural resources considered "primary" because they are mentioned in the units' enabling legislation or proclamation; are central to the parks' goals; contain T and E species and/or their habitat; or have exceptional aesthetic value. Of the primary animal and plant resources, only 14 and 19 percent, respectively, were in "good" condition, with roughly similar percentages in "poor" condition. Some 40 and 54 percent were in "fair" condition, respectively, while the remainder were "unknown."

The report identified 101 categories of "threats," with exotic plants and animals listed as two of the four most commonly mentioned. The categories Removal/Loss of Native Species and Overpopulation of Native Species were 83rd and 84th on the list. Of the 35 subcategories of threatened resources, terrestrial and aquatic animals and vegetation were seven of the ten most commonly cited.

Of the 21 major natural-resources "issues," the first five listed were:

1. Degradation of park resources due to native animal species overpopulation

2. Impacts on threatened, endangered, and other sensitive animals

3. Loss of threatened, endangered, and other sensitive plants

4. Degradation of park resources due to nonnative animals

5. Degradation of park resources due to nonnative plants

"Loss of biological diversity" was 17th on the list.

It is clear from this massive survey that NPS personnel themselves observe an extensive array of natural-resources problems in the System. In this and the following three chapters we will expand on their generalizations by providing detail on a number of problem situations that we have compiled from personal interviews, published and unpublished literature, and our personal experiences with units of the System.

As discussed in the last chapter, the management goal in those units of the System with "significant" natural resources is to preserve ecosystems that are "intact," or "healthy," or have "ecological integrity." A growing literature is defining criteria of such characteristics (cf. Karr 1993, Keddy et al. 1993, King 1993, Grumbine 1994), which generally include high biodiversity, sustainability of rare species, resistance to invasion by exotics, ability to rebound from disturbance, and freedom to fluctuate normally in the short term with environmental variation. Progressive departure from these characteristics constitutes "problems" as defined above. Where the goal for historic sites is to maintain landscapes that were present at the time of the historic events that the units represent, departure from those landscapes constitutes "problems."

There is abundant evidence that burgeoning ungulate populations, given protection inside unit boundaries, are driving both natural and cultivated ecosystems away from unit goals. Although it is the ecological changes that are the problems in the present perspective, we are discussing them here in the context of the ungulate populations. In the next chapter we suggest that it is the policies contributing to ungulate population increases that are the constraints on goal attainment.

High Native Ungulate Populations

White-Tailed Deer

One of the most widespread wildlife overpopulation concerns in NPS is the four- to ten-fold increases in white-tailed deer populations in eastern U.S. parks. Some 49 park units in five NPS regions have identified "possible resource imbalances" caused by high deer densities. It is a long-standing concern. More than a decade ago, Erickson et al. (1981) wrote: "Even the most superficial review of animal problems in the parks reveals that overpopulations are at the root of many difficulties."

Chief Park Scientist Allan O'Connell Jr. of Acadia National Park contacted us about the matter in 1989. A half-day symposium entitled Large Mammal Management and the National Park System: A Dialog, organized by NPS at the 1990 North American Wildlife and Natural Resources Conference, spent the entire period on the white-tailed deer problem. Porter (1991) was asked by the agency to review both the ecological and the policy aspects. NPS has recently issued a public-information circular describing the problem. At the 1992 Albuquerque workshop on ecological research in the NPS (Risser and Lubchenco 1992), this issue was one of seven case studies presented by NPS participants as examples of management situations needing ecological input. And Porter et al. (1994) have recently characterized it as a "dilemma" for NPS.

The actual problems are of several forms. Most clearly contrary to NPS goals is the impact of deer browsing on vegetation in certain historic cites. The goals at both Saratoga National Historical Park and Gettysburg National Military Park are to re-create and perpetuate the landscape scenes that NPS believes were present at the time of the battles. This includes restoring the prevailing vegetation, which, in the case of Saratoga, is its native plants and, in the case of Gettysburg, a mix of natural vegetation and cultivated crops. In both areas, however, vastly increased deer populations utilize the vegetation heavily and prevent it from growing and resembling the Service's reconstruction of the historic condition.

The deer situation in historical parks is further complicated by the pleasure that tourists experience in seeing the animals. According to NPS personnel, some tourists are more interested in seeing the deer, and value this experience more, than seeing and learning about the historic episodes for which the areas were established.

The eastern deer populations impact other social values as well.

The rising populations are accompanied by increasing numbers of deer–vehicle accidents. The animals were at one point thought to be reservoir hosts for Lyme disease, and there have been fears that high deer densities increase the risk of transmission to humans. Although deer are currently not considered reservoir hosts, their high densities may increase populations of the ticks that are vectors for the disease. Many of the eastern parks (e.g., Acadia National Park) are being progressively enclosed by urban development, in which the deer impact landscape plantings.

The more complex policy question to resolve once more turns on the matter of naturalness. The ecosystems in parks primarily established for their preservation (e.g., Great Smoky, Shenandoah) are clearly being altered by the browsing of elevated deer populations. The degree of alteration falls along a continuum that is correlated with deer density. The lower-density ranges may suppress or remove one or a few of the most palatable plant species, as Leopold et al. (1947) first pointed out nearly a half century ago in the case of American yew in the Lake States. The higher densities may completely alter vegetation structure.

Porter (1991) offers the following generalizations about the effects of high deer densities in eastern U.S. deciduous forests: composition of the forest overstory may be determined by browsing out the saplings of palatable tree species and leaving the unpalatable species to dominate the forest; the composition of the understory may be determined in the same way and, at the extreme, eliminated; and in some cases logged-off areas are converted to grassy openings by browsing out seedlings of woody species attempting to recolonize. Warren (1991) reviews a lengthy list of studies describing the effects that Porter generalizes. These range from elimination of plant species (in some cases rare ones) from the vegetation (Bratton 1979), to shifts in vegetation composition, to killing mature trees by bark stripping in Catoctin Mountain Park.

Fundamental changes in vegetation alter the abundance and diversity of animal species that depend on it. Mlot (1991) reported lower densities of small mammals and fewer birds and bird species in areas heavily utilized by deer in Shenandoah. Warren (1991) reviews a number of studies in which heavy deer use variously alters mammalian and avian community composition, or reduces mammalian abundance and the species richness and diversity of breeding-bird communities.

Administrators of other natural areas besides national parks are pondering the effects of burgeoning white-tailed deer populations on the ecosystems of their reserves. Diamond (1992) describes the

removal by deer of young saplings, conversion of understory vegetation, and decline in avian and butterfly populations in the
Fontenelle Forest reserve in Nebraska. Gerard et al. (1993)
describe the disappearance of "spring ephemeral herbaceous
species, destruction of woody saplings, creation of extensive browse
lines" in areas of the 204-unit Illinois Nature Preserves System,
which has as one of its major objectives: "To provide management
that will ensure the perpetuation of the preserves in as close to presettlement condition as possible."

North American Elk

There is also substantial evidence that elk are significantly influencing park ecosystems. Elk are the broadest spectrum feeders
among North American ungulates, both grazing and browsing, as
well as being large, aggressive animals with a larger food demand
than the smaller herbivores. They also have lower reproductive
rates than deer and pronghorn, and their populations consequently
grow more slowly. In addition, they habituate less readily to human
presence and activity. However, habituation does occur under food
stress, as shown by animals from Yellowstone, Rocky Mountain,
and Banff National Parks that move during winter into the yards
of residences in Gardiner, Montana, Estes Park, Colorado, and
Banff, Alberta, respectively.

The documentary record of elk influences on U.S. national parks
spans two-thirds of a century. But unlike the white-tailed deer situation, where there is reasonable accord among those who have
observed it, the elk question has generated different points of view
and a considerable amount of contention. The debate is widely con-
founded by subconscious melding of the value considerations—how
should parks be managed, what is the *proper* management policy,
etc.—with purely objective, scientific assessment of the interrelationships between elk and the systems they occupy. As Caughley
(1981a) and Porter (1991, 1992) point out, such terms as *carrying
capacity, overgrazing,* and *range damage* have both scientific and
value connotations, with resulting ambiguity.

Although the elk question is now surfacing in several parks,
Yellowstone has clearly been the focal point and scene of the over-
whelming majority of research. Hence we begin with a review of
what is now an enormous accumulation of material on the relationships between elk and the ecosystem of the park's northern
range.

Yellowstone elk management has gone through three distinct
policy phases during its history, accompanied by three responses of

the park's elk population and its effects on the park ecosystem. The first phase followed park formation and assumption of control by the military. Policy at that time decreed ungulate protection from hunting, artificial feeding, and predators. Although there was no formal research, the northern herd was censused annually, and there were subjective observations of vegetation conditions.

The second phase began in approximately 1911 with reports of heavy vegetation impacts by a burgeoning herd (cf. Beetle 1974a). The prevailing view of this phase, held by a succession of NPS biologists during this period (cf. Skinner 1928, Rush 1932, Wright et al. 1933, Grimm 1939, Kittams 1959), contended that agricultural and village developments adjacent to the park, and the threat of being shot by hunters, prevented elk from moving a considerable distance northward into what had been traditional winter range in presettlement times. In addition, hunting may have selected out those components of the population that had been inclined to migrate beyond the park's boundary. Given protection from hunting and elimination of predators, the northern herd increased to 35,000–40,000 animals by the early 1900s.

The greatly increased population now wintering on a limited area inside the boundary (the "northern range") placed heavy feeding pressure on the vegetation, altering herbaceous communities and reducing woody vegetation (especially aspen, willow along stream courses, and sagebrush). Such changes progressively reduced the "carrying capacity" for elk on the northern range, estimated by the late 1950s and early 1960s to have declined to 5,000.

Elimination of woody vegetation reduced populations of animal species that depended on such plant communities: beaver, which require aspen and willow for food and building material and which at one time had numbered an estimated 10,000 in the park, and white-tailed deer, which, in the northern Rocky Mountains, use riparian zones for their habitat. Once estimated at 100 in the park, whitetails were essentially eliminated.

Park management policy reflected the dominant value position during Phase 2 that elk effects on the ecosystem were contrary to the park's (and NPS's) goal "to protect for all times . . . from injury or spoliation . . . [the] wonders within said park." Policy now called for controlling the herd; trapping and removal began in the second decade of the 20th century through the 1920s (Erickson 1981), and shooting by park rangers began in the 1930s. Culling continued through 1967, by which time the northern herd had been reduced below 4,000. Tyers (1981) provides a useful review of the documentation and events during Phase 2.

Policy Phase 3 began in 1967 with the park's release of the one-page memorandum "Natural Control of Elk" (Anon. 1967a), and continues to the present. In its early years the new phase contained two major components: Houston's (1974, 1976, 1982) *a posteriori* reinterpretation of evidence accumulated up to the late 1960s, and "natural regulation," the ecological rationale for the new policy and a revised version of "natural control." His (1982) reinterpretation of the pre-1969 record concluded the following:

1. There had been no increase to 35,000–40,000 elk during the late 1800s and early 1900s followed by a population crash in 1917–1920. The northern herd had maintained a fairly stable level of 12,000–15,000 animals throughout the park's history and probably back into pre-Columbian times, until the reductions of the 1960s.

2. The park did not constrain elk within its boundaries during winter, stopping long-distance migration out of the area and down the Yellowstone River valley. Elk had always wintered on the northern range inside what are now park boundaries, although there was a migratory component that left the park in winter.

3. Based on his review of early park photographs, Houston agreed that there had been some decline in aspen and willow communities, perhaps a half, during the park's history. But he attributed these changes largely to secondary succession by conifers; absence of fires, which in pre-park times had burned on a 20- to 25-year frequency (Houston 1973); and climate change. Ungulate use came in a distant, and relatively minor, fourth. Houston detected what he took to be ungulate highlining on early photographs. And in total, he inferred a contemporary vegetation not very different from what prevailed at the time of park formation.

The second component of Phase 3 is the natural-regulation hypothesis. Its main points were as follows:

1. "Natural regulation of ungulate populations has been defined as regulation of numbers without human influence" (Houston 1971).

2. Cole (1971) adopted as a premise that it would be evolutionarily unstable for herbivores to increase to the point where they severely damaged their vegetation resource.

3. Cole (1971) generalized from 11 references by five authors, working on three species (elk, moose, bison) in four parks in the Rocky Mountain Region of NPS. Of the 11, one had been published, two were in press, five were unpublished intra-departmental reports, and three were presentations at professional meetings, all between 1968 and 1971. Providing no data, Cole concluded that these populations had "naturally regulated" or "self-regulated" by density-dependent, intraspecific competition for food and the "partially density-independent effects of periodic severe weather" acting on birth and death rates. With this equilibration "the native ungulates did not seem to be able to cause retrogressive or secondary succession."

4. The initial statement of natural regulation, originally termed *natural control* (Anon. 1967a), had included the influence of predation in the process. But the restatements of natural regulation four years later (Cole 1971, Houston 1971) dismissed predation "as an assisting but nonessential adjunct to the regulation of ungulate population sizes."

5. Under natural regulation, sympatric herbivorous species were hypothesized to achieve some measure of competitive equilibrium and avoid exclusion, presumably through resource partitioning.

The policy implications of Phase 3 are that elk had coexisted in equilibrium with other ecosystem components in the Yellowstone area since the Pleistocene without human manipulation of the herd. If the park's goal was to maintain the collection of ecosystem components and processes without human intrusion in as nearly the condition that would prevail without the advent of Europeans, then culling was both unnecessary and undesirable.

There were numerous skeptics about Phase 3 in the academic community, but few had any research data with which to test the paradigm. Patten (1968) had compared 1924 and 1964 photographs of the riparian zone along the Gallatin River, a wintering area for another component of the park elk population, and found sharp reductions in willows, which he attributed to elk browsing. Beetle (1974a,b) was a perennial critic of the Phase 3 interpretation, emphasizing in particular the sharp decline of aspen in the northern Rocky Mountain region, which he attributed to wild ungulates. Leslie Pengelly, University of Montana wildlife professor, while not conducting research in the park, was for many years a close observer of conditions on the northern range and of NPS personnel, and an unswerving critic of Phase 3 (Anon. 1975). Biologists in fish and game departments of surrounding states were also critical (cf. Erickson 1981).

Probably stimulated at least in part by Chase's (1986) book, Congress appropriated funding in 1986 for an expanded research effort to address the question of whether the park is "overgrazed." The ecological research of the "40 separate research projects" (Singer 1989) largely addressed the herbaceous vegetation (cf. Singer 1989, 1990, 1992, Frank 1990, Wallace 1990, Coughenour 1991, 1992, Merrill and Boyce 1991, Frank and McNaughton 1992, 1993). This work generally concluded that *production* of the herbaceous vegetation was not being impaired by winter ungulate grazing. In fact, there was evidence of compensatory increase in primary production in areas grazed by elk (Frank 1990, Frank and McNaughton 1992, 1993).

Evidence varied on the effects of grazing on herbaceous-vegetation *composition*. Coughenour (1992) and Singer (1989, 1990, 1992) generally found some differences in the native plant species between grazed and ungrazed areas. And in areas sampled by Frank and McNaughton (1992), exotic grasses (*Phleum pratense, Poa pratensis, and Bromus inermis*) were three of the five "herbaceous dominants" on the winter range, while *Phleum* (timothy) was the dominant grass in two of three transitional range sites. Wallace and Macko (1993) commented on the invasiveness of timothy over "large areas of Yellowstone's northern range." Houston (1975) had earlier commented on the dominance of *Phleum* in the understories of aspen stands. Ross (1990), too, has noted changes in herbaceous vegetation on heavily used sites.

Two other studies during this research effort were originally interpreted as supporting the natural-regulation paradigm but on closer scrutiny do not appear to do so. Engstrom et al. (1991) and Whitlock et al. (1991) sampled sediment accumulation at the bottoms of eight small lakes in Yellowstone to test the claim that the high elk densities during the 1900s had increased soil erosion. The original interpretations stressed that the evidence did not support the claim. But following a challenge by Hamilton (1994), Engstrom et al. (1994) report in a more recent paper that the methodology used was not sensitive enough either to reject or accept the claim.

Hadley (1990) examined mammalian remains in the floor deposits of Lamar Cave on the northern range. Among the 10,000 mammalian bones examined, 40 were from ungulates representing most of the contemporary species. There were 28 elk bones occurring in 7 of the 10 levels she excavated. She inferred "that the area was used by elk in the past much as it is today." However, 25 of the total were in the uppermost level, aged at less than 500 years B.P., possibly supporting the view (see below) that the current large elk population is a relatively recent phenomenon.

Concurrent with the Congressionally funded overgrazing studies, Kay (1990a, Chadde and Kay 1988, 1991, Kay and Chadde 1992, Kay and Wagner 1992) conducted research funded by the Rob and Bessie Welder Wildlife Foundation. He examined the condition of woody vegetation, including aspen woodland and its understories, riparian vegetation, and such deciduous shrubs as *Amelanchier alnifolia, Prunus virginiana,* and *Shepherdia canadensis.* Measuring vegetation inside and outside exclosures, inside and outside park boundaries, and comparing early park photographs with his own retakes of the same sites, Kay concluded that the profound reduction in these types was due to elk browsing rather than climate change and fire suppression, that the park ecosystem had not been in equilibrium since its formation, and therefore that the natural-regulation hypothesis must be rejected.

Based on his study of cottonwood (*Populus angustifolia*) stands in the northern range, Keigley (1994) concluded that normal trees were formed only in the early part of this century and during the elk population low of the 1960s. At other times, browsing pressure was so heavy that it hedged the young plants and prevented formation into trees. The long-range trend is a decline in cottonwoods along streams in the northern range as dying, older trees are not replaced.

Rosgen (1993) examined the fluvial geomorphology of the Lamar River drainage and its three major tributaries in the northern range, including measurements of streambank erosion rates. He observed the latter to be 10 to 100 times as high in the lower reaches on the winter range, where riparian vegetation had been eliminated, as in the higher reaches. The streambank erosion is producing heavy siltation.

Following a two-year study, Jackson (1992, 1993) concluded that avian densities and species diversities in the northern range were much lower in "severely browsed" riparian vegetation than in unbrowsed or lightly browsed areas. Studying winter elk distribution and movement in the park, Vore (1990) observed that December–February hunting and subsequent tourist activity concentrated elk at the "hunting/no-hunting boundary and in areas with limited public access." This was taken as support for the

Phase 2 contention that human activity since park formation was holding elk within the boundaries and preventing them from moving out to traditional, more extensive winter range.

Kay (1988, 1990a,b, 1992a,b) reviewed historical records and the entire archaeological literature on the Intermountain West. On the basis of this evidence, and the character of park vegetation in the 1800s, he concluded that prior to 1492 ungulates in general, and elk and moose in particular, were held at low densities by aboriginal hunting, possibly in synergy with nonhuman mammalian predators.

To us, the balance of evidence indicates that a large wintering elk herd during park history has profoundly altered the northern-range ecosystem, broadly reducing species, habitat, and landscape diversity. Numerous, likely ecological changes, which cannot be detailed here, are not being discussed or considered by Park Service officials. The relevant policy question is whether or not the present situation, produced by the natural-regulation policy, is meeting park and NPS goals. If those goals are to maintain a diverse, intact ecosystem in some semblance of pre-Columbian conditions, then they are not, in our judgment, being met.

Grand Teton National Park is generally considered part of the Greater Yellowstone Ecosystem. Prior to 1958 few elk summered in Teton Park (Boyce 1989:100). By the late 1980s, half of the 7,000–10,000 elk wintering on the nearby National Elk Refuge did so. Each fall this half, plus the remainder out of Yellowstone, migrate through Teton Park on their way to the refuge, where they are fed for the winter. Spring survivors travel through the park on their return migration to summer ranges. Hence there is no pattern analogous to Yellowstone's where large numbers of elk concentrate within the park and subsist on natural vegetation for prolonged winter periods.

Since 1960, the herd size (i.e., those wintering on the refuge) has remained fairly stable, in the range of 8,000–9,000, although declining a bit during the late 1970s and early 1980s (Boyce 1989:44). This stability has been maintained largely by an annual hunt, which removes from one to several thousand animals, averaging around 3,000 (Boyce 1989:75).

There have been accounts of elk effects on vegetation similar to those in Yellowstone, especially aspen, in the Teton area for decades (Beetle 1979), although the focus has been more extensive on the Jackson Hole area. But Boyce (1989:123) comments on heavily browsed aspen along migration routes and provides a photograph of a "decadent" stand in the park.

Hart (1986) investigated aspen stands in the park in which bark on the trees was chewed by elk. The wounds allowed entry of two pathogenic fungi, which increased tree mortality rates. Between 1970 and 1986, 39 percent of stems in study plots died.

Kay (1990a) reviews the results of archaeological work done in Jackson Hole, particularly that of Frison (1971) and Wright (1984). On the basis of "more than two dozen sites" excavated in Jackson Hole, Wright inferred that Native Americans subsisted mainly on vegetal foods. Of the few ungulate bones unearthed, none was from elk. These archaeologists concluded that elk were extremely scarce in the Jackson Hole area in pre-Columbian times, that local people utilized some ungulates in winter, and that they migrated considerable distances out of the area to find them. The ecological effects of elk today on the park ecosystem must be of post-settlement origin.

As in Yellowstone and Jackson Hole, there is a long history of concern over the effects of elk on the Rocky Mountain National Park (RMNP) ecosystem. Early historical accounts (Hess 1993) reported elk in the region of what is now the park migrating to lower elevations to winter. By the latter 1800s the species had been nearly extirpated by market hunting and competition with live-stock on the winter range (Braun et al. 1991). In 1913 and 1914, 49 elk were transplanted from Yellowstone to what would shortly (in 1915) become RMNP. Thereafter, the population grew rapidly. In 1933, a special task force on wildlife problems in national parks estimated the park population at 350 (Hess 1993). Herd culling began in 1944 and continued to 1968, when the park changed to natural-regulation management. The number of animals occupying the winter range in 1968 was estimated at 500 (Hess 1993).

By 1980–1982, the population occupying RMNP's low-elevation winter range had risen sharply to 2,000–2,500 (Bear et al. 1989), roughly twice the 1,000–1,500 animals that Hobbs et al. (1982) had estimated as the number that could be supported by the available forage. By 1990, the total park population was estimated at 3,000, with some animals now wintering on the summer range, including the high-elevation alpine zone (Braun et al. 1991).

Wright et al. (1933) early cited Rocky Mountain, along with Yellowstone, as one of the areas in which elk were altering the veg-etation. In 1931, Chief Ranger McLaughlin reported that "last win-ter, for the first time, the elk began tearing bark off the aspen trees." Biologist Harold Ratcliffe reported in 1941 that in Beaver Meadow, "one of most important parts of the entire winter range . . . as much as 90 percent of the annual growth of the willows along the stream . . . is eaten with resulting increase in mortality."

In 1958 Gysel (1960) measured vegetation in twelve 20-by-20-foot exclosures that had been constructed on the winter range 25 years earlier. Such woody species as *Prunus virginiana, Ribes cereum,* aspen, and willow were all well represented inside but had declined from earlier measurements outside, where grasses and forbs dominated. Even the density of the latter had declined. The photographs in his paper show bark-scarred aspen similar to those seen throughout the Yellowstone northern range.

Olmstead (1979) studied aspen-stem utilization in different areas of the park. On sites where utilization was heavy, stem densities declined from previous years and the remaining stems were uniformly in older age classes, again as occurs in Yellowstone and Teton. On sites with lighter use, trees had a wider range of age classes.

Hess (1993) has conducted the most comprehensive analysis of ecological changes in Rocky Mountain, exhaustively reviewing the published record and park files and reports, and interviewing NPS personnel who have been associated with the situation. He traces the history of aspen and willow decline, evidence of degradation in herbaceous vegetation, and increase in weedy species, bare ground, and erosion. Photographs in his book show high-lined and bark-scarred aspen in some areas, absence of aspen and willows in other areas (except in exclosures), and sloughing stream banks devoid of woody, riparian vegetation. The images are similar to those seen in Yellowstone.

Hess (1993) also reviewed the role of fire in the park. Prior to RMNP's establishment, the area had been subject to frequent fires, which maintained a vegetation mosaic. But out of concern for the urban and agricultural development closing in on the park, RMNP officials instituted a policy of fire control. This, along with removal of ground fuels by elk grazing, had virtually eliminated fires and allowed expansion of coniferous forest.

Hess examined effects of elk pressure on the fauna. Ratcliffe and Sumner (1945), as early as 1941, had observed elk occupying and grazing out winter range formerly used by bighorn sheep, which forced the sheep to winter at higher elevations. Hess also cited work on white-tailed ptarmigan, which suggested population decline due to heavy browsing on willow, an important winter food for the birds. But his greatest emphasis was on the decline of beaver (from a 1940 census of 1,865 animals, the population fell to a 1980 census of 109 in the same areas), which he attributed to elimination of aspen and willow.

Hess discussed the decline (perhaps by half) in the black bear population, which he associated with the shrinkage in early successional vegetation and the riparian type. McCutchen (1993) has also reported on the plight of black bears in the park, stressing the marginality of the habitat as reflected in low reproductive rates and body size in comparison with other North American populations. He reports that "historic fire suppression has degraded the bear habitat, [which ideally requires] herbaceous and shrub primary productivity." In total, Hess concludes:

> Fire suppression in Rocky Mountain National Park is completing what elk began—the relentless destruction of biological diversity. . . . Nearly a quarter century of experimentation has shown that natural regulation, in the absence of natural predators and historic migration routes, is no longer tenable in Rocky Mountain.

One elk herd that has received some attention and shows evidence of influencing the ecosystem of the area is in Olympic National Park. Douglas Houston (paper presented in an NPS symposium at the 1988 A.I.B.S. annual meetings) reported that Roosevelt elk in the area were reduced to low numbers by the turn of the century but have increased since, numbering around 5,000 in 1988, at which level they were thought to have stabilized.

Woodward et al. (1992) measured vegetation inside and outside exclosures in Olympic that had been established in approximately 1935 and 1955 in old-growth Sitka spruce forests. Elk had significantly affected the abundance, growth, and morphology of shrubs (*Vaccinium* spp., *Rubus spectabilis*), understory trees (e.g., *Acer circinatum*), overstory trees (e.g., *Tsuga mertensiana*), and ferns (Houston et al. 1990), all of which dominated inside the exclosures. Outside, the vegetation was converted to herbaceous forms, particularly graminoids, to form "grazing lawns" (Houston 1988 A.I.B.S. presentation, Houston et al. 1990).

One elk situation that has had very little visibility is a herd in Mount Rainier National Park. There is no historic or archaeological evidence that elk ever inhabited that area inside present park boundaries (Erickson et al. 1981, Bradley 1982). The state of Washington introduced animals on three sides of Mount Rainier in the early part of this century. The populations increased and eventually spread into the park in the 1930s, numbering some 1,500 individuals by 1976. Most of the animals use the park only for summer range, migrating outside to the adjacent national forest to winter. Hence, the park is not considered a complete biological unit for the population.

Concern has arisen over the impacts on the subalpine zone (Bradley 1982): "complete denuding of vegetative cover and the exposure of bare mineral soil. . . . The forbs were the most significantly impacted form of vegetative cover and showed responses to both foraging and trampling in all years, areas, and frequencies of use studied." This is taking place despite the fact that sport hunting outside Mount Rainier has stabilized the population.

Moose

As is well known, moose are a low-density species and occur in only a few U.S. national parks. Generally present on the continent in the 1800s and early 1900s at low densities even for this species, populations have been increasing in a number of North American areas in recent decades. Effects of moose increase on vegetation have been studied most intensively in Isle Royale National Park.

Moose colonized Isle Royale shortly after the turn of the century (McInnes et al. 1992). The population increased to somewhere between 2,000–5,000 individuals by the 1920s, then declined sharply to 200–400 animals by the mid-1930s. In Snyder and Janke's view (1976), wolf predation (wolves arrived on the island in the 1940s) has probably kept the moose population from rising above approximately 1,500. Since arrival of the wolves, the two species appear to have entered into a predator–prey cycle (Peterson 1988) with a mean period of about 38 years (Peterson et al. 1984). There is some evidence of a partial vegetation influence in the cycle as well (Pastor et al. 1993).

Effects of the moose on vegetation structure in the park have been reported for some time (cf. Aldous and Krefting 1946, Krefting 1951). More recent reports (cf. Snyder and Janke 1976, Risenhoover and Maass 1987) have described reduction in abundance of (1) mountain ash and balsam fir in the forest overstory, and (2) American yew ("near elimination") and red-osier dogwood in the understory. Other understory shrubs have been reduced in height while vascular ground cover increased. The unpalatable white spruce increased to become the dominant tree species. The overall effect was a reduction in tree density due to removal of fir and mountain ash, and a more open understory. Density of such early-successional trees as paper birch and aspen was not altered if the trees had grown beyond browsing level when the moose arrived.

Pastor and Naiman (1992), McInnes et al. (1992), and Pastor et al. (1993) extended the analysis beyond vegetation effects to the nutrient-cycling pattern. These authors pointed out that (1) coniferous foliage is more chemically defended than deciduous foliage of such fast-growing, seral species as aspen and birch; and (2) the secondary compounds that inhibit microbial action in ungulate rumens also inhibit soil–microbial action. Therefore, they hypothesized that conversion of vegetation, and associated litter fall, from deciduous to coniferous form could reduce soil–microbial action.

Pastor et al. (1993) then measured soil exchangeable cations, total carbon and nitrogen, nitrogen mineralization rates, microbial respiration rates, and above-ground net primary production in 40-year-old exclosures on Isle Royale. All were higher inside the exclosures than outside. While moose pellet deposition stimulated some mineralization outside the exclosures, it was still not sufficient to compensate for the litter effect and negate the inside–outside differences.

Pastor et al. (1993) conclude that "by changing the plant communities and the arrays of litters decomposed from them, moose browsing indirectly controls the nitrogen cycle and the long-term productivity of Isle Royale's boreal forests. Failure to consider the indirect effects of herbivores on decomposers through changes in litterfall may cause incomplete models of food webs to be seriously in error." Given the reduction in deciduous species by elk and increase in conifers in parts of Yellowstone and Rocky Mountain, it would seem desirable to examine whether the Isle Royale effect is present in these two parks.

Currently, moose are invading the upper Colorado River drainage of Rocky Mountain National Park. The animals are dispersers from a growing population of moose in nearby North Park that originated from introductions during the last decade. The situation would provide an excellent opportunity to document the effects of moose population growth on the vegetation and fauna, but that documentation would need to begin immediately in order to be effective.

Exotics and Feral Animals

In every review of major natural-resources problems in national parks, or conferences on the topic, control of exotics is considered a top priority (cf. Anon. 1988b, Risser and Lubchenco 1992). Erickson et al. (1981) highlighted five animal-management problems "meriting high-level attention." Two of the five were exotic-control situations: wild boars in Great Smoky Mountains and burros in three parks.

NPS has a clear policy on controlling, and if possible eliminating, exotics from the parks. There are some subtle matters of policy definition associated with this issue. Feral domestics and wild animals from other continents that have escaped from captivity, or been released by humans, are unequivocally considered exotics and fall under the control policy. Wild animals of the continent in which parks are situated that did not previously occur in them, but move in through their own range extensions, are considered "natural" and are not subject to control. But if such species spread into the parks from populations originating from human releases in the region, they are not considered natural and are therefore subject to control, unless there is evidence they occurred there in recent times and were eliminated by postindustrial humans. It makes no difference whether the species exist naturally in populations only a few 10s of kilometers away. Any intrusions originating from human actions are subject to elimination if they were not present recently.

One example of the Park Service's dilemmas with this policy is the matter of potential mountain goat spread into Yellowstone. Wilkinson (1990) quotes park officials as saying that there are natural goat populations to the west and northwest of Yellowstone, and populations established from human releases to the northeast and south. These officials vow that they will eliminate any animals moving in from the latter populations but will leave unmolested any animals pioneering from the west (Wilkinson 1990).

The policy has created another quandary for NPS (Colombe 1994). The wolf population in Isle Royale National Park dropped sharply in the early 1980s, possibly due to infection by the exotic parvovirus. Since the organism must have been brought to the island by humans, it is "unnatural." If the wolf population were to disappear, it would be within policy to reintroduce wolves from the mainland. But if the population's demise were due to natural causes, reintroduction would not be within policy.

The greatest success NPS has achieved in exotic-animal control has been with feral domestics. Goats and pigs have in essence been eliminated by shooting from high-elevation areas of Hawaii Volcanoes and Haleakala National Parks, and the areas have been fenced to prevent repopulation. The sensitive, native vegetation is showing marked signs of recovery. Feral domestic rabbits have also been removed from parts of Haleakala. Mongooses are ubiquitous in both of the parks, and almost certainly will never be eliminated. However, trapping mongooses, introduced rats, and feral domestic cats in Haleakala has reduced predation on the endangered Hawaiian dark-rumped petrel (Anon. n.d.).

Feral burros, as mentioned previously, have been eliminated from, or significantly reduced in number in, Bandelier National Monument and have been removed from Death Valley National Monument and Grand Canyon National Park. There was substantial animal-welfare resistance to burro shooting in Bandelier and Grand Canyon, and animals in the latter park were eventually captured and removed alive by the Fund for Animals. Death Valley burros were eliminated by live capture and removal.

One of the more recalcitrant exotic problems has been the removal of wild boars from Great Smoky Mountains. First seen there in the 1940s following escape from captivity outside the park in 1920, the population has increased and spread through most of the area (Wright 1992a). Control was first begun in the 1950s, when rooting damage to the vegetation was first observed. Early control by trapping, removal, and, on a limited scale, shooting did not alter the population. By the 1970s, there was extensive damage to the vegetation and predation on some important components of the fauna (e.g., amphibians).

Control efforts were intensified in the early 1980s, but opposition by local residents who value boars as game animals (Erickson et al. 1981) was so intense that the park stopped direct reduction by rangers on the North Carolina portion of Great Smoky. A compromise program that allowed local citizens to trap in the park and remove animals was not effective. Newer efforts will require more intensity, new approaches, stronger law enforcement, and perhaps fencing if sufficient control is to be achieved.

It is in Olympic National Park, where NPS is contending with a controversial effort to eliminate nonnatives. Mountain goats naturally occupy mountain ranges as near as 80–100 kilometers from Olympic. But the agency maintains that there is no evidence of goats ever occupying the Olympic Mountains, which it attributes to the mountains' isolation from the coast ranges of Washington and British Columbia. There is apparently evidence that other mammalian species were similarly blocked. An array of endemic plant and animal species and subspecies evolved with this isolation, producing a unique biota in the region, which Erickson et al. (1981) called a "treasure house of endemic species."

Goats were released in the Olympic Mountains in the 1920s by hunting interests to establish huntable populations. When the park was established in the 1930s, hunting was no longer allowed and the goat population increased to 1,000–1,350 animals by 1983

(Houston et al. 1986). According to NPS, by the 1960s the goats were significantly impacting the sensitive alpine vegetation and pawing out areas of the ground that became subject to wind erosion, which formed large "blow-outs" that scar the landscape.

The park began live removal of goats in the 1970s and 1980s (Wright 1992b). Carried out with helicopters in precipitous terrain, the removal is both dangerous and marginally effective, succeeding by 1992 in removing only about a third of the animals. The park now proposes to remove the remaining goats by shooting and is preparing an environmental impact statement on the proposal.

The entire operation is being challenged by the Fund for Animals, which maintains that there is evidence goats were present in the region within the last century, that the claims of vegetation damage are exaggerated, and that the blow-outs originated from goats attracted to salt blocks placed by park personnel for closer observation of the animals (R. Anunsen, personal communication, December 2, 1992, C. S. Anunsen 1993, Anunsen and Anunsen 1993).

We have discussed the matter with both Fund representatives and park biologists Bruce Moorhead and Douglas Houston but have not seen the field evidence ourselves. Hence, we have no position on the issue at this time. We will raise it again in a different context in Chapters 5 and 7.

Declining Abundance and Biodiversity

As one of the few kinds of minimally disturbed natural areas in a world of land development and alteration, national parks are looked to as one of the few means for preserving some of the abundance and diversity of the earth's biota. Yet animal abundance and diversity are declining in many parks. Much of the decline is associated with the high populations of native ungulates and exotics discussed earlier; but numerous other causes are also involved.

There is evidence of decline in all of the organizational levels at which ecology analyzes biological diversity: genetic diversity within species populations, species diversity, ecosystem diversity, and habitat or landscape diversity. In the case of genetic-diversity loss, Peterson (1994) has postulated that recent low reproductive rates in the few Isle Royale wolves surviving the 1981–1982 parvovirus decline may be the result of inbreeding depression. Introduction of new stock may be necessary to save the population.

Diamond (1992) comments on the evidence of inbreeding depression in elephants and lions in what he calls "cookie cutter" parks in Africa and speculates on the possibility in Isle Royale wolves. Soulé et al. (1979) also raise the issue for African parks.

One study of species-diversity decline in American national parks was undertaken by Newmark (1986, 1987). This investigator hypothesized that, because some parks are virtual islands surrounded by other forms of land use, and all have fixed boundaries and sizes, their faunas should behave demographically like those of land-bridge islands: they should lose species faster than they gain them, and the number of extinctions should be an inverse function of park size and a positive function of park age. Newmark then compiled records of mammalian species observations in 14 western North American parks and park assemblages (two or more adjacent parks). He confined his analysis to the orders Lagomorpha, Carnivora, and Artiodactyla.

The evidence confirmed all of Newmark's predictions. Extinctions did in fact exceed colonizations, were negatively correlated with park size (ranging from seven to zero disappearances), and positively correlated with park age. He concluded (1987) that:

> The natural post-establishment loss of mammalian species in western North American national parks indicates that virtually all North American national parks were too small to maintain the mammalian faunal assemblage found at time of park establishment. To reduce the potential loss of mammalian fauna in the future will most probably require that the mammalian fauna within the parks be more actively managed and that the parks be "enlarged" either through the acquisition or cooperative management of lands adjacent to the parks.

Newmark's results were challenged in a manuscript that was submitted to *Ecology* by J. Quinn, C. van Ripper, and H. Salwasser but eventually withdrawn and never published. Quinn et al. questioned Newmark's results on two grounds: (1) Responses from their interviews with officials in 12 of the U.S. parks in Newmark's sample indicated that some of the species originally reported to him as extinct were in fact still in the parks; and (2) most of the parks in the study are surrounded by national forests or Bureau of Land Management lands with similar habitat, in which the species in question often still occur, although they have disappeared from the parks.

Newmark (personal communication, April 7, 1993) told us that he had responded to the criticism by rechecking the species records with park officials and verifying most of his original conclusions. There were one or two updates, but the basic inverse correlation between park size and species disappearance remained. On the matter of the surrounding land types, he pointed out that this was not a contradiction of his conclusions. The basic question is species disappearance in relation to area size. If species are more prone to disappear from small areas, irrespective of their persistence in surrounding habitat, it merely bears out the principle. Their presence in surrounding terrain only affects the probability of their recolonizing the area from which they disappeared, something less likely in isolated parks without comparable surrounding habitat.

Since his original study, Newmark has also analyzed species persistence in East African parks and found a similar inverse correlation between park size and disappearance. And as we will discuss in Chapter 7, Soulé et al. (1979) have observed the same effect with islands on the Sunda Shelf in Southeast Asia.

One of the most extreme and widely publicized declines in wildlife abundance in the American parks has been the drastic decline in Everglades National Park of the vast wading bird populations for which the park was established. A recent, massive treatise (Davis and Ogden 1994) analyzes in great detail the Everglades ecosystem.

The freshwater input from the north, which is the lifeblood of the ecosystem, has been seriously reduced by extensive hydrological development and contaminated with agricultural chemicals from intensive farming on the north and east. The result has been a profound ecological change in park ecosystems and a decline of more than 90 percent in the wading bird population. One estimate places the decline in roseate spoonbills between 1980 and 1990 alone at 50 percent. Other species have been equally impacted: American crocodiles, which once nested as far north as West Palm Beach, are now endangered and relegated to the Florida Bay area and adjacent mangrove swamps (George 1987).

McCullough (1989) reconstructed trends in desert bighorn sheep populations of the area now established as Death Valley National Monument. He postulates population decline between arrival of the first Europeans in 1850 and approximately the time of the monument's establishment in 1933. The decline was attributed in part to alteration of waterholes, introduction of burros, mining activities, and perhaps legal and illegal hunting. He detects some population recovery—burros have been removed and some work has been done on waterhole development. But the population may never be restored to 1850 numbers because the physical facilities and infrastructure of Death Valley have been constructed around the most important waterholes.

Although Mintzmyer (1990) comments that recent evidence indicates improvement in the status of Yellowstone grizzly bears, and that "recovery . . . depends on public support and understanding rather than biological information. We basically know what we need to know," it seems desirable to touch on the subject.

The decline of the bear population in Yellowstone following closure of the garbage dumps on which the animals had been feeding has been widely chronicled (cf. Craighead 1979, Schullery 1980, Chase 1986). A National Academy of Sciences study (Cowan et al. 1974) concluded that the population declined between 1967 and 1973 from a "conservative" 234 to 158 (about one-third). McCullough (1981, 1986) reported evidence of density dependence in the bear population and pointed out that the Craigheads' population projection model had not had this feature programmed into it. And the National Academy report commented, "We believe that the compensatory processes discussed above have resulted in, or will lead to, replacement of bears that were removed from the ecosystem in 1968–73."

However, the evidence shows continued population decline, at least through the mid-1980s. In a January 1983 memorandum, an Ad Hoc Committee for Population Analysis ([Knight et al. 1983a]) of the Interagency Grizzly Bear Steering Committee estimated a minimum 1980 population of 139, and possibly 183–207 when corrected for estimated sighting efficiency. These numbers were based on the observed number of unduplicated females with cubs (UFC) and expanding for observed sex ratio, age composition, and survivorship.

The committee also regressed UFC on time and concluded that "no significant trend is indicated for 1974–1980." However, in a one-page "errata sheet" ([Knight et al. 1983b]) distributed in October 1983, the committee reported that it had erred in its regression, recalculated it, and corrected the conclusion to "a significant downward trend is indicated for 1974–1980."

Hence the post-dump decline reported by Cowan et al. (1974) continued. Applying the Ad Hoc Committee's regression equation to the National Academy's 1973 number of 158 bears suggests a post-closure decline by 1980 of more than 40 percent. Subsequent publications conclude that decline continued for at least several more years (Knight and Eberhardt 1985, 1987, Eberhardt et al. 1986).

Why the compensatory tendencies in the population did not stimulate the recovery that the National Academy report anticipated is not clear. But one possibility is that these tendencies were overridden by the animals' reduced nutritional plain following deprivation of the garbage food source. The animals' body weights and litter sizes declined following closure, and the minimum age of female breeding rose.

Park news releases in the late 1980s and early 1990s reported some population increase. But the currently used population indices are based on casual sightings. Since the bears' visibility varies with annual, weather-related variations in food supply (Gaillard and Wilcox, 1993, C. E. Kay, unpublished manuscript, Mattson and Craighead 1994)—when food is short the bears forage more widely and therefore are more likely to be seen—there is some unease about how well the indices are reflecting population trends. Adding to the unease is the fact that the late 1980s and early 1990s have been a drought period, and the 1988 fires destroyed substantial areas of whitebark pine, an important source of bear food (Mattson and Craighead 1994). On the positive side, Knight and Eberhardt (1985, 1987) comment, on the basis of computer simulation, "that the risk of extirpation over the next 30 years is small if the present population parameters continue to prevail."

Thus, while Mintzmyer (1990) states that there was some recovery in the 1980s, Mattson and Craighead (1994) hold out much less assurance. Amato and Whittmore (1989), writing for the Greater Yellowstone Coalition and paraphrasing Knight and Eberhardt (1987), report that "the current population . . . is teetering between an increasing and decreasing population and . . . this delicate balance can potentially be upset if more than two adult females are killed per year" (p. 20). Economic development proceeds around the outside of Yellowstone, where bears are forced to forage, creating disturbance and impairing food supplies and habitat, and occasioning bear–human interactions, which often result in bear deaths. And Kay (1989) discussed elimination of food and cover vegetation by the large elk population, thereby exacerbating the bears' need to forage more widely.

Little attention has been paid to black bears in Yellowstone. Park numbers on the species have for years been conjecture. The fact that park reports placed black bear numbers at exactly 500 each year from 1962 to 1975, then increased them to exactly 650 each year from 1976 to 1978 (Schullery 1980), reflects the lack of any factual content in these numbers.

While the numbers allege no significant change in the black bear population since the 1930s, the species at one time used park garbage, is affected by many of the same forces that impinge on grizzlies, and may have been influenced by increased aggression or predation from food-deprived grizzlies (Mattson et al. 1992). Black bears are now seldom seen in the park. Craighead (1991) recently commented that "The black bear population is the lowest since scientific records have been kept." Population trends and numbers need to be examined more fully.

There are also significant declines in habitat and landscape diversity. The changes described above for the Yellowstone northern range (Kay 1990a, Chadde and Kay 1991, Kay and Wagner 1992) constitute the disappearance of the entire riparian shrub zone, aspen as a woodland type, and the upland, deciduous-shrub habitat type. As mentioned earlier, Yellowstone biologist Richard Keigley (manuscript submitted 1995) has observed suppression of reproduction in streamside cottonwoods (*Populus angustifolia*) by elk browsing as the northern herd has increased. As the older trees mature and die, the woodland type shown in early photographs is disappearing. He has also observed similar effects in conifers of the northern range with the process hastened in those areas hit by the 1988 fires that killed the mature trees. Hess (1993) describes a similar simplification of the landscape in Rocky Mountain. We infer similar changes in eastern parks under influence of deer browsing as described by Bratton (1979), Mlot (1991), Porter (1991), and Warren (1991).

Kay (1994a) argues that the reduction of beaver numbers in Yellowstone since park formation—attributed to the decline of willow and aspen—has significantly reduced habitat and landscape diversity. Calling beaver a "keystone species," he contends that their actions increase the area of riparian zones and the associated aquatic and riparian biota. Their effect is also to raise the water table in flooded areas, while their decline results in the disappearance of these landscape features and altered hydrology.

The changes are not universal in the System. Numerous parks exhibit striking vegetation recovery: in Big Bend and Shenandoah through protection from commodity use, Sequoia-Kings Canyon and Yosemite through prescribed burning, and Haleakala and Hawaii Volcanoes through removal of exotics. Landscape diversity in the higher elevations of Yellowstone was increased by the 1988–1989 fires. Intact prairie vegetation is being maintained in Wind Cave by prescribed burning and animal-population control.

In Glacier, grizzly bear management has recently been declared to be highly effective. The cutthroat trout population in the Yellowstone River and Lake has been restored through limitation on the sport fishery, which is providing an enhanced food resource for park grizzlies. More than a dozen parks and monuments—including Acadia, Shenandoah, Isle Royale, Dinosaur, Rocky Mountain, and Yosemite—are restoring peregrine falcons through hacking (Anon. n.d.). Captive-reared red wolves have been released on Gulf Island National Seashore, and release of grey wolves in Yellowstone appears imminent as this is written.

But there are numerous cases of declining diversity, and additional examples will be cited in the next chapter.

Concluding Comments

We offer the above examples as value-neutral descriptions of changes, as best we can evaluate the evidence available to us within the time constraints of this study. As we commented at the beginning of this chapter, whether or not these changes should be considered problems depends on whether or not they are contributing to achievement of System and park goals based on public values.

We conclude that the changes reviewed in this chapter are taking the natural resources of numerous parks away from the long-standing goal of preserving "intact" or "healthy" ecosystems. This is occurring in numerous eastern parks; in Everglades and Great Smoky; in Yellowstone, Grand Teton, and Rocky Mountain; and probably in others. Moreover, the resources in a number of these parks are diverging from the newer System goals of preserving biodiversity and protecting T and E species.

In these senses, there are significant problems in a substantial number of parks, many of them the flagships of the System. In the next three chapters we will enumerate these problems and attempt to identify the constraints operating on the System that prevent goal attainment.

4

Constraints on Attainment of Natural-Resources Goals

Introduction

The National Park System, drawing over 300 million visitations each year, holds enormous cultural and educational value for the American people. It is also an international asset. The parks have become major stopping points for foreign tour groups. Languages from all over the world can be heard in park facilities, and multilingual menus and signs appear.

There is no significant disagreement in any quarter over the merit of the System's general natural-resources goals that we inferred in Chapter 2: preservation of "natural" or "intact" ecosystems (both in the parks and in those areas of other units that have ecological resources), biodiversity, and T and E species, and of natural settings in historic sites attempting to recreate images of past events. Indeed, Freemuth (1989) comments that the Park Service has the highest public-approval rating of any of the federal resource-management agencies.

However, we have seen that the condition of the resources in numerous parks is diverging from System goals. In essence, the values of this asset are in decline in many areas.

At the beginning of Chapter 2 we listed four contingencies that determine whether or not the National Park Service succeeds in its ultimate charge of satisfying social values. Regarding the first, we have concluded that System goals generally address the values, although in Chapter 7 we will discuss the problem that lack of goal specificity poses for clear direction of individual park policies and management programs. In Chapter 2 we concluded in our second contingency that policies faithfully address goals at the System level but fall short at the park level. How clearly policies prescribe appropriate management programs, contingency 3, will be addressed in part in this chapter, in part in the next two chapters. And we will also address contingency 4 in this chapter: how effectively management programs carry out policy directives. A complex of constraints and pressures operates on both policies and management, deterring goal attainment.

Constraints of External Threats

Much has been written in recent years about forces that operate on parks from outside their boundaries. The Park Service is powerless to fend off many of these, in which case mitigation policies and programs may be the only means for goal attainment. In other cases the only approach may be new organizational arrangements and even legislation.

Broad-Scale Environmental Impacts

There is a common impression, encountered both outside and inside NPS, that the parks are isolated, pristine islands surrounded by a sea of economic development and environmental degradation. In fact, even the largest parks exist in more extensive ecosystems in which park boundaries have no ecological reality. Mobile park animals move across those boundaries to interact with outside environments, and an array of environmental forces arising outside the parks transcends the boundaries to impact the systems within.

Among the most pervasive forces are air-pollution effects. The risk of damage from ozone and acid deposition to ecosystems in the arid and semiarid West is generally considered to be low because of the sparse human population and generation of acid precursors, compared with the eastern United States, and because of the buffering capacity of highly basic western soils. However, a 1988 workshop (Mangis et al. 1988) reported that contaminants in western parks and monuments near the more populous areas (e.g., Joshua Tree and Saguaro National Monuments) were above background levels. Some desert plant species are sensitive to air pollutants, and foliar damage was reported in some shrub and tree species. Lichen damage has been observed in a number of areas, and concern was expressed for cryptogamic soil crusts so important in desert ecosystems. Vulnerability of aquatic systems, especially ephemeral pools, was also examined.

Armentano and Loucks (1983) evaluated air-pollution threats to ten national parks, monuments, and lakeshores between northern Minnesota and the southern shore of Lake Erie. They concluded that pollutant output from the midwestern industrial complex and large, coal-burning power plants in the Ohio River Valley "show evidence of significantly threatening the resource qualities protected in these parks." That evidence includes premature loss of foliage from the most sensitive coniferous tree species, reduced visibility during high sulphate periods, and increased acidity of sensitive streams and lakes during spring snowmelt.

Changes occurring in Great Smoky Mountains National Park suggest only one of what must be a myriad of indirect interactions between air pollution and other ecosystem components. Watershed measurements in the park have shown a rise in nitrate concentrations in stream runoffs in recent years (H. Van Miegroet, personal communication, October 18, 1992), and soil studies over the past 50 years have shown a rise in soil acidity in some areas (Joslin et al. 1992).

Coincident with these changes has been a deterioration in canopy cover and loss of foliage in red spruce at the higher elevations. More extreme has been the sweeping mortality of Fraser fir at all elevations in Great Smoky (Samuel B. McLaughlin, personal communication, April 27, 1993). A 1988 U.S. Department of Agriculture Forest Service report concluded that 91 percent of the firs larger than five inches in diameter at all elevations in the park were dead. Mortality has continued since the report, and hence very nearly all of the mature trees must be dead as this is written (Samuel B. McLaughlin, personal communication, April 27, 1993).

Research by Oak Ridge National Laboratory biologists showed tree-ring growth declines in red spruce beginning in the 1960s, and decline in the calcium–aluminum balance in the wood chemistry (Joslin et al. 1992, Van Miegroet et al. 1993). Calcium is important in trees' respiration and has been shown to be leached out of the soil by acid precipitation. Amendment of soils with calcium and magnesium in greenhouse plantings of young spruces improves their vigor, and calcium amendment to soils around free-growing saplings increases calcium content of needles (Van Miegroet et al. 1993).

Research has also shown that the Fraser firs are attacked by a small, exotic, aphid-like insect, the balsam wooly adelgid. Inserting a stylus through the bark, the adelgids suck the trees' sap, which blocks water transport by the stems. A current hypothesis suggests that the trees have been rendered more vulnerable to the adelgid (i.e., are less able to chemically defend against them) because they have been weakened by acid precipitation. The result is the virtual elimination from the forest of the mature trees in a codominant tree species.

These are but a few of the situations with which NPS must cope. From visibility impairment in Colorado Plateau parks due to effluent from the Navajo Power Plant (Freemuth 1991), impacts on the coastal ecosystem of Kenai Fjords National Park from the *Exxon Valdez* oil spill, to the almost certainly ubiquitous but largely unpredictable effects of global warming, no parks escape these problems. Thus, no parks are true islands in an ecological sense despite Freemuth's (1991) metaphor. As Sax and Keiter (1987) put it, "modern environmental knowledge and concerns increasingly reveal conventional borders to be dangerous irrelevancies, mocked by acid rain and the perils that confront migratory wildlife."

Human Actions on Adjacent Lands, Private and Public

One set of external pressures that complicates the parks' efforts at managing their natural resources is outside economic developments that impact park biotas. Some of these developments occur on private lands adjacent to parks or near enough to affect them. The prototypical case is the Everglades problem discussed earlier. The park is situated in the southern tip of a huge hydrologic system that drains a large portion of southern Florida. The water flow of that system is essential to the functioning of the ecological subsystems within park boundaries. The southern Florida hydrology has been profoundly altered to divert most of the water to extensive and lucrative agricultural areas of that part of the state and to the Greater Miami megalopolis.

Urban expansion around, and up to the boundaries of, eastern parks (e.g., Acadia) and historic sites complicates a number of natural-resources problems, including control of white-tailed deer populations. Expansion of the town of Estes Park, Colorado, along the boundaries of Rocky Mountain National Park is causing an analogous problem of elk control in that park. Urban expansion around both units of Saguaro National Monument threatens to block necessary population interchange by deer and peccary between the two units.

A religious sect, the Church Universal and Triumphant, has

acquired a large tract of land in the Yellowstone River Valley adjacent to the northern border of Yellowstone Park to develop a farming and ranching community. In addition to fencing, which influences ungulate movements, the church has considered developing geothermal resources on its property. There is great fear that this would affect the underground hydrology of the park and alter its geothermal features. On the other hand, there are some positive developments. The Montana Department of Fish, Wildlife, and Parks and the Rocky Mountain Elk Foundation are aggressively buying land north of the park to expand winter elk habitat.

Sax and Keiter (1987) describe the natural-resources management tensions between Glacier National Park and the adjoining Blackfeet Indian Reservation. Concerns from the perspective of park managers include reservation cattle that wander into the park and compete with wildlife for forage, and the Blackfeet encouragement of oil and gas development, with its attendant disturbance of wildlife, near the park boundary. From the Blackfeet perspective, the park lands are part of their traditional tribal domain. They claim use rights under an 1896 agreement with the U.S. government. According to park senior scientist Clifford Martinka (personal communication, August 24, 1993), although efforts have been made to achieve some rapport, tensions still exist due to the differing perspectives of two different cultures.

For the most part, NPS has little power to control development activities on private land outside park borders that threaten park wildlife. Coggins (1987) concludes that "present NPS power is wholly inadequate to combat the ever broader range of threats to park resources, including wildlife. If the Park Service is to lead such an effort effectively, legislative authorization must first be forthcoming."

More attention has been directed to threatening land-use actions on adjacent public lands, both because the administrative potential should exist to arrive at intragovernmental solutions and because so many of the western parks are surrounded by public lands, where so many problems arise. However, the record to date gives little optimism for many effective solutions in this class of problems.

Sax and Keiter (1987) analyzed the "federal interagency relations" surrounding Glacier National Park, much of whose boundary is adjacent to remote wilderness terrain in two national forests. This terrain, together with the park, forms a larger ecosystem for wide-ranging park wildlife requiring freedom from human disturbance (e.g., elk, grizzly bear, timber wolves).

The adjacent national forests also have rich timber resources and likely oil and gas deposits, and park officials consider logging, energy exploration, and road construction around the peripheries to be serious threats to wildlife. Park officials negotiated with the two forest supervisors in an effort to gain some consideration for park wildlife in the national forest plans. One supervisor expressed some interest in coordinating forest programs with the park's management goals for their mutual benefit. But in essence, he was accommodating on "low stakes" issues while avoiding commitments on highly valued, commodity resources. In the other forest, the supervisor showed little concern for park problems and was determined to press forward aggressively with what he considered to be his responsibility in developing the energy resources. Here again, recent efforts at achieving mutual understanding have been partially successful, but differences in philosophy remain.

A number of authors (Schneebeck 1986, Keiter 1989, Clark et al. 1991, Clark and Minta 1994, Primm and Clark n.d., Mattson and Craighead 1994) explore the same issues surrounding Yellowstone. The problems are much the same, with the regional ecosystem defined in terms of the home ranges of its grizzly bears, bald eagles, and elk, extending beyond the margins of the park into adjacent national forests, Teton National Park, the National Elk Refuge, and private and state land. Over much of this area the predominant land-use goals are such extractive industries as mining, timber production, livestock grazing, and urban development, most of which are detrimental to varying components of the ecosystem. Ongoing efforts to coordinate activities require action at the ecosystem level and need to be intensified in order to be fully effective.

During the 1960s, a number of coordinating and information-exchange committees were formed to facilitate regional approaches to wildlife-management problems. Keiter infers that there is "an emerging 'common law' of ecosystem management" to which the agencies have given de facto recognition. But he concludes that:

> Whether the agencies—given their divergent management principles and the strong passions of their constituent groups—are capable institutionally of transcending the boundary mentality to articulate a regional vision that fully integrates ecological imperatives with individual human interests remains uncertain. Moreover, whether the agencies can overcome their traditional preoccupation with managerial discretion to establish meaningful ecosystem-based management standards remains unclear.

One indication of the agencies' difficulties with transcending the boundary mentality may be shown by the recent effort at agreeing to a "regional vision." This was the Vision for the Future initiative directed out of the NPS Rocky Mountain Regional Office and entered into by the supervisors of six national forests, three regional foresters of the Forest Service, two national park superintendents (Teton and Yellowstone), and NPS regional director Lorraine Mintzmyer. A draft document was issued that received a cool reception in the White House, according to Goldstein (1992) and an account given us by Rocky Mountain regional chief scientist Dan Huff. In the White House view, the balance between commodity use and preservation in the Yellowstone ecosystem was tilted too strongly to the latter. The document had to be revised.

Steven Whitney, director of The Wilderness Society's national parks program, testified before the House Subcommittee on National Parks and Public Lands in 1989 about external-threat problems around several parks. He expressed concerns about what effect logging and road construction around the boundaries of Olympic National Park will have on the well-being of Roosevelt elk, bears, mountain lions, fishers, and spotted owls. Logging in six national forests around Great Smoky is cause for concern about that park's wildlife as well. Over objections of NPS, EPA, and the Fish and Wildlife Service, the Bureau of Land Management (BLM) approved development of a cyanide-leach gold mine within seven miles of Death Valley National Monument. The mine will require huge amounts of water that is thought to feed springs in the monument that sustain bighorn sheep and endangered desert pupfish.

There are numerous other cases of difficulties in reaching interagency accord to benefit park resources. Freemuth (1991) discusses differences between NPS and BLM over tar-sands development in the Glen Canyon National Recreation Area, a dispute on which Secretary of Interior Hodell would not render a decision within his own department. The common thread through all of these is the difficulty of arriving at political and land-use compromises among interest groups that hold conflicting land-use values and missions.

One final example illustrating how profoundly a park ecosystem can be changed by developments outside the boundaries has been described for us by Grand Canyon National Park biologist Larry Stevens (personal communication, February 5, 1992). Construction of Glen Canyon Dam on the Colorado River encouraged downstream buildup of rainbow and brown trout, which spawn in tributary streams feeding the Grand Canyon. Because these fish have attracted wintering bald eagles, the canyon now holds one-fourth of the southwestern U.S. wintering population of eagles.

The altered hydrology has produced environments that facilitate increases in chironomid midge populations, which have attracted larger resident numbers of swifts and swallows. The latter have attracted an increase in peregrine falcon populations, which are peripherally preying on other avian species.

Dam construction has damped seasonal variations in river flow. Before impoundment, sharp, seasonal variations each year scoured out the canyon and limited development of riverine vegetation; and the sediment load deposited a shifting network of sandbars. Now with a muted range of flows and no sediment load, an abundant riverine habitat and associated enriched avifauna have formed. But now that the river no longer has its fringe of sandbars, the numbers of some avian aquatic species may have been reduced.

Prior to impoundment the meager riparian zone provided enough habitat for the southwestern subspecies of willow flycatcher, and the birds were common along the Green and Colorado Rivers. Today, the altered river flow has allowed formation of more habitat, but flycatchers are still scarce and being considered for T and E listing. It is not clear what all of the factors contributing to the birds' scarcity are, but one major one appears to be large increases in parasitism by brown-headed cowbirds, which have greatly increased their numbers to take advantage of the expanded riverine habitat and associated avifauna.

As though all of that were not enough, the Arizona Department of Fish and Game introduced desert bighorn sheep near the park. The sheep have now extended their range into the park and are grazing on pristine vegetation that, according to archaeological investigation, has not been used by sheep for approximately 1,000 years.

Structural Features of the National Park System

If external threats pose serious constraints on natural–resources goal attainment, certain built–in characteristics of the System are equally or more problematic. A number of reviews have pointed out these effects, and we have encountered them in the course of our studies.

Founding Mechanisms and Resulting Balkanization

Yellowstone (established in 1872 as the first park in the System), Sequoia, General Grant (later Kings Canyon), Yosemite, Mount Rainier, and other flagship parks were established by separate acts of Congress prior to passage of the Organic Act of 1916, which created the National Park Service. Since passage of the Organic Act, Congress has retained the prerogative of establishing new national parks.

The Antiquities Act of 1906 gave the president authority "to proclaim and reserve 'historic landmarks, historic and prehistoric structures, and other objects of historic or scientific interest' on lands owned or controlled by the United States as 'national monuments'" (Mackintosh 1991:13). Between 1906 and 1978, 12 presidents established 99 national monuments under this act. Many of the monuments, such as Grand Canyon and Grand Teton, were later converted to parks. Others were subsequently added to existing parks. Thus, as Mackintosh's excellent history of the System points out, nearly a third of the National Park System was established under this provision of the act.

Establishment of Grand Teton National Monument by President Roosevelt in 1943 aroused considerable Congressional ire over the Executive Branch prerogative of setting aside land, and only five monuments were authorized between 1943 and 1978. After 11 more were established in 1978, largely in Alaska, the presidents have deferred to Congress any further additions to the System (Mackintosh 1991).

This history is outlined here to emphasize the primary role of Congress in establishing the parks and most of the monuments, and how the mechanism influences formulation and execution of policies. Foresta (1987) has contrasted this political procedure with the more measured, professional, executive process in Canada for adding units. Mackintosh (1991:107) discusses the ease with which legislators' proposals for new parks pass through Congress.

Once established, the parks and monuments become part of a senator's or congressman's state or district, and proprietary relationships commonly develop (Frome 1992). Commercial interests and gateway communities that develop around a park, concessionaires within, and the local public's attachment to it become important constituencies for the legislators. And the fact that many of the superintendents are expected to submit to the will of the respective members of Congress may influence their actions more than the Service's administrative structure, dilute their responsiveness to Service policies, and virtually make them autonomous administrators over independent System units. In our contacts with persons both inside and outside NPS, we have repeatedly heard superintendents referred to as sovereigns of various kinds.

The end result produces the most decentralized agency among the federal land-managing bureaus and sets up a balkanized system of decision making that frequently contravenes centralized, agency policy structure. According to Carol Aten, chief of the NPS Office of Policy Development in Washington (personal communication, July 17, 1992), "at the park level there is no System view." And Larry Stevens, biologist at Grand Canyon, described (February 5, 1992) the independence of the parks and the lack of communication between them.

This decentralization has both positive and negative consequences for resource management. On the positive side, the superintendents justify their independence on the grounds that every park is different, and each needs its own specialized program to address its unique management and political problems. Indeed, problems arise that need prompt attention by individuals on the spot who are familiar with the details and circumstances. And in defense of the superintendents—we have met many very capable ones deeply committed to NPS goals—theirs is the extremely complex task of managing the parks for the flow of millions of tourists each year, along with the associated subsistence, educational, medical, traffic, and law-enforcement problems that this entails. Their responsibilities approach those of mayors and governors. As we will discuss in Chapter 5, their task is something of a difficult tightrope walk between discharging these responsibilities while maintaining some degree of equanimity with their local Congressional surrogate masters.

On the negative side, the decentralized structure of NPS and associated autonomy of parks and their superintendents influence the quality of resource management in a number of ways. One is that management policies may be set "ad hoc" (Pring 1987) at the park level, ignoring System policies. We quoted Rockwood (1988) in Chapter 2 describing the parks as "autonomous sub-units" that have limited communication with the regional and Washington offices.

One result of the decentralization, according to Foresta (1984), is that NPS has lost control of policy. Another result, reported by a number of our contacts, is that without firm backup and recourse to strong systemwide policies, parks are more vulnerable to the local pressures we described earlier and decisions contrary to the welfare of the resources.

The balkanization, along with the myriad of pressures applied to the parks, produces a high degree of park and agency insularity. Sax and Keiter (1987), referring to the "notoriously insular agency," found this to be a deterrent to the interagency negotiations needed to address the external-threats problem. Pring (1987) noted "The failure to look outward. . . . [T]he ostrich approach."

We have encountered this insularity in our own interactions with park personnel, and it has been pointed out to us by a number of our interviewees. One NPS employee told us about a Yellowstone biologist who was unwilling to step outside the park boundary to examine aspen and riparian zones, which were not subjected to the elk pressures sustained inside the park. Comparisons of vegetation inside and outside the park would have broadened his perspective for the inferences he was drawing about the park vegetation. A Forest Service official told us of attending a Park Service conference in Florida in 1989 in which an NPS employee commented that birds migrating north from Central America in spring stop off in the Everglades and then are forced to fly all the way to Great Smoky for the next stop. The implication was that there were no stopping areas but the parks, and no sense of intervening rural wooded areas, national forests, state parks, etc.

One result of this insularity is that there is insufficient communication and exchange of information on management programs between the parks. We have been told this by a number of NPS employees and have encountered it ourselves. For example, Saratoga and Gettysburg once had deer studies under way at the same time, yet neither was aware of the other's projects.

Balkanization and Vulnerability to Political Pressures

Wright (1992a) discusses at some length his view that the balkanized structure of the System renders the individual parks vulnerable to a variety of political pressures. He refers (p. 181) to "situational decision making," which has the effect of making it

> extremely difficult to undertake controversial management programs. Political factors rather than formalized rules and procedures are generally the key elements considered before a specific management action is implemented. . . . In the final analysis, the process contributes

to a strong desire to avoid situations that might cause problems. The lack of reliance on precedents and procedures also contributes to inconsistencies in policy and management between parks, making legal challenges to administrative actions possible.

We have observed numerous examples of such pressures.

Gateway Communities and Businesses. Tourists provide gateway communities, through which they enter and leave parks, important, sometimes the major, economic sustenance. Hence these communities have a strong vested interest in management actions in the parks. Private businesses around the fringes of parks may also be affected economically by park management. Because of their strong vested interests, these towns and businesses often exert political pressures on park management.

A much publicized case of gateway-community influence is the Fishing Bridge campground incident in Yellowstone (Chase 1986, Keiter 1989). The campground on Yellowstone Lake is situated in prime grizzly bear habitat. As a result, the associated human activities to some degree deter bear use of the area while at the same time encouraging unwanted human–bear confrontations. Park officials decided in the 1970s to close out the campground by 1985 in the interests of grizzly bear management. But business interests in Cody, Wyoming, outside the eastern entrance to the park feared that campground closure would reduce tourist flow through their town. With assistance from the Wyoming Congressional delegation, pressure was applied to the NPS, resulting in a compromise that retained part of the campground.

Keiter (1989) concludes, "Indeed, the Park Service has not consistently followed a strict natural process management approach. Nor, as the recent Fishing Bridge campground controversy proved, is it clear that Yellowstone officials can implement a management philosophy dominated by an exclusive concern for nature."

An example of pressures brought to bear by a local business (W. F. Porter, personal communication, August 30, 1993) is the case of a man who owned a peninsula of land extending into Saratoga National Historical Park. The man became concerned over his inability to grow crops in the area because of large deer numbers dispersing out of the park into his fields. He convinced his local congressman to prevail on NPS to reduce the herd. Although the agency declined to do so without an environmental impact statement, it did allocate a large sum of money for an extramural research project to investigate the nature and magnitude of the problem.

Another example of political pressure by a vested interest is the influence that the livestock industry exerts directly and through its Congressional delegations on park formation and management. As new parks are formed and existing ones are expanded in areas where ranchers are grazing livestock, continuation of grazing use may be grandfathered into the enabling legislation establishing the park. That grazing may damage park biota. This was the case with the new Great Basin and Canyonlands National Parks and with the expansion of Capitol Reef National Park. Elsewhere, livestock interests have long opposed some aspects of grizzly management in the Greater Yellowstone Ecosystem and currently are opposing reestablishment of wolves in the park.

Park Concessionaires. A second category of pressure groups, whose influence Frome (1992) discusses at considerable length, is the park concessionaires. These interests enlist the help of local Congressional delegations to press superintendents to make decisions that often are detrimental to park resources. We have encountered several during the course of our study and will give two examples.

One currently disputed issue involves tourism management in Katmai National Park. The park was established initially to protect brown bears, of which it has the highest density anywhere in the world. Within the park's resource-management plan, bear management is accorded top priority among the resource-management programs.

A fall salmon run up the Brooks River, which flows through the park, attracts large concentrations of bears accumulating important fat reserves for winter hibernation. The major tourist-management effort by the park is facilitating bear viewing near the river. Research by bear behavioral ecologist Barrie Gilbert and graduate student Tammy Olson has shown that human presence both delays the autumnal dates on which bears begin feeding on the stream and shortens their fishing time—in the case of nonhabituated females with cubs, by 93 percent. Gilbert and Olson surmise that this could be detrimental to bear survival, especially the cubs, and to the females' subsequent reproduction (Olson et al. 1995).

The Sierra Club Alaska office reports (Anon. 1991b) that, in an effort to enhance tourist flow, Senator Ted Stevens (R-Ark.) pressured the park into building an inappropriately situated bear-viewing platform and extending the tourist season and the concessionaires' services in the park to a later fall closing date. The park currently places no limits on the number of people allowed into the viewing area, which has been growing in popularity, and has no plans in place for regulating this flow. By contrast, the Alaska Department of Fish and Game, which operates a similar bear-viewing platform at its McNeil Falls State Game Sanctuary, rigidly controls tourist flow, allowing only one-tenth of the applicants in by lottery. Thus a state department, with a major mandate to administer fishing and hunting, is doing a better job of protecting the bear resource than the agency vested with a purely protection mandate.

The second example of catering to concessionaires at the expense of resources involves Everglades National Park. Biologist John Ogden told us at the time of our 1992 visit that the park was not enforcing boating speed limits, enacted for the protection of manatee, in the Florida Bay area. A major source of manatee mortality is severe laceration of the animals by the screws of high-speed boats passing above. Boating concessions sailing out of Flamingo at the southern tip of the park cater to fishermen using the bay.

Hunting Interests. Allan O'Connell, chief of the Division of Science and Natural Resources in Acadia National Park, told us of difficulties encountered in controlling deer populations. At one point the state department of fish and game threatened to take NPS to court if the park assigned rangers to cull deer rather than allow public hunting. Frome (1992:107–108) recounts the plight of a Great Smoky Mountains superintendent, whose predecessor had provided a number of special favors for a small group of local, "politically privileged North Carolinians." The new superintendent moved to terminate these favors and hired professional shooters to eradicate wild boars, which local hunters had been hunting in and around the park. The hue and cry over these actions eventually got the superintendent transferred.

Yellowstone is the prototype for this category of political forces, the hunting interests, and is particularly noteworthy because its responses eventually became de facto System policy. As Chase (1986) describes, the park's efforts at controlling the elk herd in the 1960s were opposed by hunters, who wanted to do the culling themselves, and by outfitters and guides, whose livelihood from guiding hunters around the park boundary to shoot exiting elk was sagging because of low client success. These groups sought the help of the Wyoming Congressional delegation. The March 1967 hearings, convened in Casper by Senator Gale McGee, then a member of the Senate Appropriations Subcommittee which funded NPS, and the senator's innuendo that park funding would be cut if it did not stop culling, are all a matter of public record (U.S. Senate 1967). Although Chase's (1986) allegation that the park stopped culling because of this threat was met with indignation when his book appeared, that motivation is now acknowledged matter-of-factly by persons in or close to NPS (Boyce 1991, Wright 1992a).

As discussed in Chapter 3, this policy reversal was the beginning of the natural-regulation policy that, as Wright (1992a) comments, eventually became System policy. There was no new scientific evidence to support the policy change (Barmore 1968), and as reviewed in Chapter 3 there was considerable skepticism in the scientific community outside the Park Service and some contrary evidence.

As NPS biologist David Stevens has pointed out to us (personal communication, July 7, 1993), Service response to hunting interests was given policy status in the 1960s, when Secretary of Interior Hickel ordered parks to coordinate their wildlife-management actions with the state wildlife agencies. Since that time the states have had significant influence on wildlife management in the parks. Although many of the efforts have been unsuccessful, a number of states still contend that population control in the parks should be carried out by public hunting within the borders.

Animal-Welfare Interests. We have found a number of cases in which animal-welfare groups, our fourth category of pressure groups, interceded in animal-control situations, both native and exotic. NPS allowed a public hunt on Fire Island National Seashore in order to reduce a burgeoning white-tailed deer population. However, the Fund for Animals protested and stopped the reduction. The same organization protested burro control in Bandelier and Grand Canyon and ended up capturing and removing most of the canyon animals itself. There has been similar reaction to Yellowstone bison control as a measure to prevent brucellosis spread to cattle on surrounding lands.

As discussed in Chapter 3, representatives of the Fund have expressed concern over the proposed elimination of mountain goats from Olympic National Park. Aside from opposing on principle the elimination through lethal means, Fund representatives C. S. Anunsen and R. Anunsen (1993) have conducted thorough, in-depth research of records and literature sources on goats in the Olympic Peninsula. Their efforts have pointed up insufficient care and thoroughness in scholarship by Park Service employees and evidently have delayed a park vegetation report promised since 1990 and a draft environmental impact statement promised for 1992.

Environmental Organizations. Foresta (1984) comments at some length on the influence of the environmental movement on Park Service directions. In his view a coalition of environmental organizations has "met periodically in Washington to hammer out common positions on national park matters and to act, as much as possible, as a policy directorate for the National Park System" (p. 71). The result has been to accent "resource preservation and . . . [depress] the importance of visitor access in its park development and planning. . . . Both the idea of a national park as a park and the idea of a park in a democracy seem to have gotten lost, or at least obscured, in debates about the National Park System in recent years" (pp. 127, 268).

It must surely be true that the environmental philosophy, the background of which Foresta analyzes in some detail, has permeated much of the Park Service. And Chase (1986) argues the same point at length, somewhat pejoratively. However, despite this ideological tilt, the reality of Park Service operations is strong testimony to a huge, residual imbalance toward managing for public use. Sudia's (1989, personal communication) assertion that NPS is 90 percent a tourism agency and the Service's budget structure, with only 8 percent of 1993–1994 funding allocated to resource management, are the strongest indicators of the imbalance.

What we do see from some spokespersons of the environmental community are statements advocating no management of any kind in national parks (cf. DeWitt 1989, Boyce 1992b, Willers 1992, Carter 1994, Macfarlane 1994, Wuerthner 1994a,b). These sentiments seem to us to be based on two views or concerns. One is that the term *management* to many in the environmental community is associated with management for consumptive uses of natural resources: wildlife management for hunting and fishing, forest management for timber production, and range management for livestock grazing. Those uses have so altered North American landscapes that only a small fraction of the United States—national parks, wilderness areas, certain other forms of natural areas— remain sufficiently unaltered to allow the emotional and spiritual experiences of "wildness" or "naturalness" that we recognized in Chapter 2 as one of the values of national parks. To engage in management in the parks would, in the view of these individuals, intrude on and dilute those values and, conceivably, be a step in the direction of allowing commodity uses in the parks.

The second view or concern appears to be based on the complexity of ecosystems, the frequently unforeseen and unpredictable results of management efforts, and previous management fiascos. The safest approach, in this view, is to avoid any action.

It is our contention that the NPS policy emphases on naturalness, natural regulation, and nonmanagement in the parks are in part driven by these views held by some members of the environmental community, and their embrace by NPS personnel. In this sense, we agree with Foresta's contention on the influence of the environmental movement.

Political Pressures in Perspective. One of the main themes of this book is that the National Park System belongs to the American people, and it is they who should determine what its goals should be. Those goals should then be converted to policies that prescribe management programs for achieving the goals. Policies are set at different levels of government: Congress and the administrative hierarchy of the Department of Interior and National Park Service.

Goal setting and policy articulation are political processes in a democratic system. Politics is the proper means by which the public makes its values known and translated into goals and policies. The term is in no way used pejoratively here. Moreover, the interest groups that we have discussed are perfectly valid components of American society. As such they are fully entitled to have their wishes heard and considered in the political processes of establishing national park policies.

Thus National Park System policy setting is indeed a political process, and properly so. As Freemuth (1989) quotes Yellowstone superintendent Barbee as saying in connection with the Fishing Bridge incident:

> The political bottom line was underestimated. It's as simple as that. The parks are very much the children of politics. It is naive to think that politics doesn't have an influence on policy. . . . [Compromise over the campground closure is] not something the Park Service would have chosen.

The process malfunctions, however, when one or more of the interest groups exert sufficient pressure to drive ad hoc management decisions that are contrary to established policy, damaging the resources that are the foundation value of the American pub-

lic's asset. And it malfunctions when it renders the agency dys-
functional by threatening jobs of Service employees and preventing
their acting in the best interests of the resources.

As we have seen, a wide range of political pressures is exerted on
resource management in the parks by a variety of groups pursuing
their own agendas. When those pressures are exerted through local
Congressional delegations, they can alter or stop management programs and imperil the tenure of superintendents. Everglades biologist John Ogden told us (personal communication, April 2, 1992)
that a major difficulty with solving his park's resource problems
lies in the rapid turnover of superintendents. The strong ones who
address the problems are soon transferred because of political pressures applied by the local Congressional delegation. When we visited there in April 1992, there was only an acting superintendent
in this, one of the flagship parks in the System, and the scientists
were carrying most of the public-relations and policy activities.

We have been told about one park in which an incoming stream
was being polluted by a nearby town, but the superintendent assid-
uously avoided saying anything to town officials for fear of incur-
ring their displeasure. Frome (1992:129–132) describes an incident
in which the superintendent of Shenandoah National Park
declined to stand up to local citizens who were violating wildlife
laws in the park. Facing the problem of what to do with elk in
Yellowstone, Superintendent Barbee commented in a November 24,
1987, letter to former Assistant Secretary of Interior Nathaniel P.
Reed: "If the current case of experimental management fails, the
next most logical hypothesis to test is the effect of a virtually ungu-
late-free ecosystem. I hope I am employed elsewhere when that
option is chosen."

Whether NPS could successfully stand up to these kinds of pressures is debated in a number of circles. Wright (1992a) comments:
"It seems clear that many of the problems are self-imposed. Park
managers often refrain from imposing policies in the face of opposition from special-interest groups. Even though clear evidence of
biological damage exists, managers are sometimes reluctant to
take action."

Sax and Keiter (1987) were surprised to find that Glacier
National Park did not avail itself of perfectly valid, established
legal procedures to protect park resources against external threats
on surrounding public lands. Nor did it call on a substantial, supportive constituency to help with opposition or search for a "structural solution" to thwart damaging development. "Is Glacier simply
too timid?" Sax and Keiter asked rhetorically. They answered their

own question by concluding that the reason for the reticence was that park officials did not wish in any way to curtail their freedom of action by entering into formal arrangements to address the problems. They seek maximum discretion: "Law is a shackle, only discretion liberates. . . . Glacier is constrained by bureaucratic prudence and timidity."

As the above examples indicate, the pattern extends far beyond Glacier, beyond the mere concern for preserving discretion. It is the manifestation of a deeply risk-averse organization. In fairness, NPS is not alone. All public, land-management agencies in a democracy must chart a course through conflicting public demands. Inevitably some will be heeded while others will be ignored. Navigation was particularly difficult for these bureaus during the highly politicized 1980s and early 1990s, oriented as they were to economic development.

But the bottom line remains: Decisions are often pressured that are detrimental to the natural resources and contrary to park and System goals.

Imbalance in the Dual Mission

A great deal has been written about how the Service's dual and conflicting statutory mission—to preserve the resources while at the same time facilitating their use by the public—affects its operation. The schizophrenia began at the very start of the System's history with the Yellowstone Act ("a pleasuring ground for the benefit and enjoyment of people in order to protect for all times") and the Organic Act ("to conserve . . . and to provide for the enjoyment"). Rockwood (1988) considers this duality to be the major force producing what Foresta (1984) calls a "confusion of purpose."

As we discussed earlier, Sellars (1992, 1993a,b) attributes the early momentum toward the scenery and tourism side of the dichotomy to Director Mather. And that momentum carries to the present, with only 8 percent of the 1993–1994 budget committed to resource management.

If success is measured by number of visitations, the tourism emphasis is clearly successful, with over 300 million visitations per year. But that success incurs a number of problems for the resources that attract the visitors in the first place. One is resource damage by excessive tourist use. Damage to sensitive alpine zones in Rocky Mountain National Park has been described by Hess (1993) and in Glacier National Park by Frome (1992:143–148), who also discusses use damage in Great Smoky. Sellars (1989) describes the chaotic, uncontrolled growth of tourism in Yosemite and its impacts on resources.

Harrison and Dyer (1984) evaluated the effects of lead accumulations from the combustion of leaded gasoline on mule deer foraging adjacent to roadsides in Rocky Mountain. The lead content of deer forage adjacent to roadsides was 30 times greater than similar forages from control areas. The authors estimated that mule deer need consume only 1.4 percent of their total daily forage intake from roadside forages to exceed a safe level of lead intake. Since lead produces significant detrimental effects on learning and behavior, Harrison and Dyer suggested that the high automotive traffic volume in the park might conflict with resource preservation that strives to maintain the park system "in its natural state."

McCutchen (1993) pointed out visitor impacts on black bear populations in the same park. Heavy visitor use in the east side of the park tends to frighten bears away from using habitat in this area. According to McCutchen, the habitat in this high-elevation terrain is already marginal for black bears—as shown by their small body size and low reproductive rate—and to deny them a major segment of habitat places even more pressure on their marginal survival prospects.

On the positive side, Denali, Yosemite, and Zion National Parks have taken a long stride toward resource protection by providing vehicles to transport tourists and control their movements. Yosemite is moving to reduce visitor accommodations in order to reduce tourist impacts on resources.

A second problem posed by the emphasis on heavy tourism is insufficient protection of resources caused by lack of funds. A Department of Interior audit between November 1991 and April 1992 by its Office of Inspector General (Bloom 1992) examined protection of natural resources in 33 units of the System. It concluded that:

> The Park Service did not ensure that known threats to natural resources were addressed or corrected on a timely basis, did not have a complete natural-resources inventory to identify potential threats, and did not have a monitoring program sufficient to assist park managers in managing their natural resources. . . . The deficiencies occurred because the Park Service gave greater priority and emphasis to visitor-related issues and consequently was not able to provide adequate oversight and funding to protect and conserve natural resources. As a result, natural

resources in some parks have deteriorated or have been irreversibly damaged or destroyed, and the Park Service has a backlog of 4,700 projects, with an estimated cost of about $477 million, that need to be completed in order to prevent or mitigate known threats to the parks.

That the Service's dual mission should have been heavily weighted in its early years to visitor use is understandable, given the early directions imparted to it. But the System today continues to reinforce that emphasis, for it is built into the reward system. As one park biologist told us: "In the performance evaluation reports of superintendents, whether or not they address public complaints (like road conditions) and those of congressmen is important. But the public does not have much understanding of resource issues, so there is not much reinforcement for them to do well in resource management." Wright (1992a) points out this same predisposition.

Carol Aten, chief of the NPS Policy Office in Washington, has commented to us that the momentum toward development in the parks is also driven by the empire-building ambitions of superintendents in synergy with the pressures from concessionaires discussed above. Total visitations are a measure of success, a rationale for getting more funds to expand facilities, and a means of expanding constituencies. A proposal to build an aerial tramway to the top of Guadalupe Peak in Guadalupe National Park was argued on the grounds that it would increase park visitations from 60,000 to 500,000 (Sax 1979).

A recent proposal by the superintendent to expand cross-country skiing and snowmobile use in Yellowstone to increase winter visitations raised concerns among biologists that it would further disturb wildlife already under winter stress. Such disturbance has been documented by Cassirer et al. (1992). According to Freemuth (1989), a Yellowstone Park Preservation Council, consisting primarily of park resource specialists, formed to counter what it considered an excessive "pro-development bias" of park management.

A senior NPS scientist wrote us in 1990:

> Park visitors come to parks largely to enjoy themselves— not find fault with the NPS. . . . [W]e don't get a lot of criticism. This should not be interpreted as meaning the NPS is carrying out its mandate. Few people, including many in Congress, seem to remember that the NPS was intended to do things beyond just providing for basic visitor health and welfare.

And NPS historian Richard Sellars (1989) remarked:

> Science has challenged traditional views of park manage-
> ment for more than half a century, yet interest in the
> scenery—the national parks as pretty places to visit—con-
> tinues to dwarf real concerns for the parks' ecological sys-
> tems and the threats they face.

Insufficient Technical Training of NPS Personnel

Much has been written about the lack of or minimal technical
training for rangers, from whose ranks many superintendents and
resource managers rise. Its most general effect, as Chase (1986),
Sellars (1989), and Wright (1992a) point out, is that there is often
insufficient appreciation for the role that science can play in decision making and management. Another result is that animosities
arise between biologists and managers, and between biologists and
rangers. More generally, it does not seem likely to us that an organization lacking very many personnel with advanced knowledge of
ecological systems will develop a broad and pervasive sense of the
values of those resources to the System, of the stresses they are
experiencing and their consequent declines, and what measures
will be needed to stem those declines.

Another effect, in our view, is that personnel without such knowledge do not have a basis for setting quality standards for research
and management of complex systems or for making discriminating
judgments in the employment of new technical personnel. We have
seen cases in which persons were employed for research positions
who did not have the background or credentials for doing the work
they were assigned. We see cases where public-relations personnel
with no scientific training are given the task of writing publications
on complex ecological subjects. Not infrequently, the result is scientifically naive statements.

The agency has emerged from an era when its management horizons were largely administering tourism, and protection was
enough management for resources. These two contingencies
required personnel with a particular set of capabilities to staff the
organization. And they have built and now run a system that is
admired around the world, and to which they are deeply committed
and loyal. But the System's natural resources are now in decline,
and their restoration and protection depend on complex scientific
understanding and management for which many of the agency's
personnel do not have the background.

A Park Service conference in Vail, Colorado, in fall 1991 (Briggle et al. 1992: "The Vail Agenda") gave considerable attention to this issue. It concluded:

> It is also apparent that the resource issues facing parks are too complex to be handled by resource management generalists forced to deal with a multitude of issues and problems. As a result of this problem, parks have a limited ability to: interpret existing information, detect changes resulting from external and internal threats, implement resource management plans, monitor trends in resources, recover from environmental catastrophes, and place resources in their proper ecological, historical or archaeological context.

The Vail agenda followed with the recommendation to:

> Substantially increase the number of National Park Service resource professionals, emphasizing subject matter specialists currently lacking in the agency and the placement of individuals in parks which lack sufficient resource management expertise.

Mattson and Craighead (1994) have also explored the implications of this problem in relation to saving the threatened grizzly bear in Yellowstone.

Discussion

The government's own analyses stress a bewildering array of problems affecting the attainment of natural-resources goals. We mentioned earlier the 1980 NPS report to Congress, which identified 4,345 specific threats to park resources, and the Natural Resources Assessment report, which also identified numerous problems. At the NPS conference in Vail, EPA administrator William Reilly was asked to address the group. He charged that out of 350 units in the System, only 50 superintendents are actively protecting resources. And now we have the 1992 inspector general's audit (Bloom 1992) chiding the superintendents for not protecting the resources.

The problems appear to resolve into five basic difficulties that constrain attainment of natural-resources goals. Obviously a major one, perhaps the most influential, is the field-level political constraints. These produce the balkanization and insularity of parks, which appear to render them more vulnerable to political pressures, result in Wright's situational decision making, and incur deviation from sound System-level policies to nonconforming park-level ones. They also contribute to the imbalance toward tourism, which in turn produces decisions detrimental to the resources.

Somehow the political constraints have to be reduced and superintendents given more freedom, security, and support to protect the resources. The complex of political forces that shackle NPS conjures up an image for us of a giant NPS Gulliver, tethered to the ground by a mesh of political "ligatures" and rendered immobile by a swarm of Lilliputian interest groups. A central aspect of the problem would seem to be the manifestation of a much broader governmental conundrum: the tensions and equities between local/regional and national values. Help will almost certainly have to come from Congress in the form of balancing the desires of local representatives with those of other representatives who are not personally involved. We will suggest another possible measure in Chapter 7.

A second and equally threatening difficulty is environmental threats from the outside. In many cases these are beyond the capability of the Service to prevent and to mitigate. The realities surrounding this matter are that there is no such thing as a "natural" park or an island park. All park ecosystems are being, and have been, altered by a complex of influences, and they are all parts of larger, regional ecosystems. To assume that park ecosystems can be left alone to manage themselves is to be oblivious to ecological reality. The management challenges are to articulate appropriate park goals; to determine whether or not, and to what extent, mitigation is possible; and to devise appropriate policies and management measures to achieve the goals. That achievement will only be possible if accommodations are reached with outside influences. There is no room for insularity.

A third difficulty, vying with the first two for preeminence, is the program imbalance. Resource management is now, and will be increasingly, expensive. The public's resources cannot be adequately protected by relegating them to a minor budget line. And the tourist flow must be controlled in order to prevent further resource damage.

A fourth difficulty is the need for stronger professionalism. The comments in the Vail agenda indicate that the agency is well aware of this problem.

The fifth, to be discussed in the next two chapters, involves science in the agency. In brief at this point, there is not enough of it, it is not of high enough quality, and it is often improperly used in policy and management processes.

There is progress and hope. We detailed at the end of the last chapter numerous cases of improvement in the status of natural resources. What appears to be a strong administrative accomplishment is the Office of Natural Resources *Assessment.* Surveying the problems of the whole System, and calling for design of five-year action programs detailed at System, regional, and park levels may help in bringing the organization together. Completion of *NPS-77* (Anon. 1991a) was a major accomplishment. It may well have the same effect by prompting units of the System to think about common problems and concentrate more on resource issues. It obviously entailed a huge effort.

Moreover, the agency is staffed by a large number of personnel who have the best interests of the System at heart and who have committed their lives to its welfare. Thus there is a large, collective desire, will, and commitment.

The new (mid-1994) administrators of the Department of Interior and Forest Service are determined to dissolve the barriers between and isolation of their agencies and promote common concern and cooperation in the solution of each other's problems. In addition to the intentions of these individuals, the move is being stimulated by the new management paradigm, ecosystem management, to which all of the agencies are subscribing and for which agency boundaries are often irrelevant and deterrents.

There is even optimism. Everglades biologist John Ogden told us, in reference to what seem like insurmountable problems of that park: "We are going to win in the restoration battle. It may take us 15 to 20 years, but we're going to win it."

5

Science Administration for and in the System

Introduction

Reviews of science in the National Park System—e.g., the Leopold study (Leopold et al. 1963), the Robbins report (Ackerman et al. 1963), the Gordon Commission (Bishop et al. 1989), and the 1992 National Research Council (NRC) study (Risser et al. 1992)—have all emphasized that effective management of natural resources requires a scientific understanding of those resources. Ecosystems are too complex to be managed by guess, intuition, superficial day-to-day impression, or rule of thumb. And that understanding can only come from a carefully planned, well-executed research program that is free to seek and report the objective reality of park ecosystems and the effects of ongoing or contemplated management programs on those systems.

The 1992 NRC review (Risser et al. 1992) commented that there have been "a dozen major reviews" of science in the Park Service since the early 1960s. At our first meeting with NPS officials in Washington (November 6, 1989) at the beginning of our study, John Dennis, Science Branch chief in the Wildlife and Vegetation Division, told us that Yellowstone research chief John Varley had found 30 reviews in Service files repeatedly urging the Service to develop a strong, high-quality research program to enlighten policy formation and management programs. Haskell (1993) comments: "We have had every blue-ribbon advisory group, every major national conservation organization, thousands of concerned citizens, and even the Congress tell the USNPS that the agency must get on with the job of building a scientifically credible resource-management capability so that management of parks is driven and supported by sound science." He concludes by quoting the NRC study: " 'unfortunately, these repeated exhortations . . . have gone largely unheeded, even though they are all the more relevant today. . . . ' "

While the progress has been slow and the accomplishment limited, NPS had moved through 1993 to develop a research program. Although Haskell (1993) notes that the impetus was from the ground up rather than strong policy direction from the top down, there has been some progress. At the February 1992 Ecological Society of America and National Park Service workshop, M. Ruggiero reported that the in-house NPS research effort consisted of 91 scientists from a variety of disciplines, and 2 percent of the agency's 1991–1992 budget.

This growth trajectory in the Park Service changed abruptly on October 1, 1993, when the agency's researchers were transferred into the newly formed National Biological Survey (NBS). During the course of our review we gave special attention to the issue of research in the Park Service, and our early drafts of this book devoted considerable space to it. It might seem something of an anachronism to include that material in this book now that the Park Service research program no longer exists as such. However, we believe that some messages emerge from that part of the agency's history that are worth considering for the new NBS program. Hence we review the Park Service science program briefly in this chapter and consider the role and prospects of NBS research in the Service's science need.

Research in the National Park System

Prior to its transfer into the National Biological Survey, research in the Park Service was divided among several weakly coordinated functions. It is not yet entirely clear how research for the parks will be organized in the NBS. That structuring is taking place as this is written.

Pre-NBS Administrative Structure

As the NRC review (Risser et al. 1992) pointed out, research administratively was part of Resource Management: "Because there is no separate research authority, all scientific studies are funded as part of management." As a result, research and resource management competed for funds.

Research and resource management were organized administratively at three levels: Washington office (WASO), the ten regional offices, and in the individual parks (Risser et al. 1992). WASO developed general policies and priorities, but in fact research was planned and directed from the regional offices. "As a result, there is not one science program in the NPS, but ten separate programs, each different in form, function, and effectiveness" (Risser et al. 1992). In some regions, research was in fact directed out of the regional offices by the regional chief scientists while resource management was administered in the parks by the superintendents. In other regions, research and management were both administered by the superintendents who thereby exerted strong influence. As one regional chief scientist told us, "there is no model."

According to the NRC review (Risser et al. 1992), "The absence of a distinct science program hampers research planning, tracking of expenditures, and accountability for results." Regional chief scientist Dan Huff told us that there was not even a single, complete listing or roster of all the research under way in the System. As a result, it was not possible even to determine accurately the amount of money allocated to NPS research.

Hands-on research in the System was carried out by three categories of investigators. The first were NPS scientists who were either assigned to the parks or operated out of research offices like the Water Quality office in Fort Collins, Colorado. In general, only the larger parks had research staffs. Many parks did not have any researchers posted in them. There were two formal research centers based in parks in Indiana Dunes and the Beard Research Center in Everglades. The latter had a staff of around 40 and substantial computer facilities. Presumably these centers are now part of the NBS program.

The second category was personnel attached to the Cooperative Park Study Units (CPSUs) based on university campuses. In early 1992, there were 23 CPSUs (Risser et al. 1992), and these generally reported to the regional chief scientists.

The third category was research carried out on extramural grants and contracts by scientists from academia and from private research firms. In the former group, the research was funded in some cases by NPS, in other cases by grants from other agencies. The extent to which research was conducted by NPS scientists and by extramural investigators varied between parks and probably with the availability of funds. Prior to 1986, most of the Yellowstone research was done in-house. But when Congress appropriated major funding in 1986 to address the question of whether the Yellowstone northern range is overgrazed, a large number of projects were contracted out.

NPS research quality was variable and depended in part on training and research experience of the investigators and administrators. There was excellent science in Everglades, Glacier, and the Sierra Nevada parks. Freemuth (1991) emphasizes the high standards of the air-quality work done in the Colorado Plateau parks. The monitoring and associated research in Channel Islands (Davis et al. 1987) are exemplary and should set the standard for the entire System.

But we observed, and NPS scientists pointed out to us, that in some parks research on complex ecological problems is assigned to personnel with no more than M.S. degrees and limited research experience. In some cases, as Service personnel also commented to us, park research supervisors and regional chief scientists had no more than an M.S. NPS employees in Yellowstone and Alaska reported that field research observations, rather than being made by biologists, were often assigned to temporary or seasonal aides or to volunteers who had no technical background or sense of the discipline, care, and objectivity necessary for scientific research. Moreover, technical publications and reports on complex ecological subjects, and semipopular interpretations of technical materials, in some cases were and still are written and presented orally by individuals with little or no background in the natural sciences.

We encountered numerous criticisms of research planning. One West Coast NPS biologist, who sought us out to relay his impressions, pointed out that "research needs within any park unit are identified in the park's natural-resource management plan. The plan is normally prepared by resource-management specialists lacking research experience and tends to focus on high-profile (heroic) species or species guilds." More often than not, the plans are not subject to internal or external review. The same point was conveyed to us by one CPSU leader. A 1989 audit by a Department of Interior assistant inspector general for audits (Bloom 1989) found that no study plans had been prepared for 23 of 41 research projects in Yellowstone. Plans for the remaining 18 were "deficient with respect to content." One park biologist commented on the "tyranny of charismatic megafauna" and scarce attention to whole-ecosystem questions and perspectives.

Although Service policy has recently prescribed that publication in peer-reviewed journals is expected and a basis for advancement, productivity is still low. On a poster at the 1989 Ecological Society of America meetings, University of Idaho CPSU leader

Gerald Wright reported that of 8,000 research projects on which he checked the history, only a small fraction resulted in publication. One NPS scientist and another CPSU leader commented that most research ends up in "gray literature" (internal reports and technical summaries), largely not peer reviewed. The 1989 inspector general's audit criticized Everglades and Glacier for inadequate publication, the results from some studies dating back to 1960 not yet seeing the light of day.

In fairness to the scientists, in many parks they were spread too thinly over the research needs and often were assigned to a variety of nonresearch management, administrative, and public-relations tasks. In April 1992, Everglades biologist John Ogden told us that Research Chief Michael Soukup had spent virtually all of his time for the past three years in litigation on water-quality inflow into the park. When asked in 1989 how much time he spent on public relations and political matters, Yellowstone research chief John Varley replied, "about two-thirds."

At a 1990 meeting of NPS personnel with members of the NRC committee and members of our committee at the Ecological Society of America annual meeting, agency scientists pointed out that some parks only had a single biologist who was assigned to address the full range of ecological problems—aquatic, vegetation, vertebrates, insects—which extended well beyond his/her educational background and research experience. Isolation was a related problem, many of these individuals spending their time in remote parks isolated from other ecologists, adequate library resources, and in general the mainstream of science.

Science, an Uneasy Stepchild

The NRC committee concentrated on the quality of science in the agency. But the problems surrounding the role of science in the System extend considerably beyond the issue of scientific quality to the question of what role science does and should play in the policy process.

High quality, though an essential ingredient in a science program intended to serve the formulation of well-conceived policies and management programs effectively, alone is not sufficient. The System must be committed to an open, objective research program in which investigators are free to pursue truth uninfluenced by the policy and bureaucratic predispositions of the organization. And furthermore, the System must be willing to consider research results openly and objectively in the course of policy formulation.

In saying this, we are not suggesting that policy should be based solely on scientific evidence and recommendations by researchers (cf. Wagner 1989b). Scientific evidence is but one of the several influences that shape policy. Of necessity, policy may at times be contrary to research recommendations for political, economic, organizational, or other reasons. But free and unbiased science is essential for accurate portrayal of the consequences of policy alternatives and for truly enlightened decision making. Hence we consider it useful to go beyond the NRC's concern for scientific quality in NPS to examine the administrative environment in which science operates in the agency.

As we discussed in the last chapter, much has been written about how science does not fare better in the System because the original and continuing purposes of the organization did not foster an understanding of what science could contribute to management and most of the personnel employed have not had that understanding. The NRC report makes these points as does NPS historian Sellars (1989, personal communication, March 22, 1990). And University of Idaho CPSU leader Wright (1992a:179) comments: "Real reform in the NPS science program can only occur by changing the ways the agency thinks about the role of science. This implies a long-term evolving process requiring the placement of more individuals trained in the sciences in key management positions."

Given the traditions and backgrounds of personnel in the organization, the resulting climate for research in parks depends very much on personnel in each, particularly the superintendents. Former superintendent Roland Wauer of Big Bend created a very hospitable climate for extramural researchers in that park, and the current superintendent, Robert Arnberger, has continued this tradition; Yellowstone has had a vastly increased research program since 1986; Glacier formed an advisory science council comprised of non-NPS scientists; and Everglades has developed excellent rapport with the Corps of Engineers in addressing the park's hydrologic problems.

But we have received numerous complaints from both NPS and extramural investigators over the difficulties of conducting research in some parks. One was the insecurity of funding. Funds earmarked for research were diverted to other uses considered to be of higher priority. In Saratoga and Acadia, money allocated for resource monitoring was diverted to interpretation and other functions. In another park, $10,000 of $15,000 granted for research to an NPS scientist by a foundation was taken by the superintendent for other purposes. We have had a number of concerns expressed by NPS scientists over the lack of long-term stability in research funding, abrupt changes having been made almost on a year-by-year basis.

Another difficulty is the tensions or outright belligerence that develops in some parks between administrative or ranger personnel who do not have a background in science and extramural and NPS researchers. A highly respected ecologist at one Intermountain university told us of unwillingness in Capitol Reef to cooperate in extramural research. Another faculty member at a Midwest university who has worked with NPS for a number of years in several capacities wrote of one case in which a superintendent refused to move a park biologist into research grade because the biologist would then have a higher GS rating than the superintendent. In another park a superintendent and a biologist, both with the same GS rating, had difficulty working together until the superintendent was promoted to a higher rating. One NPS scientist wrote us, "When I first began working in the Park Service I was amazed by the distrust of science and scientists inherent in many park managers."

In some cases, rangers impose constraints on research activities that hamper effective investigation. In one park, the chief ranger established a policy that only rangers could immobilize animals for research purposes, not the biologists. In another, the rangers' permission was required to set up exclosures, and it was granted only with some difficulty. The 1989 U.S. Department of Interior inspector general's audit (Bloom 1989) chided Glacier for prohibiting researchers from attaching neck collars on grizzly bears. The report considered the risks of bear–human encounters to be of such great concern that these kinds of impediments should not be placed in the way of getting more effective research information.

However, these strictures on research go beyond park personalities to being systemic in the Service. The 1988 *Management Policies* document (Anon. 1988a) stipulates that "Manipulative or destructive research activities generally will not be permitted within a park." In an era when experimentation is routinely considered essential to effective ecological research, and some granting agencies will not even consider research proposals that do not have an experimental component, this prohibition places an a priori hobble on investigations in the parks.

While the lack of a strong science tradition and the prevalence of personnel who do not come from a background stressing the values of science to policy formation and management contribute significantly to the uneasy atmosphere in which science operates in NPS, the problem is much deeper although evidently similar to that encountered in other agencies. From its inception, NPS has had to set policies and initiate management programs in order to address its mandate, whether or not it has had an information base to inform these actions. As science was first brought into the System it was, in the view of some observers, expected to support existing policy. Rockwood (1988:53) comments, "A theme has emerged within most, if not all, of the research done on the National Park Service that Park Service personnel are committed to the agency and its purpose." And Chase (1987) comments:

> Government research in the national parks, the Service decided, would be "mission-oriented." That was interpreted to mean that the role of scientists was to provide "service to the superintendents." Scientists in the major national parks reported to the superintendents, were graded by the superintendents, could only do research approved by the superintendents, and had every incentive to publish only those findings that pleased the superintendents.

We have been told by two different individuals of two instances (one is in correspondence) in which a park biologist commented negatively on proposed research because it might challenge existing policy.

When newer research enters the picture a posteriori and, operating under proper standards of objectivity, finds that policies and management that have been in place and advocated publicly for a long period are for whatever reason unwise or inappropriate, science assumes an adversarial position. Administrators are placed in a position of having made erroneous public statements and/or having practiced faulty management. If, in addition, alternative policies and management implied by the new findings are likely to arouse public animosity or buck the tide of political forces, administrators are placed in particularly dangerous positions and science definitely becomes the unwanted stepchild. Wright (1992a:191) quotes a former superintendent of Olympic as saying, when a new biologist was assigned to his park, "don't get me in trouble."

We have seen two types of responses to these science–policy confrontations. One is belligerence toward research and, at the extreme, attempts to abolish it. One ecologist at a midwestern university found officials at Isle Royale lukewarm almost to the point of belligerence. They refused him permission to do any experimentation, in his view out of fear that it would show something contrary to policy, and were considering removal of his moose exclosures. He commented, "They have made up their minds on what is happening." An NPS scientist in one park told us of a threat to his position by an administrator when he began finding and reporting research results contrary to park policy.

Hess (1993) describes the tensions between biologists and superintendents at Rocky Mountain over impacts elk were having on the park ecosystem. But in our conversations with two of the three biologists, the difficulties were more broad-based, generally turning on the superintendent's and regional director's sensitivity to a number of the scientists' recommendations. Finally in 1991, the three park biologist positions were abolished, two of the scientists were transferred elsewhere, and the third was moved to a nonresearch position in the park. By 1992 the latter individual asked for transfer because he felt that he was being ignored and was not serving a useful purpose. Hess (1993) points out that the replacement for this individual has been assigned to investigate global climate change. Hence, at that point in time, there was no longer any concerted research attention to, and institutional memory of, the elk problem.

According to Hess and one of the biologists, Rocky Mountain regional director Mintzmyer, who had worked up through the ranks without a technical background or experience in research, was involved in these actions. Moreover, we were told by one NPS scientist that the director closed out a biologist's position at Wind Cave in 1988 and transferred the incumbent to another park when tensions arose there. Chase (1992) reports that the director, before her own transfer from Denver, had made a number of such transfers in cases where scientists "dared disagree with her or . . . showed any innovation." According to Hess (1993), "science and research positions" in four parks and two CPSUs were eliminated during this period.

Since appearance of Hess's book, an extensive research project has now been proposed by personnel in the National Biological Survey to evaluate the elk situation in Rocky Mountain. The research prospectus specifically refers to Hess's criticisms and comments that the issue needs to be addressed.

The other type of response to the science–policy confrontation that we have observed is an effort to shape science to support policy. This may take the form of selecting findings that support the agency position and ignoring those that contradict it. Chase (1986) first called attention to this approach when Yellowstone changed its ungulate-management policies within months after a documented threat from Senator McGee to cut off funding if NPS did not stop culling elk. In Chase's view, park biologists in the 1970s rewrote the history of Yellowstone elk in order to conform to the new policy, changing and reinterpreting what had been the prevailing view and research data accrued over more than 30 years.

In our experience, this selective science has continued in Yellowstone. Park researchers have studied aspen and proposed untested hypotheses that are in concert with park policies. They have ignored northern Rocky Mountain research conducted by an entire aspen-ecology team in the Forest Service's Intermountain Forest and Range Experiment Station. The team has challenged the Yellowstone views. Arizona State University ecologist Duncan Patten, who himself has studied riparian ecology in Yellowstone, has told us of urging park officials to initiate research on heavily browsed northern-range riparian zones, and drafting research prospecti in 1987 and 1989. These were ignored. Bonnicksen (1989a), in criticizing fire management in Yellowstone, comments, "the Park Service ignores a large body of scientific knowledge, and it often spends precious research dollars to fend off criticism rather than to answer critical management questions."

In a strong plea for scientific ethics and objectivity, Finley (1983) commented on the actions of the Interagency Grizzly Bear Study Team, formed immediately after garbage-dump closure in Yellowstone, to suppress disagreement and deny one team member access to original data. He concluded, "Administrative decisions are accepted as infallible and require no further examination of the natural world. . . . The Department of Interior was more interested in suppressing disagreement than in finding the truth or saving grizzlies." The National Academy of Sciences report (Cowan et al. 1974) expressed concern over this mode of operation.

Data suppression apparently continues on the Yellowstone bear situation. In 1993, former Yellowstone bear biologist David Mattson reported that when his studies on grizzly bear population trends contradicted the official position, his superior seized his files from his office, erased files from his computer disk, and ordered the office secretary to open and examine his mail before giving it to him (David Mattson, personal communication, November 2, 1993, Clifford 1993, Welch 1993). Mattson and Craighead (1994) present a powerful and damning portrayal of the entire history of bear research and management in Yellowstone.

Richard Keigley (personal communication, July 6, 1993, Clifford 1993, Welch 1993) has reported publicly, also without denial, about his research on Yellowstone cottonwoods. His evidence indicates that the species is in decline on the northern range due to elk browsing, a result that challenges the natural-regulation policy. A manuscript he wrote for submission to a scientific journal was held up for several months by superiors until he removed verbiage pointing out the implications of his results for the policy.

Kay (1992b), in reviewing the book *The Jackson Elk Herd*, criticizes the author (Boyce 1989), who was heavily involved in Grand Teton National Park research, for his scholarship. Kay points out that the author cited results from a single, distant archaeological study to support his contention that elk have always been abundant in Jackson Hole and did not cite a large amount of research carried out precisely in Jackson Hole which concludes that elk were scarce. Kay also charges that the author misrepresents results from aspen research in the area and goes on to quote from a 1984 letter veteran archaeologist Gary Wright wrote to University of Montana wildlife professor Leslie Pengelly:

> Keep in mind that I have [been] battling wildlife biologists from Grand Teton and Yellowstone Parks for some years. One told me, after a seminar I gave at the Jackson Hole Biological Research Station on the faunal resources of the region, "Even if you demonstrate that no elk were here, we would still continue to argue for them because our management policies require a herd of at least 10,000 elk by the end of the Pinedale ice."

Another case of alleged selective use of evidence to support a policy position has been brought to our attention. As discussed in Chapter 3, Olympic National Park officials aver that there is no evidence of mountain goats ever having occupied the Olympic Mountains prior to the early 1900s, and that the population now in the park originated from transplants and releases in the 1920s. By NPS criteria they are nonnative, and the park has been attempting to eliminate them.

A 1987 environmental assessment (EA) by the park stated, "there is no evidence to suggest that they (the goats) ever inhabited the Olympic Peninsula" (as quoted in Anunsen 1993). Yet R. Anunsen (personal communication, December 2, 1992) and C. S. Anunsen (1993, Anunsen and Anunsen 1993) discovered that park officials at the time had two references in their files to reports of mountain goats on the peninsula prior to 1907. The Anunsens had already searched out these references themselves and, since then, have turned up two more accounts—one an archaeological study—of goat presence on the peninsula. The Anunsens also charge that park officials repeatedly refer to the dangers of goat grazing to endangered plant species when in fact there are no federally listed plant species in the park. And an earlier report on a vegetation study by a park biologist states that there is no significant threat to any of the plant species.

We contacted Olympic biologists for further information on the matter. Bruce Moorehead informed us that they had not considered the reported instances valid scientific evidence. He did not explain the unequivocal statement in the EA, and we did not discuss the details of the vegetation's status. Douglas Houston told us that a thorough, external, professional review of goat history and prehistory has now been completed. And he agreed with us that it would have been more open and prudent if the early observations had been mentioned in the EA and the rationale then given for not considering them valid records. Whatever the resolution, the handling has made the local press critical of the park and prompted it to charge that the park selects scientific evidence to support its policy position (cf. Judd 1993a,b).

We do not claim that data selection has or has not occurred in this case, nor do we suggest that it is the norm in NPS research. There is certainly a great amount of high-quality, objective work under way in the System. But we have found enough cases of data selection to argue for restructuring research in the agency to protect investigators and the parks themselves from this risk.

In fairness, it must be said that data selection is not unique to NPS science. An abundant literature now agrees that there is no such thing as perfect objectivity in scientific research—it is always "context laden" (Longino 1990). And students of research in public agencies now generalize data selection as a general principle of bureaucratic behavior (cf. Downs 1966, Bella 1987, 1992, Smith 1988, Wagner 1989b, Mattson and Craighead 1994). In a lengthy and detailed analysis, Schiff (1962) describes how the Forest Service for years ignored and suppressed solid research evidence that controlled burning was a beneficial silvicultural practice in southeastern U.S. forests, and that forest stands were less effective deterrents to soil erosion on steep slopes than the agency claimed. Both were contrary to Forest Service policy positions at the time.

But to add this caveat is not to condone the practice. It is to emphasize once again the need to be alert to the tendency and to protect research administratively so that it can approach objectivity as nearly as possible.

The other means of shaping research has been to hire employees

and award extramural contracts to investigators who, to say the
least, are not likely to produce research that challenges current
policies and paradigms. In our experience, there are, at times, tendencies for some extramural researchers supported by NPS funding to incline toward park positions. Three different NPS employees have told us of observing this effect; and Chase (1987) and Hess
(1993) both comment on the tendency.

This may in part explain why some parks tend to favor certain
universities with their contracts. One faculty member from a midwestern university commented in a letter to us of an "old-boy network." A faculty member from another university has complained
to us of a tendency in one CPSU toward sole-sourcing contracts,
especially to its own institution. Although the introduction to
Yellowstone's *Interim Report on Northern Range Research* (Anon.
1992) states that the park did not "influence" selection of investigators for the overgrazing studies, we have been told of two cases
in which major projects were sole-sourced for the research. One
case was reported to us by the principal investigator, who was the
recipient of one of the contracts. The other one was recounted by a
high-level NPS official who saw the paperwork on it.

Here again, a caveat provides some perspective. A growing literature is examining effects on the objectivity of university research
of unrelenting pressures on academia to find grant funds. Bella
(1985) cites President Dwight D. Eisenhower's famous 1961
farewell address, in which he warned of the dangers of the mili-
tary-industrial complex. Largely overlooked in President
Eisenhower's address was a concern about "the free university . . .
[as a] fountainhead of free ideas and scientific discovery. . . . [A]
government contract becomes a substitute for intellectual curios-
ity" and, Bella adds, "critical inquiry."

In conclusion to this stepchild discussion, two important points
emerge from the information we have presented. One is to firmly
underscore the NRC recommendation that NPS research critically
needs to be separated out into an independent administrative
entity. This is not a new recommendation, several earlier science
reviews having urged it. But it cannot be reiterated too often.
Research needs administrative and budgetary security.

And park researchers need to be freed from administrative coercion, fears for the security of their positions, and distanced from the
current policy predispositions of the organization. In our experience, there is in some parks a pronounced atmosphere of tension
and defensiveness toward any contrary evidence or criticism. Some
park investigators cannot interpret evidence detached from its

implications for existing policy. In these situations there is no relaxed atmosphere that encourages balanced assessment of the evidence on all sides of a question and detached inferences on where scientific truth lies.

The second point was made at the beginning of this discussion. No matter how effective a park research program might become, there is still uncertainty about how much influence it could have on policy in an organization that is so constrained politically, or at least fearful of repercussions. There is no shortage of definitive, scientific evidence on the Rocky Mountain elk situation. Yet, as Hess (1993) passionately points out, there has been no significant remedial action.

Although again beyond the scope of this study, the solution to this second problem will somehow need to extract NPS from its Lilliputian strands and free it to act definitively in protection of its resources. This is not to suggest that it should be sterilized from politics. As discussed in the last chapter, NPS is a public agency charged with public service, and politics in a democracy is the medium by which public values are communicated and satisfied. But unless the Park Service is given a sufficiently free hand to manage effectively the park resources with which it is entrusted, there is the distinct prospect of losing invaluable public assets. The real losers will then be the American public and the values which make the parks unique.

The Move to NBS

Now that Park Service research has been transferred to the National Biological Survey, and the latter agency assigned the responsibility of providing the research service for NPS, we would be remiss in this review if we did not give our prognosis on how effectively that arrangement may function. As this is written, the arrangement is not yet a year old and the NBS director, Ronald Pulliam, is relatively new. Hence our comments are largely surmise. But we offer them nevertheless.

We see both advantages and disadvantages in the new arrangement. Among the positives, formation of the agency should lend stature and visibility to the preservation end of the resource-management spectrum in an executive department (Interior) that has had a strong orientation toward the consumptive-use end. The Park Service is clearly part of that preservation end. As public values are increasingly concerned with preservation, such a policy shift in Interior moves its posture along with those value changes.

This, of course, is more an influence on the Department of Interior than on the Park Service.

Pulliam, a former president of the Ecological Society of America, is a highly regarded scientist. He will undoubtedly demand high performance standards and quality in his agency's research and promote a sense of the ecological complexity of the nation's natural resources. Both enhancement of research quality and a stronger, basic ecological focus will benefit the wildlife field (Wagner 1989a) and the other resource-management areas; and it could strengthen research on national-park problems.

The arrangement will also provide the administrative distance that the NRC study and we believe is necessary to free the scientists to seek truth irrespective of whether it supports the agency's policy positions. Quality science is impossible without that freedom. Research must be free to question, debate, and challenge policy; and it needs to be able to state openly in the organization, without fear of reprisal, when policy is contrary to fact. In NBS, research is no longer under direct supervision of the park superintendents.

But there are also uncertainties associated with this separation. The same investigators who worked under the policy pressures of the Park Service are now in NBS and in many cases are still working in the same parks and conducting research on the same or related problems. The superintendents still have a voice in what research is done in their parks and, as one NBS biologist pointed out to us, can control that research through issuance or non-issuance of collecting permits. To the extent of these controls, the same scientific capabilities they brought from NPS, and the degree to which the biologists still personally subscribe to the policy positions, their scientific horizons might not be any more open in NBS.

Moreover, there are questions as to the appropriate distance between research and management. There are always tensions between the two. Proximity can foster interpersonal relationships and perhaps a better chance of trust and acceptance by management of research recommendations. At the same time, proximity of research to management increases the likelihood that researchers will be fully cognizant of and sensitive to the management problems and thus will keep their efforts relevant to them. But the cost may be the lack of intellectual freedom and objectivity discussed earlier. Administrative distance between research and management should promote that freedom.

What, then, is the appropriate distance? There is no clear answer. Before its transfer to NBS, we were prepared to recommend a separate research division in the Park Service with its own associate director and administrative and budgetary lines. But there is no certainty that this arrangement would have been successful. It seems to have been effective in the Fish and Wildlife Service but considerably less so in the Forest Service (Wood 1994). Nevertheless, there is real uncertainty as to how ready the Park Service will be to accept research recommendations from an entirely different executive agency, especially in view of its spotty history in accepting recommendations of its own research. One high-level Park Service administrator has already told us of indecision on the part of some park superintendents to cooperate readily with NBS biologists working in their units. Cooperation will take firm direction from the top in the Department of Interior and effective liaison at the field levels.

Another uncertainty is how long, and to what extent, NBS will be able to provide the research service needed to support the management efforts. As Zeide (1994) comments, the new mission of the fledgling agency—said by its director at the 1994 American Institute of Biological Sciences meeting in Knoxville to be determination of the status and trends of the American biota, and the causation of those trends—is enormous, in fact hardly less than the whole of American ecology. Prior to the change, the 1,800 scientists transferred from seven Department of Interior agencies were fully occupied with the research needs of their organizations. As they change course to NBS's demanding new mission, it seems highly probable that less effort will be applied to the traditional needs of the donor agencies, one of which is the Park Service. This seems likely even if allowance is made for some complementarity of function between the two agencies.

The result may be that the donor agencies will need to rebuild their scientific personnel. While some observers might see this negatively as duplication, the positive perspective would be that it would increase the total scientific personnel in resource management and environmental sciences, something that has been sorely needed. Yet in an era of governmental downsizing and fiscal restraint, one could not be optimistic about this eventuality.

Finally, Haskell (1993) points out that, at a time when reviews of NPS science were urging the agency to employ more individuals with advanced scientific training in order to strengthen the scientific atmosphere within the agency, NBS has removed the research personnel who had the strongest scientific backgrounds in NPS. Haskell comments that many of the superintendents have relied on these individuals for counsel on technical matters, which is another argument for replacing the departed scientists.

In total, there are potential gains and losses from the move to NBS. Maximizing the gains will take concerted and creative administrative effort on the part of both agencies. Resource management can only proceed effectively with strong support from research. If the move to NBS means less scientific effort in the parks, resource management in the latter will suffer.

Closing Comments

The realization that the complexities of managing renewable natural resources requires a strong science base goes back more than two-thirds of a century for the management of fisheries and wildlife, rangelands, and forest resources. Federal agencies responsible for managing these resources—the Forest Service, Fish and Wildlife Service, and shifting agencies responsible for marine fisheries—have long had strong research arms and have depended heavily on the progressive accumulation of research data to illuminate and update their policy and management actions.

Early on, the responsibilities of these agencies for managing consumptive uses may have raised concerns for the resources' sustainability. Scientific knowledge of the resources' structure and function has been essential to understanding the effects of harvest on them.

Whatever the driving force, from the beginning the agencies hired employees with strong scientific training. As they moved up the administrative ranks, employees assumed leadership positions from which they were able to foster a continuing favorable environment for science and its essential role in policy and management.

With its dual mission of resource protection and visitor management, there has not been the strong rationale for an active research program through much of the Park Service's history. And the upward movement into leadership ranks of rangers and landscape architects, whose major career concerns have been with the dual mission, has produced little impetus toward building a research program and scientifically enlightened policy. Nor has impetus been given by directors (Frome 1992), who have changed every three to four years, many of whom were political appointees without scientific backgrounds. Thus research development has been meager despite the prescience of George M. Wright in the 1930s, and the studies of Leopold and Robbins at the beginning of the 1960s.

It is in the last quarter century, with the impacts of exploding numbers of visitors, manifold influences from outside the parks, and distortion of biotas, that active management of the resources has become increasingly recognized as a necessity for many parks. Even so, the laissez-faire imperative of the natural-regulation policy is a continuing damper on this recognition.

The increasing turn to management has been accompanied by growth in the research program. But as we have seen, the growth has been very limited, administratively disparate, and not recognized as a central priority. The 2 percent allocation in the 1993 NPS budget hardly reflects a strong commitment.

With park research now transferred to the National Biological Survey, we hope that research planning in that agency will recognize and address the considerable research needs of the National Park System. If NBS gives it a high priority, the parks may for the first time receive attention that expert panels have been urging for decades.

6

Ecological Terms and Concepts That Influence Policy Directions

Policies As Verbal Constructs

In the wildlife field, and more broadly in ecology, words and terms are used as abstract symbols of the concepts we form about ecological entities in the real world: processes, components, and states. The terms are used to facilitate thought and communication. How effectively they do this depends on how faithfully our concepts accord with the real-world entities, and how explicitly we define the terms that represent the concepts. Needless to say, problems occur with both thought and communication.

Terms used in ecology may be assigned early in our understanding and perception of the objects and happenings they symbolize. Our scientific grasp of these phenomena grows more precise and congruent with reality over time, yet the terms used to communicate about them stay the same. Hence, individuals with earlier understandings may use the same terminology as those with newer understandings but have in mind quite different concepts or mental pictures of the same aspects of the real world. Moreover, as is common in science, different individuals may hold different mental pictures of the same aspects of reality even though they are equally conversant with the latest evidence. Yet they assign the same words to their differing concepts of those aspects. Finally, some observers may use the same terms to represent quite different real-world entities or processes. The upshot is that ecology has been racked through most of its history with fruitless, semantic arguments.

When ecology is applied in natural-resources policy formation and management, communication can take on even more ambiguity. To begin with, policy statements and management objectives based on vague ecological terms take on the same semantic imprecision of the science itself. As a result, it may not be clear precisely what management objectives are, or when they have or have not been attained. Management programs must move forward, and in many cases do so effectively. But in other cases, they flounder or even mismanage for lack of clear direction.

Resource management has the additional problem of distinguishing between scientific and human-value connotations in its thinking and communication. Since policies are conceptualized and management programs are put in operation to satisfy human values, terms often take on an additional value connotation that further adds to their ambiguity and the problems of setting and achieving clear management goals.

Two steps are needed to address these problems and help resource management more clearly conceptualize and achieve its goals. First, there is a great need for ecology, the central foundation science of renewable-resource management, to adopt a set of explicit definitions, in many cases mathematical, for its terms. This recommendation is not new with us, other ecologists already having advocated it. Boyce (1991:186–187), for example, recognizes the problem and points to the need for explicit definition of such terms as *regulation and stability*. Coughenour and Singer (1991) wrestle with the term *overgrazing*. Moreover, there is the further need for ecologists to accept these definitions and base their communications on them. Unfortunately, however, the ecological community has not been enthusiastic about submitting to this discipline. But until there is some concert on this matter, it will continue to pose a problem for the science and for resource management.

The second needed step is for resource management to draw a clear distinction and separation between value judgment and value-neutral scientific description—Decker et al. (1991) make a cogent case for this distinction—and between analysis and advocacy (cf. Wagner 1994). Resource-management agencies are constituted to advocate the social values that they are chartered to satisfy. In this day and age they also employ science to enlighten their policy decisions. If science is to serve management effectively, it must strive for objectivity, which requires distancing itself from management's value positions, as discussed in the last chapter.

When analysts adopt strong, public advocacy positions, there is a distinct risk that their image of objectivity will be tarnished, if not in fact compromised. Attorneys in environmental litigation now

routinely question expert scientific witnesses about their member-
ships in environmental-advocacy organizations in an attempt to
undermine their credibility. While we make no claim to absolute
objectivity, it is because of the analysis–advocacy tension that we
have attempted to avoid advocating park goals in this report in the
hope of approaching objectivity as nearly as possible.

Ambiguities and Misconceptions
As Bases for Policies

In this chapter, we will attempt to explicate a number of ecological
terms in the hope of clarifying the national-park policy issues on
which they turn. And we will try to dissect out the value connotations of terms where appropriate so that this aspect is evident.
Macnab (1985), Boyce (1991), Coughenour and Singer (1991), and
Porter (1991) have provided some of this clarification in connection
with national-park management, and we will attempt to extend it
further. In the process we hope both to make more evident the role
of these scientific concepts in driving policy and to comment on the
facility with which science is often used in the agency.

Carrying Capacity

The term and concept of carrying capacity are frequently used as a
basis for wildlife-management policies. In 1977, the Western
Region of Parks Canada (Anon. 1977a) proposed "To maintain large
mammal populations [in Elk Island National Park] at a level
slightly below the carrying capacity of the range through herd
reduction or transplant programs." Caughley (1976a, 1981a),
Houston (1982:62), and Macnab (1985) have opined that "ecological
carrying capacity" is the appropriate objective for ungulate management in national parks; and a fall 1993 NPS research proposal
(Anon. 1993) requests a large sum of money to, among other things,
develop an understanding of "ecological carrying capacity of ungulates" in Rocky Mountain National Park and Bighorn Canyon
National Recreation Area. In a seminar in Pocatello, Idaho, on
November 3, 1991, Yellowstone research chief John Varley commented that the northern elk herd was somewhere near the 16,000
calculated to be the carrying capacity for it; hence the system was
in a favorable state. Yet, in a recently published glossary for the
Forest Service, Lyon and Christensen (1992) defined carrying

capacity and then commented, "This is a well-established biological concept, but is too imprecise for any useful application in elk management. . . . Avoid using this term in relation to elk."

What precise management objectives *are* prescribed by a policy that turns on the term *carrying capacity?* How does one determine what the carrying capacity for large mammals is in Elk Island Park and what is "slightly" below? What is ecological carrying capacity and is it the appropriate objective for national parks? Can one be sanguine about the northern range if the elk population is at carrying capacity? Or is the concept too imprecise to allow answers to these questions?

McCullough (1992:968–969) comments that the term "is a slippery shibboleth [a metaphor originally posed by Macnab (1985)] . . . because different and distinguishable ideas, each with merit, have been given the same label. . . . A morass of scientific confusion surrounding the concept of carrying capacity makes communication difficult." He then lists seven definitions representing as many different ways in which the term has been used, most implying biologically quite different mechanisms.

We believe it is useful here to analyze at further length the implications of different uses of the term. But before doing so, it is desirable to review briefly some of the key ecological findings surrounding that complex process herbivory, with special attention to ungulate effects. We will then examine definitions of carrying capacity which are posed as parameters of herbivory. It is useful to consider the latter in order to judge whether or not the definitions are useful or meaningful descriptors of any real-world aspect of the process.

Ecology at present does not have a single, comprehensive theoretical construct of herbivory (Wagner 1987). Rather, it has a collection of empirically derived generalizations for different areas of the world, some abstract conceptual models, and some hypotheses based on modeling studies, many of them addressing different parameters of vegetation and herbivore response. These are worth reviewing briefly to give some sense of the complexity of herbivory in ecosystems, and the consequent problem of forming any simple carrying-capacity concept that can serve as the basis for policy statements and management programs.

- Probably the earliest ungulate–herbivory theory was developed in the early stages of the range-management field in North America in the latter 1800s and early 1900s, and coincident with F. E. Clements' emerging concepts of plant succession. Assigning an 1899 date, Clements (1928:225) credits J. G. Smith with giving "the first clear recognition of grazing as a fundamental field for investigation." The era witnessed a large number of grazing studies in the southwestern United States, the western national forests, and the central North American grasslands; and produced a stream of publications (e.g., Sampson 1913, 1919, Wooten 1916, Jardine 1917, 1919).

These early studies clearly used a terminology and viewed ungulate-vegetation interrelationships in a Clementsian, linear-successional context. That context was later formalized by E. J. Dyksterhuis (1946, 1949) in a range-management model that still has influence today.

These authors' concern was with retrogressive changes in plant-community *composition* from a climax, ungrazed form down through progressively greater compositional changes with increasing grazing pressure. Total primary production was considered to change little, if at all, until retrogression well down the scale. But of course its distribution among the constituent species changed as the community composition changed. The concept assumed that the system could be equilibrated at any point along the scale with the appropriate stocking rate; and that easing, or release from, grazing would allow the system to move back toward, or to, the climax condition.

• Working in an equatorial grassland with wild ungulates, McNaughton (1979, 1983) has proposed an optimality paradigm of the response of vegetation *production* to grazing. With a variety of physiological and morphological responses, East African grasses produce more herbage with some measure of grazing than with none. There is an optimum grazing intensity for maximum production beyond which production falls off. Attempts at finding this pattern in North American grassland have been less successful (Wagner 1987), although Frank's (1990, Frank and McNaughton 1992, 1993) recent two-year Yellowstone studies suggested it for that area. Wallace and Macko (1993) comment that overcompensation has been shown in Yellowstone grasses, presumably with Frank's work, but not in grasses of the central North American prairies. Elsewhere, there is a considerable school of demurral over the overcompensation idea (Belsky et al. 1993, Patten 1993, cf. exchange of papers in *Ecological Applications* 3[1]); and whether or not, and if so how, it might function in forbs and shrubs is entirely unclear (Wagner 1987).

* Based on studies of ungulates introduced into New Zealand, time series of domestic sheep numbers in Australia, and numbers of reindeer introduced on St. Matthew Island in the Bering Sea, Caughley (1976a) generalized that ungulates introduced into an area erupt and then undergo damped oscillations in numbers, eventually settling on a stable equilibrium density. The sheep and reindeer time series that he showed did in fact erupt initially but did not make a convincing case for damped oscillations, although the sheep numbers did fluctuate over time, probably with annual variations in rainfall.

Caughley adapted simple predator–prey equations to serve as a model for the behavior of vegetation–herbivore systems and simulate what he inferred from the empirical evidence. The parameter values that he chose for the model generated reciprocal damping oscillations in the herbivore (predator) and vegetation (prey). But if the empirical evidence for damping oscillations in a newly introduced ungulate is meager, no evidence has been presented of such time series in vegetation.

Caughley (1976a), as had May (1973) before him, pointed out that the predator–prey equations he used would generate qualitatively different time series, depending on the values he assigned to their parameters: oscillations damping to equilibrium values simulating the empirical cases he inferred, stable limit cycles, and widening oscillations that diverged eventually to zero. He commented that the latter two behaviors are not observed in real-world ungulate–vegetation systems for the probable reason that they are selected out during evolution. Hence his range of parameter values and the generalization of damping oscillations are put forward on deductive, not empirical, grounds. But in another paper in the same year (1976b), he hypothesized that elephants and woody vegetation in East Africa might cycle in a 200-year periodicity.

Finally, Caughley surmised that the function describing the relationship between ungulate numbers and plant biomass at equilibrium is an inverse linear one (Fig. 6-1). The midpoint in the function, termed "economic carrying capacity," is that plant biomass and ungulate density at which the maximum sustained yield of ungulates can be removed. Points along the line are potential equilibria if human exploitation and/or nonhuman predation take enough animals to stabilize the population at those points. The point representing the maximum number of animals and least plant biomass is that density at which the ungulates' reproductive and mortality rates are equal and the population stabilizes itself without human removal. He termed this point the "ecological carrying capacity." Here again Caughley has presented no empirical record of this relationship.

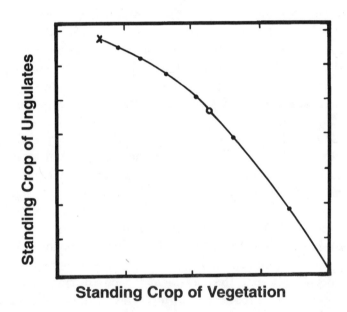

Standing Crop of Vegetation

Figure 6-1. Caughley's isocline of equilibrium values between ungulate numbers (or biomass) and associated vegetation standing crop (phytomass or density). The circles are equilibria only if animals are removed at regular intervals, with the open circle defined as "economic carrying capacity." The x, defined as "ecological carrying capacity," is a self-imposed equilibrium without animal removal. Redrawn from Caughley (1976a).

• Noy-Meir (1975) adapted predator–prey graphs devised by Rosenzweig and MacArthur (1963) for simulations of vegetation–herbivore behavior. Depending on the pattern of herbivore consumption, and the response of plant growth rate to its own standing crop, the simulations predicted a wide range of behaviors: single stable equilibria; no equilibria leading to extinction; multiple equilibria—some stable, some unstable—with the potential for the system to be perturbed among these. While emphasizing that his approach was simplistic and that grazing systems are more complex than his simple models, his survey of the literature turned up cases in which real systems behaved in ways suggested by his theoretical forays.

• Noy-Meir's simulations, like McNaughton's and Caughley's paradigms, treated vegetation as though it were a single entity—in fact a single species in Caughley's predator–prey equations and Noy-Meir's graphs—and focused on vegetation production and phytomass. But range ecology in semiarid and arid areas, where there is a diversity of vegetation life forms, was finding profound shifts in vegetation type (Wagner 1987). Some of these shifts were thought to be irreversible (Westoby 1979/80) and, along with Noy-Meir's predictions of discontinuous stability, have evolved into the newer multiple-equilibrium paradigm (Westoby 1979/80, Ellis and Swift 1988, Westoby et al. 1989) mentioned in Chapter 2. Thus range ecology has moved away, or at least diversified its thinking, from the Clementsian, linear-succession model.

Research in Africa, Australia, and North America has now shown numerous examples of browsing ungulates converting woody vegetation to herbaceous and grazers changing herbaceous vegetation to woody. Broad-spectrum feeders such as elk, while subsisting largely on herbaceous vegetation, can eliminate woody species from the system, as apparently has occurred in Yellowstone. Some of these changes are thought to be irreversible, either because of alteration in site conditions and/or shifts in competitive balance between the different vegetative components (Westoby 1979/80, Ellis and Swift 1988).

• Additional factors complicate real-world herbivore–vegetation systems further. Fire, both lightning-set and anthropogenic, have been part of the natural scene for millennia and add to the competition–herbivory milieu in structuring vegetation. Herbivory is not a monolith because animals have feeding preferences, concentrating first on their preferred species and impacting them, then moving progressively down the preference scale as the more preferred are suppressed. Often preference scales coincide with nutrition scales. Constraints on the herbivore population can set in at points along this scale and before significant reduction in total phytomass.

• Yet another complication arises with ungulates occupying different summer and winter ranges in temperate regions. With summer range more extensive, of higher nutritional value, and fully available in the absence of snow, and with mild temperatures prevailing, animals recover weight lost in winter and store up fat, with which they enter the next winter. They survive the winter in part by drawing on this stored fat, and in part by consuming forage on the winter range. Thus the number of animals that can survive on a given winter range is not determined alone by the available winter forage, nor does the ungulate population adjust solely to that forage. The end result is larger populations, and heavier impact on the winter range, than would be the case if survival rates and population size, and in fact "carrying capacity," were keyed solely to the amount of winter forage.

Utah State University range ecologist Philip Urness has suggested to us that one result of the 1988 Yellowstone fires could be an improved forage base on the summer range, from which elk would migrate to the northern range in better condition. The result could be higher natality and survival, population increase, and even heavier impacts on the northern range. That the prefire summer range exerted some measure of constraint on the northern herd is indicated by the Merrill and Boyce (1991) evidence, which shows the population's rate of change varying with weather conditions that affect summer forage production. Boyce (personal communication, March 1993) has told us that variations in summer vegetation conditions may account for somewhere around a third of the variation in annual rates of change in the Yellowstone northern herd.

What part of all this complexity can be represented by an explicit, quantifiable carrying-capacity concept that can be used as a goal for national-park policy and management? We will consider five concepts or definitions of carrying capacity in the context of the above review of herbivory. One is the traditional range-management concept and the other four are subdivisions of two in McCullough's (1992) list. We consider the other five in his list to be too general for the present discussion, or are subsumed by the others, or have largely been applied to species other than the herbivores under discussion here.

1. Coughenour and Singer (1991) associate the origins of the carrying-capacity concept with Malthus' 1789 concern for how many humans the earth's resources could accommodate and Verhulst's nineteenth-century proposal that the logistic equation is a general law of population growth. However, the term itself actually originated in the early days of the discipline of range management. All of the early range scientists mentioned above (that is, Smith, Sampson, Wooten, Jardine) were using the term in their publications, sometimes interchangeably with "grazing capacity."

   Some of these authors merely took carrying capacity as the number of livestock for which a given vegetation could provide forage, without consideration for the condition of that vegetation. But as early as 1919, Jardine (1919) redefined the concept as the potential of a site (its capacity). The essence of Jardine's definition was repeated by Hadwen (1922) for Alaska reindeer, was subsequently formalized in range-management texts, and ultimately became a central principle and credo through much of the profession's history. Sampson (1923), author of the first text in the field, provided a definition similar to Jardine's. Stoddart and Smith (1943) used it in the first edition of their text, but did not define it until the second (1955):

   > *Grazing capacity,* then, has come to be regarded as the maximum animal numbers which can graze each year on a given range, for a specific number of days, without inducing a downward trend in forage production, forage quality, or soil.

   This is essentially the same definition as Sampson's and is similar to the one in Heady's (1975) text.

   Leopold (1933) introduced the term into wildlife management in his classic text *Game Management.* But the generality of his definition ("the maximum density which a particular range is capable of supporting . . . a property of a unit of range"), while implying that it was a property of the resources of an area, left the conceptual specificity to the sister discipline of range management.

Three specific points or implications of the traditional range-management concept bear emphasis. The first is that when numbers are at carrying capacity, there is no significant impact on the system and its sustainability. It is in this characteristic of a population at carrying capacity not seriously impacting the system that generalization of the idea in ecology often implies, in both a scientific and value connotation, a system that is in some sense "healthy" or "in balance." This appears to be implied in Varley's comment, cited above, that we can be sanguine about the Yellowstone northern elk herd at the time reportedly numbering around 15,000–16,000, the calculated "carrying capacity."

Taken literally, the range-management definition poses something of a contradiction for the profession since, as Macnab (1985) points out, Stoddart et al. (1975) discuss elsewhere in their book the continuum of changes in range conditions that different stocking intensities elicit. And the Dyksterhuis (1946, 1949) paradigm, which has had a strong and continuing influence on American range management, is a Clementsian concept that portrays a continuum of vegetation response over a spectrum of grazing intensities. It is not clear that there is *any* moderate stocking level that will have no effect on either vegetation production and/or composition.

A second implication of the range-management concept is that the number of animals at carrying capacity has not reached any self-induced equilibrium. Animal numbers may in fact not be increasing, but that equilibrium is imposed by the annual removal of an animal crop by humans, or what Macnab (1985) calls a "contrived equilibrium." Sampson's term "maximum grazing capacity" implies that the number of animals could increase to higher levels, *but with ultimate reduction of the carrying capacity.*

A third implication is that carrying capacity is a function of the vegetation resource of an area. Hence the significance of the word *capacity,* or what the area *can* support.

In sum, the range-management concept is (a) a combined view of both animal numbers and vegetation state, (b) the implication that the vegetation state is sustainable (in fact an equilibrium state) without significant alteration, (c) maintained by extrinsic control of the animal population size, and (d) is a function of the resources of an area. It is presumably calculable if the nutritional needs of animals are known and the productivity of the vegetation is known in terms of the plant species and their ecophysiology, and the climatic and soil conditions.

There is of course no question that vegetations in different ecosystems, with different plant species, soils, and climate, can and do produce at different levels of primary production. In this sense, different systems have the "capacity" to support different numbers of herbivores. What is not clear to us is, as stated above, whether there is any significant number of animals that can be supported without any effect on vegetation production and/or composition.

2. As described above, Caughley (1976a, 1981a) generalizes the equilibrium relationships between ungulate standing crop and vegetation standing crop as a roughly linear, inverse correlation between the two (Fig. 6-1). He proposes two carrying-capacity concepts within this model. The approximate midpoint of the relationship is what he calls the "economic carrying capacity." This point, which can only be maintained by continued removal of animals to stabilize their numbers (Macnab's contrived equilibrium), is the population size allowing the largest sustained yield of animal numbers or biomass.

What Caughley refers to as "ecological carrying capacity" is that extreme point in the relationship at which ungulate standing crop is at its maximum and vegetation is at its minimum. This state is self-determined, the herbivore reproductive and survival rates having declined to the point where the population has stabilized itself.

Like the traditional range-management model, Caughley's is a two-dimensional one, expressing both ungulate numbers and vegetation state. And like the successional Clementsian and Dyksterhuis models, it poses a range of vegetation effects by a range of ungulate numbers.

However, we have difficulties with the reality of Caughley's (1976a) concept of ecological carrying capacity and with the conversion of it into explicit and measurable management goals. One problem is that his plant measure is standing crop. While he mentions plant density, his discussion of his Figure 17 and conversion to units centers on plant biomass.

Plant biomass is a problematic parameter for relating to potential ungulate numbers. It is a highly variable vegetation-state parameter that varies seasonally between the end of the growing season and beginning of the next, even without herbivore use. And it varies with the timing and extent of use. At any point in time, a highly productive and a poorly productive vegetation may both be grazed down to low biomass, but the former will carry large ungulate numbers and the latter few. Thus the more appropriate vegetation parameter, and the more realistic determinant of how many herbivores a vegetation can support, is production. And while Caughley may have been using biomass only as an abstract or symbolic indicator of vegetation condition or function, his discussion of it in relation to the X-axis of his Figure 17 creates some confusion.

More substantively, we have problems with the linearity of the relationship (cf. our Fig. 6-1). It gives the impression that ever lower plant biomass, or whatever parameter, supports ever higher ungulate numbers. Yet there must be some point below which vegetation abundance supports fewer and fewer animals. The relationship is more likely parabolic, somewhat similar to McNaughton's model.

As a third difficulty, it is questionable to us that ecological carrying capacity can be an equilibrium state. As the above herbivory examples show, herbivore–vegetation interactions are typically dynamic, with the vegetation shifting composition, life form, and equilibria. Heavy vegetation use by a given herbivore can drive its food species out of the system, thereby reducing its own food source. There is reason to believe that the high mule deer populations of this century in the Intermountain West have severely reduced their own winter-range browse species and contributed in part to the deer declines of the last few decades.

A single biomass measure alone does not reflect all this dynamism. Phytomass can actually increase under grazing pressure. For example, mesquite or pigmy-conifer woodlands and perhaps even creosote-bush and sagebrush deserts can carry many times the total phytomass of the grasslands from which they were driven.

Beyond these purely biological considerations, it does not seem consistent with national-park goals to set ecological carrying capacity, even if real, as a management objective. The stated NPS goal is to preserve maximally diverse, intact, natural ecosystems, natural being defined as what would prevail today had Europeans not come on the scene. A natural system would include a full complement of nonhuman, large mammalian predators and hunting by preindustrial humans. In all probability these limited ungulate populations at lower levels than those occurring today, as we will discuss below. It is contrary to the agency's own goals to allow ungulate populations to rise to densities at which they alter their ecosystems, reduce diversity, and threaten survival of T and E species in ways that would not have occurred in the absence of postindustrial humans eliminating major checks on their numbers.

3. McCullough (1992) poses two other carrying-capacity concepts in his list, which are derived from the logistic-equation population model (Fig. 6-2). One is the population size at which the growth curve goes to equilibrium, K (Fig. 6-2a) of the equation, and given the notation "KCC" by McCullough. The other is the midpoint of the growth curve (Fig. 6-2b), variously termed the inflection point, or maximum-sustained-yield density (MSY), and dubbed "ICC."

McCullough equates these two concepts with Caughley's ecological and economic carrying-capacity concepts, respectively. There is in fact a partial analogy in that the pairs of concepts do serve as parameters of herbivore population size. But they differ in that the logistic-curve values are one-dimensional, serving only as measures of animal-population values. Caughley's concepts are descriptors both of animal numbers and vegetation state.

Avoiding most of the complexity and confusion inherent in the subject of herbivory, many of the contemporary, general-ecology textbooks simply equate the term *carrying capacity* with the logistic K. But this simplification abandons most of the meaning implicit in the original range-management, and in many cases more broadly ecological, sense of the term. It connotes nothing about the condition and sustainability of the system, again being only a one-dimensional parameter of population size.

Moreover, it abandons the implications of the word *capacity*. This word is usually taken to imply in some sense the numbers of animals that an ecosystem has the capacity to support. But if we consider animal populations to be constrained by varying combinations of limiting influences—weather/climate, predation, competition, etc.—then a given population can be limited at different densities, depending on the kinds and intensities

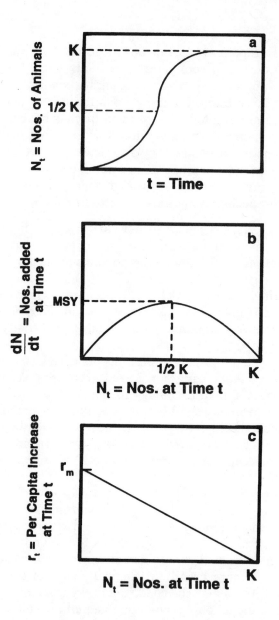

Figure 6-2. Representation of the logistic equation $dN/dt = r_m (1 - N/K)$. Figure 6-2a is the population increase over time to K, the size at which growth stops. Figure 6-2b is the relationship between numerical increase (dN/dt) and population size at time t (N_t). MSY is the maximum sustained yield of the population, achieved at population size ½ K. Figure 6-2c is the relationship between per capita rate of increase at time t (r_t) and population size at time t (N_t). The value r_m is the maximum per capita increase rate of which the population is capable.

of influences, and therefore at different Ks. A K value for a population held at low density by stringent constraint from such factors says nothing about what the resources of that system have the *capacity* to sustain. Hence, to equate carrying capacity with the logistic K so simplifies the concept as to strip off most of the meaning originally attached to the idea.

In our view the complexities of herbivory are so great that the concept can only be usefully applied in the sense of a general or qualitative abundance of animals that the resources of a given system can support. And unfortunately it does not give clear direction for specific and well-designed management programs.

Natural Regulation

The term *natural regulation* is used in two ways in NPS policy. One is as a modifier of the agency's nonintrusive, animal-management policy. As we quoted Wright (1988) in Chapter 2, natural-regulation management is a reliance "on natural processes to regulate herd size." The implication, of course, is nonintervention by human action.

The second way in which the term is used is as a label for the population process which it represents, that process becoming a premise for the management policy. Hence it is useful to examine both the biological reality of the process, and the way it is conceptualized in NPS science and policy. We will address the scientific question first.

Each of the two words in the term carries a meaning, and we will dispense at the outset with the word *natural* by accepting pro tem Peek's (1980) definition: regulation "in the absence of human influence." This leaves it unspecified whether the reference is to technological humans, leaving preindustrial peoples as "natural," or whether it refers to all human influence. We will address this issue below, and for the present only for purposes of discussion, we adopt the latter, more inclusive position. We wish to concentrate here on the term and the process *regulation.*

Unlike carrying capacity, there is a mathematically precise population process that can be defined unequivocally and represented appropriately by the word regulation. Paradoxically, the term and the process have been at the center of what probably has been the longest and most extensive controversy in ecology. As Boyce (1991:186) points out, there have been hundreds of papers written on the subject. In our view, the problem is a semantic one, with investigators failing to conceptualize explicitly the population process and either using the term ambiguously or using it for a different, although related, process. These problems are inherent in the term's use in NPS policy.

Population ecology has devoted a major portion of its research and theoretical effort to two aspects of animal population behavior over time. The first aspect in many populations is a net absence of change, or equilibrium, over a specified time period. There may be short-term fluctuations, but these tend to vary around a mean density, the equilibrium density, for the period in question and the net change for the period is zero. This state is sometimes termed a *dynamic equilibrium,* and the process effecting it is the *maintenance* of equilibrium.

Not all populations are at equilibrium. The favorability of environments may decline or improve over time, and associated populations may decline or increase. And no population remains at the same density indefinitely. Indeed, Botkin (1990) argues for the obsolescence of the idea of equilibrium. But the question is a matter of time scale. Climates change, as do other environmental variables over extended time periods, so that on a climatological, geological, or evolutionary time scale, there is no population equilibrium. But for periods scaled in years and decades, many populations do remain at roughly the same densities through these periods (cf. Ehrlich and Roughgarden 1987:91–94, Pimm 1991).

The second aspect is a qualitatively and demographically different process. Equilibrium can be maintained at different densities, and its analysis does not focus per se on the density at which it occurs. But the second aspect focuses on the *assumption* of equilibrium, *and the density at which that occurs.* The two aspects are demographically related, but nevertheless distinct. They are more explicitly and unequivocally defined in terms of a population's rates of change. Equilibrium is that state in which the mean, per capita rate of change r is equal to 0 over a specified period of time. Assumption of equilibrium at some density (K) is the *reduction* of r from its genetic maximum to a mean of 0 at K. The ecological questions of interest are the demographic processes that produce these two behaviors, and the kinds of environmental variables and their modes of action that drive the processes.

There is now widespread agreement in the population literature that equilibrium is *maintained,* or otherwise stated a population is stabilized, by positively density-dependent factors (hereinafter simply density-dependent factors or density dependence). Somewhat confusingly, these actions are also termed *negative feed-*

back. The process of density-dependent maintenance of equilibrium is termed *regulation*. The term has been used in this sense by a sequence of authors for nearly a half century (cf. Solomon 1949, 1964, Klomp 1966, Varley et al. 1973, Begon and Mortimer 1981, Begon et al. 1986:548, Hassell and May, 1990).

The *assumption* of equilibrium at some mean density is achieved by the action of all factors reducing the rate of change r at K: positive, inverse, and time-lagged density-dependence, and density independence. Equilibrium can be assumed through the action of density dependence alone, in which case it is both assumed and maintained (regulated) by density dependence. But most populations function in multifactorial environments that have complexes of the different forms of density influence.

Unfortunately this second process has been assigned a number of terms over the years which doubtless has contributed to the confusion: "limitation" (Franz 1962, Wagner 1981a, Messier 1991), "control" (Solomon 1949, 1964), and more generally in recent years "determination" (Varley et al. 1973) or "determination of abundance" (Wagner 1969, Begon and Mortimer 1981, Begon et al. 1986:548). Wagner (1969) presented a graphical model to explicate the process. For simplicity, we will hereinafter use the term *limitation* for it.

The distinction between the two processes has been articulated in the ecological literature for 60 years. Nicholson (1933) first used the term *balance* for what is now generally called equilibrium, and argued that balance could only be maintained by density-dependent action. That part of his argument is clearly regulation. But he also recognized that density-independent influences, operating in conjunction with density dependence, could influence the density at which balance is achieved. All of the above authors have recognized the distinction.

It is true that all of the above authors but Wagner, May, and Messier are insect-population specialists and have published much of their work in the media of that subdiscipline. Caughley (1976a) points out that many of the most important theoretical advances in population ecology have been made by insect specialists. In failing to be conversant with these conceptual advances, the wildlife profession has, in his tactful words, "slipped behind." But the distinction between regulation and limitation has been in the wildlife literature for three decades (cf. Wagner et al. 1965, Wagner 1969, Connolly 1978, Messier 1991, Sinclair 1991). And Caughley's point does not explain the confusion in the broader ecological community.

The confusion has been caused by two problems. One is the failure of other ecologists to perceive the distinction, often treating the two processes as some imprecise combination of the two. The other is the familiar semantic problem of using the same terms, most often *regulation,* for both of the processes or more commonly for the vague hybrid.

Three major players in the early years were Nicholson (1933) and Andrewartha and Birch (1954), who have been cast in many contemporary ecology texts as espousing contrary views on the same issue, regulation. Indeed, they did challenge each other, but it is in fact a classic case of three individuals arguing two different entities and thereby debating past each other without communicating. Nicholson (1933) was focusing on balance, what we now call equilibrium, and arguing that it could only be maintained by density dependence. He recognized peripherally that density-independent factors could influence the *level* of the equilibrium density. But his emphasis was on balance and its maintenance. Andrewartha and Birch (1954) were impressed with the importance of climatic variables, commonly assumed to operate density independently, *on insect abundance* (limitation). Consequently they challenged, irrelevantly, what they considered to be Nicholson's overemphasis on density dependence.

More recent examples show the same confusion. Peek (1980) begins his discussion of natural regulation by citing other authors who state "that wild populations fluctuate within limits regardless of the potential rate of increase, and the task is to determine causes that confine a population within these limits." This is a valid, alternate representation of regulation. But then in the same paragraph he defines natural regulation "as that set of controlling mechanisms that serves to limit or control population density in the absence of human influence." Depending on what he means by "limit" and "control," he could now be describing what we here are calling limitation. And later in this paper on natural regulation he weighs the evidence for predation as a determinant of mean ungulate density, clearly a limitation question.

In a discussion of regulation, Boyce (1991:186) appropriately comments that "The word *regulation* is similarly burdened with semantic baggage." He concludes that the controversy is largely behind us, resolved by Horn's (1968) model. Horn's paper is entitled "Regulation of Animal Numbers: A Model Counter Example." In fact, Horn's logistic model simulates explicitly how the equilibrium density N_e can be set at different levels, depending on whether the population is being influenced only by density dependence, density dependence and weak density independence combined, or density dependence and strong density independence combined. The simu-lations are precisely addressing *limitation*. The confusion is not yet behind us.

This has been a detailed, and perhaps daunting, discussion of what may seem like esoteric points. But as Wright (1992a) states, the central theme of NPS wildlife management is natural-regula-tion management. Hence the scientific nuance of this issue had to be clarified in order to examine this aspect of NPS policy.

As discussed in Chapter 3, the NPS concept of natural regulation was, to the best of our knowledge, first posited by Cole (1971) as an established ecological phenomenon for a number of ungulate species in a group of northern Rocky Mountain parks. In the same year, Houston (1971) presented essentially the same idea as a *hypothesis* for Yellowstone to be tested with the research under way in the park. He concentrated on elk but generalized to five other ungulate species. Houston's hypothetical stand was the more appropriate since, in 1971 when he spoke, the Yellowstone north-ern herd was still at low numbers, increasing from the stringent reductions of the mid and late 1960s, and therefore not at equilib-rium or regulated. And, as discussed in Chapter 3, the Rocky Mountain National Park elk herd, one of the populations from which Cole generalized, was also increasing at the time and not at equilibrium or regulated. Since 1971, a number of NPS presenta-tions and publications have reiterated the paradigm and inferred natural regulation in individual populations (cf. Meagher 1971, Cole 1974, 1983, Houston 1975, 1982).

In addition to addressing the above publications and reports on our own initiative, we were asked by Washington NPS official Dr. John Dennis at the beginning of our study to respond to the question "Can ungulates self-regulate in an area the size of the Yellowstone ecosystem?" Hence, we will examine the issue in the context of the above discussion.

To begin with, the terminology problem. The papers generally discuss the combined effects of intraspecific competition for forage, severe winter weather variously said to be "density independent" or "partially density independent," and in some cases predation, in determining the density of the populations. The concern is clearly with limitation and not regulation. The latter term has been mis-applied for more than 20 years. The suggestion that weather oper-ating density independently would regulate is an oxymoron.

Beyond this, the publications and Dr. Dennis' question state or imply three corollary questions: (1) Will the populations stop grow-ing without human intervention? (2) If so, will they do so without significant impact on their vegetation? (3) Can predators, or would they if present, influence the density at which the populations do/would equilibrate?

The answer to the first question has to be yes on several grounds. First, deductively, there are limits to the food resources in any area. No population can continue growing indefinitely. At some point the amount of food available per animal must decline to the point where nutritional states depress reproductive rates, increase mortality, and reduce rates of change to zero. If the population were spatially constrained, the lack of emigration would also play a role.

Second, there is abundant evidence of density-dependent declines in natality, and increases in mortality, in a variety of ungulate species: African buffalo (Sinclair 1977), Michigan white-tailed deer (McCullough 1979), Scottish red deer (Clutton-Brock et al. 1982), Yellowstone elk (Houston 1982), and Colorado mule deer (Bartmann et al. 1992), to name a few.

There is some debate over the form of these density-dependent functions, Fowler (1981, 1987) arguing that the curves for large mammals are convex, indicating no density-dependent resource constraint until populations approach their equilibrium densities. However, Sinclair, McCullough, Clutton-Brock, and Houston all show density dependence in natality and mortality rates at low densities. McCullough's relationship spans densities almost to zero deer. The other three authors' populations were recovering from low densities—Houston's elk from the herd reductions of the 1960s, Sinclair's buffalo from the suppressive effects of rinderpest, and Clutton-Brock's red deer from a period of more stringent culling— and had not reached equilibrium densities at the time of their studies. Hence, some form of density dependence operates over a wide range of densities down to low numbers in these populations, and linearity in ungulates is not uncommon.

Whatever the forms of the functions, natality rates will eventually decline and/or mortality rates will rise until the two are equal and the populations stop growing at some density. This may already have occurred in Yellowstone as discussed above, Merrill and Boyce (1991) finding very nearly logistic growth in the Yellowstone northern herd with K on average approximately 15,000. And using the park census figures, we calculated annual, per capita rates of change r and regressed these on population size for the northern herd as of 1986. The relationship is essentially linear, implying logistic growth (cf. Fig. 6-2c), with r declining on average to 0 at approximately the same numbers found by Merrill and Boyce. Houston et al. (1990) surmise that the elk in Olympic

National Park may have reached their equilibrium density, and Cole (1983) believed this to be the case with an elk population in western Yellowstone.

The second question of what effects an equilibrium, ungulate population has on its vegetation is more complex. Cole (1971) equated excessive impacts with causing "retrogressive or secondary succession" without stating what this implies in terms of specific vegetation effects. He also reasoned on evolutionary grounds that ungulates that seriously impacted their food base could not have survived over evolutionary time. The implication is that they must somehow limit their population growth below any extreme effects on the vegetation.

But we have discussed in the previous section the complexity of ungulate interactions with vegetation that cannot be encapsulated in a simple, abstract concept derived from linear, Clementsian succession. Vegetation types are converted from one life form to another. Broad-spectrum feeders eliminate some components of the vegetation (and their associated fauna) while subsisting on others. Plant-community composition is changed and opened to invasion by exotics. At the extreme, there is soil erosion and altered hydrology. There is evidence for all of these changes, as discussed in Chapter 3, due to white-tailed deer in the East and elk in the West. There is no convincing evidence that ungulate populations will limit their own increase short of these kinds of impacts if the only constraint on their numbers is intraspecific competition for food plus some involvement of weather.

The description of the reality and nature of these effects is a scientific function. Whether or not these changes are acceptable for park management is a policy question. As Boyce (1991) comments, some vegetation effect is to be expected with any presence of ungulates. Any "healthy" or "intact" or "natural" ecosystem (whatever these terms connote, a question we will discuss at a later point) with ungulates will experience some effect. The policy question is how much is acceptable.

The answer to the policy question, in our view, depends on the management goals of the parks. And management can only proceed knowledgeably with clear direction if those goals are formulated in precise, ecological statements. Porter (1992) comments that "An unambiguous test of the natural-regulation hypothesis is not at hand" and concludes that it is premature to discard it. But if there is no unambiguous basis for falsifying the hypothesis, it is equally true that there is no unambiguous basis for sustaining it. What is premature is employing the management approach in the first place without a more thorough scientific analysis and prognosis of its likely ecological effects; an explicit set of criteria, coupled with careful monitoring, to measure its effects along the way; and precise decision criteria by which to decide on continuance or termination.

In fact, Houston (1971) did propose a set of qualitative criteria with which to test the hypothesis of natural regulation in Yellowstone. Kay (1990a, Kay and Chadde 1992, Kay and Wagner 1992, Chadde and Kay 1991) evaluated these criteria and concluded that the hypothesis should be rejected.

Boyce (1991:193) also notes, "Existing evidence suggests that each of these premises has been violated, and therefore, one might think that the natural-regulation hypothesis should be rejected." However, he goes on to conclude that each of Houston's rejection criteria is inappropriate because one expects ungulates to affect vegetation and sympatric herbivores. But this demurral misses the key, implicit point in the hypothesis that we pointed out in Chapter 3: the elk and the northern range were considered to have been in equilibrium for millennia, and no changes of the kind that Boyce concedes were to have occurred under natural-regulation management. The herd had, after all, presumably been under de facto natural-regulation management prior to park formation, so its continuance should not have elicited significant change after 1872.

Porter (1992) opined that it was premature to discard the natural-regulation hypothesis on the grounds that there was not yet enough scientific evidence. Yet, he continued, "A case can be made that . . . [deer and elk] populations in some parks are too high. . . . Where high ungulate populations are causing changes in vegetation which conflict with clearly articulated, and broadly accepted management objectives, there is reason to intervene." We are fully in accord with this latter contingency statement, and we will return to the question of scientific adequacy in the next chapter.

We will address the third corollary question of the NPS natural-regulation approach, the role of predators, next.

What Role Predation?

There is embedded in the NPS natural-regulation policy the presumption that predators did not play a significant role in limiting North American ungulate populations before their extermination during the European era. Ungulate species are presumed to have evolved self-limiting mechanisms that would enable them to curb their population growth below densities at which they would damage their own resources to their disadvantage. To do otherwise would be evolutionarily unstable (Cole 1971). Moreover, the presence of several species of sympatric ungulates implied that no one species had increased to the point of competitively excluding the others.

As mentioned in Chapter 3, this rationale was not the first one proposed. The first version of the policy (Anon. 1967a), "Natural Control of Elk," stated: "In summary, periodic severe winter weather, native predators and the elk population itself interact to naturally control elk numbers within limits set by winter food. . . . The occurrence of uncompensated predation deaths relieves grazing pressure on vegetation and severe food stresses on elk populations at critical times." Why the policy was changed has never been clear. Chase (1986) suggested that the first version did not square with the fact that wolves had been exterminated and other large predators were reduced to low numbers. The paradigm had to be revised to provide for population limitation without predation.

Whatever the circumstances surrounding the development of the new policy, any critique of it carries the need to assess what constraints could have operated on ungulates in pre-Columbian times and prevented them from impacting their resources excessively. Predation by large predators is one obvious factor.

American wildlife management has been ambivalent over the question of whether predation is a significant limiting influence on wildlife populations. While European gamekeepers in the first part of this century were producing bumper crops of small game with intensive management that included stringent predator control, American wildlifers were generally accepting the principles proposed by Paul L. Errington (1946). These held that predation did not significantly influence small-game population levels. Rather, the levels were said to be determined by the nature of the habitat and the territorial behavior of the animals. Predation reportedly took just the excess over what that habitat could sustain, an excess that could not survive even in the absence of predators.

Connolly (1978:378) surmised that these ideas were readily accepted in wildlife-management circles because they provided a theoretical rationale for recreational hunting. We would add that American wildlifers also value predatory species, and the Erringtonian ideas provided an argument against hunters' demands for predator control as a wildlife-management measure. Modern ecological research has gradually altered the earlier American predation views, the results of some studies and reanalyses of Errington's own data leading to different interpretations of predatory effects on small game.

Often overlooked in the mass of Errington's writing is the fact that he exempted ungulates from his general paradigm in his seminal 1946 papers:

> Intercompensations in rates of gain and loss are evidently less complete in the life equations of the ungulates than in the muskrats. There is vastly more reason that I can see for believing that predation can have a truly significant influence on population levels of at least some wild ungulates. (Errington 1946)

One year after appearance of that statement, Aldo Leopold et al. (1947) published their classic paper on overpopulated deer ranges. These authors, as Connolly (1978:375) discussed, reviewed evidence on approximately 100 North American deer irruptions and found that all those in the western United States followed the institutionalization of federal predator control in the early part of the century. Eastern irruptions had occurred previously following earlier predator elimination. Irruptions had not occurred in Canada and Mexico, where the full array of predatory species was still present.

Since then, a number of authors have published evidence of predatory effects on individual ungulate populations, while others have reviewed the accumulated evidence on the matter. Keith (1974) reasoned, on the basis of his survey of the accrued evidence, that pre-Columbian predator populations could have been a major constraint on ungulate numbers. Connolly (1978) reviewed the subject and listed 31 North American ungulate populations that showed evidence of predatory effect. Of these, 22 were deer and pronghorn populations, with coyotes and/or bobcats implicated as the constraint in 16 of the total. Peek (1980) reviewed a number of North American cases that showed evidence of predatory limitation on ungulate populations. He concluded that the reality of natural regulation, as he perceived it, could not be evaluated unless native predators were restored.

Yet despite these indications, wildlife ecology in the United States still did not have a clear and concerted position on the question. Wolves had been almost totally eradicated from the lower 48 states, and cougars and bears had been reduced to low numbers in some areas and eliminated in others. This left only coyotes and bobcats in appreciable numbers in many areas. And while Connolly's overview showed some evidence of limitation by these species on the smaller ungulate forms, there was no way of knowing what the collective effect of the intact, pre-Columbian, large-carnivore fauna had been on the full range of ungulate species in North America.

During the 1970s and 1980s, however, research in a number of Canadian provinces and territories, and in Alaska, where wolves and bears remained in substantial numbers, began to converge on a consistent picture (cf. Carbyn 1983, Bergerud et al. 1983, Messier and Crete 1985, Gassaway et al. 1992) that included elk, moose, and caribou as well as deer. Seip (1992) summarized this picture at a 1991 conference. And then the Second North American Symposium on Wolves, held in Edmonton in August 1992, brought together the principal players for three days to present evidence and discuss these issues. Most participants concurred on an emerging paradigm.

Although there is now a great deal of evidence from Canada and Alaska on ungulate and predator densities and population trends, estimates of kill rates by prey age classes, fractions of prey populations killed, and prey preferences, the real strength of the evidence lies in its quasi-experimental nature. There have been enough studies in different areas to where it is now possible to show inverse correlations between ungulate densities and predator numbers across a diversity of areas. And there are enough time series on individual ungulate populations where predators were not controlled, were then controlled, and then again were not, which show associated ungulate responses. The view now prevails among most of the biologists who have worked on the problem that, where there are naturally occurring wolf populations and certainly if accompanied by significant bear populations (blacks or grizzlies), ungulate numbers more often than not are maintained at low densities.

Two other lines of investigation bear on the influence of large-carnivore predation on ungulate densities. The first, an exception that apparently proves the rule, is the extremely high densities that some ungulate populations attain in the presence of natural carnivore communities. These are the large herds of barren-ground caribou and plains bison in North America, and the spectacular increase of wildebeest populations on the Serengeti Plain following relief from rinderpest (Sinclair and Norton-Griffiths 1979). Researchers on both continents are converging on a common hypothesis. All of these species migrate extensive distances between seasonal ranges. Bergerud (1992) hypothesizes that migration serves to move the animals away from sedentary predator populations and ease predatory pressures. Fryxell et al. (1988), proposing a similar function for migration, present evidence showing that migratory ungulate species in a number of African areas attain densities that average an order of magnitude higher than sedentary forms. And with computer simulation, they showed how migration could reduce predation constraints and produce high population densities.

The other avenue of investigation is Boyce's (1992a) simulation modeling of the effects of wolf reestablishment in Yellowstone on the Greater Yellowstone elk population. His simulations predict an average 10–30 percent reduction in the elk population with a hypothetical wolf population ranging from 90 to 140 animals. The predictions, of course, depend on the assumptions on which the model is built, and the degree of elk population reduction may differ from 10 to 30 percent, depending on how closely the model corresponds to the real world. As Boyce concludes, "We cannot know the consequences of wolf recovery until it actually takes place." But the qualitative conclusion that wolf predation will reduce the elk population by some fraction is probably a strong one.

To conclude this section, in our view there is now extensive and persuasive evidence that large-predator communities unconstrained by human action, and functioning with other factors in the ecosystem, can and do limit ungulate densities at levels below what would prevail in their absence. We agree with Peek (1980) and Caughley (1981b) that predatory effects operate in concert with other constraints, such as vegetation and weather. We do not suggest that all ungulate populations at all times were, in the absence of European intercession, held at low levels by predation and other effects. But we suggest that predation was a ubiquitous influence, perhaps fluctuating in effect over time like climatic variation, but on average applying a significant, general limiting influence on ungulate numbers.

Moreover, the evidence cited above on density dependence at low densities implies less predation force needed to limit populations at low population size than would be the case without density dependence. If natality and survival rates are already reduced somewhat through density dependence at low densities, less reduction in r by predation is needed to achieve equilibrium at those densities. If, as appears to be the case, predation frequently operates in an inversely density-dependent manner, the probability of its adding a significant suppressive effect at low densities is even stronger.

Two other limiting influences on ungulate populations—dispersal and aboriginal hunting—have yet to be considered and will be addressed next. When these are added to the ones already discussed, it will become clear that a complex of constraints must have operated on pre-Columbian ungulate populations that likely were sufficient to hold those populations, and their impacts on their ecosystems, below what we see today in the national parks.

"Natural"

It is clear by now that the term and concept *natural* have figured prominently in NPS policy throughout the history of the System. The enabling legislation establishing Yellowstone decreed preservation of the "natural curiosities, or wonders . . . in their natural condition." Since that time, a stream of policy statements has reiterated this general theme:

> National parks, preserved as natural, comparatively self-contained ecosystems, have immense and increasing value to civilization as laboratories for serious basic research. Few areas remain in the world today where the process of nature may be studied in a comparatively pure natural situation. (Anon. 1968)

> The primary purpose of Yellowstone National Park is to provide present and future visitors with the opportunity to see and appreciate the natural scenery and native plant and animal life as it occurred in primitive America. (Anon. 1977b)

As with the other terms and concepts discussed above, it is necessary to know unambiguously what the term connotes if it is to give clear direction to park management. Two meanings of the word natural can be inferred from other statements, although by no means unambiguously. One meaning involves the influence of humans:

> A portrayal of primitive America is defined as having natural conditions where scenery and "balance of nature" in ecosystems are not altered by man. (Anon. 1967b)

> National parks were founded on the principle of . . . natural processes, and the importance of minimizing human interference. . . . [M]anagement's primary purpose is to maintain the area's pristine condition to the fullest extent possible. . . . This includes the perpetuation of natural processes in the absence of human interference— processes essential to the existence of a healthy ecosystem. (Varley 1988)

The natural-resource policies of the National Park Service are aimed at providing the American people with the opportunity to enjoy and benefit from natural environments evolving through natural processes minimally influenced by human actions. (Anon. 1988a)

The ambiguities in these statements lie in the variations between "minimal" and "no" human actions, and in whether they are referring to the effects of post-Columbian Europeans or Native Americans or both. Later statements, to be cited below, do exclude Europeans, but there is still no clear indication of whether aboriginal effects are included or not. We are inferring that the effects of pre-Columbian humans are presumed in these statements to be inconsequential on the basis of the 1967 statement ("primitive America is defined as having natural conditions . . . not altered by man") and Varley's ("natural processes in the absence of human interference").

Until quite recently, North American ecologists, often without a thorough reading of the archaeological and anthropological literature, have tended to dismiss the effects of preindustrial humans on the continent's ecosystems as inconsequential. But in all parts of the world, archaeologists studying prehistoric human uses of natural resources, and anthropologists studying those uses by contemporary subsistence cultures, along with a burgeoning literature, are forcing on ecology the realization that such effects have been dismissed too lightly. Borrowing such questions of ecological theory as the degree to which resources limit (human) populations, the effects of humans on their resources, and optimal-foraging theory, these scientists are finding significant exploitation effects on animal populations and alteration of landscapes with fire, deforestation, and cultivation (cf. Diamond 1986a, 1988, Redford 1990, Simms 1992, Gómez-Pompa and Kaus 1992, Birkedal 1993, Wagner and Kay 1993, Kay 1995 for reviews).

The universality of these influences prompted archaeologist Simms (1992) to generalize that:

All human societies have played a role in shaping ecosystems, [and] there are many cases of hunter–gatherer behavior that . . . would be classified as having negative impacts upon wilderness environments. The evidence suggests that simple societies may be as susceptible to causing significant environmental damage as more complex societies. To be sure, there is a difference of scale.

And according to Redford (1990):

> The recently accumulated evidence . . . refutes this concept of ecological nobility. Precontact Indians were not "ecosystem men"; they were not just another species of animal, largely incapable of altering the environment, who therefore lived within the "ecological limitations of their home area." . . . Evidence of vast fires in the northern Amazonian forests and of the apparently anthropogenic origins of large areas of forest in eastern Amazonia suggests that before 1500, humans had tremendously affected the virgin forest, with ensuing impacts on plant and animal species. These people behaved as humans do now: they did whatever they had to to feed themselves and their families.

Skeptics of the idea that Native Americans significantly altered North American ecosystems prior to 1492 protest that human populations were too low to have had much impact. This view is based on the assumption that pre-European human populations were similar to those encountered on the continent by the first immigrants. But recent authors (cf. Dobyns 1983, Ramenofsky 1987) are concluding that European diseases were introduced by the first Spaniards arriving in the West Indies. The diseases are thought to have been carried to the mainland by the natives and then swept across the continent, decimating populations up to two centuries before Europeans arrived in many parts of the mainland. The pre-Columbian North American population is now thought to have numbered as high as 100 million.

These newer insights raise very real questions regarding appropriate goals for national-park management and what constitutes natural conditions. Following the extensive archaeological investigations of Frison (1971, 1978) and Wright (1983, 1984), who concluded that ungulates in general, and elk in particular, were scarce in pre-Columbian Jackson Hole, Kay (1990a,b) analyzed the ungulate species composition in both published and unpublished data on the remains of more than 200 archaeological sites in Washington, Oregon, Idaho, Montana, Wyoming, Utah, and Nevada. These contained over 52,000 identified ungulate bones. The total evidence indicated that ungulates (and animal resources more generally) made up less than 5 percent of the aboriginal diet. Moreover, elk remains were only 3 percent of the ungulate total, including sites near Yellowstone, where today they comprise roughly 80 percent of all ungulates.

From these and other sources of evidence, Kay (1988, 1990a,b, 1995) hypothesized that low ungulate densities and very different species composition in the pre-Columbian western United States were maintained by aboriginal hunting, possibly in synergy with carnivorous predators. The low numbers would include areas now in national parks.

The pre-Columbian, anthropogenic role of fire also bears on the question of what is natural. Bonnicksen and Stone (1981, 1982a) describe the patchwork, mixed-age character of the giant sequoia–mixed conifer forests of Sequoia-Kings Canyon National Park that prevailed near the end of the last century. They ascribed this character, and the shrub and hardwood understory, to periodic burning by Native Americans. Park managers now engage in prescribed burning to simulate this effect.

Houston (1982) found evidence of a 20- to 25-year fire frequency, quite possibly anthropogenic, on Yellowstone's northern range, which the park has not attempted to simulate with prescribed burning. Pyne (1989) blamed park management for this failure, to which he attributed in part the severity of the 1988 fires:

> To exclude anthropogenic fire and rely on lightning fire alone did not restore an ancient environment but created landscapes that probably had never before existed. . . . The norm is the human use of fire everywhere and for every conceivable purpose. Both natural fire and suppression [policies] are anomalies because they propose alternatives to anthropogenic fire. Yet Yellowstone purged this middle terrain—deliberate fire usage—as interventionist.

To sum up at this point, there is abundant and increasing evidence that Native Americans significantly influenced the character of North American ecosystems prior to European contact. If the NPS policy is to preserve the ecosystems of national parks in some semblance of their pre-Columbian structure and function, the agency can no longer ignore these anthropogenic effects and must as a matter of policy simulate them as some parks are now doing. If it chooses not to do so, it is incumbent on the organization to propose a credible, ecological rationale for omitting from the systems those constraints, relationships, and processes with which the constituent species coevolved for 10 millennia or more and accept the consequences for thus altering the systems. Either way, the Service can no longer afford to ignore the issue.

On a related note, Anderson (1991) proposed a set of three criteria by which to judge naturalness: (1) the degree to which the system would change if humans were removed, (2) the amount of cultural energy required to maintain the functioning of the system as it currently exists, and (3) the complement of native species currently in an area compared with the suite of species in the area prior to settlement.

Anderson appears at one point to exclude all human influence from his concept of natural when he states, "The most common usage of 'natural' in the ecological literature is understood to mean a process, situation, or system free of human influence . . . a usage applied in the context of aboriginal as well as technological humans." But elsewhere he speaks of assessing the ecological changes that would follow removal of humans by addressing "the extent to which key ecosystem processes and components have been modified by *modern humans* [emphasis ours]," and "the extent that it is possible to reconstruct the assemblage of species just prior to exploration and settlement of the region by European settlers."

Anderson is one of the few authors to at least raise the question of influence by preindustrial people and to provide a set of explicit, ecological criteria with which to measure naturalness. But in our view his criteria could be clarified further. They are all conceptualized in terms of human effects, and it would be helpful if they were posed in a dual scheme: one set in terms of removing European effects while accepting aboriginal, and another in terms of removing both.

A second meaning of the word natural that appears in some definitions involves concern for continued evolution of species in the parks. This is evident in the above quotation from the NPS 1988 *Management Policies* document, and in the following from the same source:

> Managers . . . will try to maintain all the components and processes of naturally evolving park ecosystems. . . . The National Park Service will strive to protect the full range of genetic types (genotypes) native to plant and animal populations in the parks by perpetuating natural evolutionary processes and minimizing human interference with evolving genetic diversity.

And Walker (1989) articulates the same theme in speculating on what the manager of a conservation area should do in the next century: "the persistence of any particular species depends on its maintaining a high (intraspecific) genetic diversity, with an associated diversity of physiological and behavioral traits enabling it to be an adapted and adaptable species."

In our judgment, this is a worthwhile ideal but almost impossible to realize given the contemporary isolation of parks. Major selective factors such as predation and human exploitation have been removed. At the same time, the very isolation and absence of genetic exchange with other populations almost certainly increases inbreeding and reduces heterozygosity. The smaller a population the greater this risk. Managers of Kruger National Park in South Africa recognize the risk with their small, remnant population of roan antelope and have resolved to give the species as much protection as can reasonably be given. Accordingly they vaccinate the animals each year against anthrax (Younghusband and Myers 1986). Advocates of the current U.S. park-management philosophy might argue that nature should take its course, and if the animals are eliminated by the disease, that would simply be natural. But the risk was induced by human action in the first place: the park has been fenced, and genetic exchange prevented, for decades. Given the park goal of preserving biodiversity, South African scientists argue that extreme measures are required to counter the modern human influences that have brought the system to its present state, if the goal is to be reached.

Finally, the most recent definitions of natural carry some new policy implications:

> "Naturalness" is defined as those dynamic processes and components *which would likely exist today,* and go on functioning, if technological humankind had not altered them. (Philpot et al. 1988)

> As a point of reference, *natural conditions* [*sic*] are defined as those *that would have existed today* in the absence of the effects of European man. (Anon. 1991a)

The emphases are ours in both cases.

We find this an impossible goal to reach. To begin with, the issue of the aboriginal effects is still left unconsidered. But beyond this, to know what is natural by this definition, and therefore a management goal, would require an impossible, complete understanding of the structure and function of the system at European contact and an equally complete understanding of changes that would have occurred (but never did) in the absence of Europeans, including:

1. Native American effects that would have occurred from their unknown and never-eventuated population trends, changes in

geographic distribution, new and abandoned patterns of resource use

2. Biological trends such as species extinctions, evolution, changes in geographic distribution, etc., that would have occurred if Europeans had not altered the North American landscape

3. Climatic and geological events, and their interactions with the above.

The agency has, in our view, set a goal for the parks that is both unknowable and unattainable.

Walker (1989) has commented, "Before we reach the year 2100, the changes in the world's atmosphere and the human pressures on conserved areas will have highlighted the futility of trying to maintain completely 'natural' areas as they exist today." We noted in Chapter 4 that, given the plethora of external pressures on the parks, there are no truly "natural" ones. We now add to those external effects the removal of aboriginal influences; fragmented biotas, including disappearance of predators; addition of exotics; and constraints on animal movement, which eliminate both population release and genetic exchange. We could not agree more with Walker's comment. If the parks are to have seriously attainable, wildlife-management goals, they will have to be more realistic and less idealistic. We will consider those in the next chapter.

Might the Systems Cycle?

Several observers have postulated an alternative to the natural-regulation Caughley-esque paradigm of ecological carrying capacity. Boyce (personal communication), Coughenour and Singer (1991), and G. Belovsky (personal communication) have suggested that the ungulates and their vegetation might undergo cyclic or other nonequilibrial fluctuations over time. Porter (1992) commented that there may be time lags in these ungulate–vegetation systems. And Caughley, while concluding that the empirical record does not show such systems cycling (1976a), hypothesized elsewhere (1976b) that elephants and their vegetation in East African parks might cycle on a 200-year periodicity.

The policy implication of such a happenstance is that, if the systems cycle naturally in this manner, and park-management goals are to preserve natural systems, then extreme alteration of park ecosystems, like those induced by elk in Yellowstone and Rocky Mountain, are simply part of nature's scheme. The systems can be expected to cycle out of the current altered states some decades or centuries in the future and back to what we currently and stereotypically consider to be intact or healthy systems.

The mechanism for such a cyclic phenomenon would be that of a herbivore population rising with few or no constraints until it exhausted and seriously suppressed the vegetation. At that point the herbivores, deprived of food, would decline to low densities. With the grazing pressure off, the vegetation would gradually recover until at some point the herbivores could increase again and repeat the sequence. Theoretical models, actually predator–prey models adapted for the purpose, have been used by Caughley (1976a, Caughley and Lawton 1981) and Crawley (1983) to generate dynamics similar to those postulated and give some theoretical credence to the hypothesis.

Our reactions to this idea are two-fold: one is a scientific judgment on the likelihood of such behavior; the other is a consideration of the value aspects. In our scientific judgment, the likelihood of limit-cycle behavior in these ungulate–vegetation systems is remote for both theoretical and empirical reasons. First, it is necessary to examine the reality of the biological assumptions with which the models are structured, for the same biological relationships must abstractly drive oscillations in the models and in actuality drive the real-world systems.

The original predatory–prey models are those constructed and analyzed by May (1975, 1981). The starting points are the overly simplistic, Lotka-Volterra (L-V) predator–prey equations, which drive cyclic time series on a constant period and amplitude if unperturbed. The prey (or vegetation) model is made more realistic by replacing the exponential-growth term and straight-line predator functional response on the right side of the L-V prey equation with a logistic term and a Type II functional-response term, respectively. An asymptotic numerical-response term is added to the right side of the L-V predator (or herbivore) equation.

The time series generated by these two new equations will cycle if they are assigned the appropriate parameter values. As May (1981) points out, the prey logistic term and the Type II functional response work in opposition to each other, the density dependence of the logistic term tending to stabilize and the inverse density dependence of the functional response tending to destabilize. If r_m of the logistic is small and/or K large, the density dependence is weak, the functional response will overpower it, and the system will cycle or, even at the extreme, go chaotic. But with large r_m and/or small K, the density dependence is strong, and the system will damp to stable equilibrium values.

There are three reasons why we consider cyclic or chaotic behaviors of this form unlikely in the ungulate–vegetation systems for which we have evidence. First, there is density dependence in real-world ungulate populations. If a term for it is added to the predator (herbivore) equation, it adds to the stabilizing force of the prey (vegetation) logistic term and makes stability highly probable (Crawley 1983).

Second, the cyclic behavior depends on the Type II functional response. Recent herbivory research shows functional responses in ungulates to be considerably more complex than the simple curves used in most predation theory (Spalinger et al. 1988, Spalinger and Hobbs 1992). The more complex responses may not induce cyclic behavior.

Third, the predator–prey equations are structured to represent the behavior of one predator and one prey species. Wagner (1981b) has shown that cyclic behavior depends very nearly on this level of simplicity. The Lotka-Volterra equations can be rearranged algebraically to show that all of the variation in the prey's rate of change is associated with predator N, while all variation in the predator's rate of change is associated with prey N. Any alternate predator species that prevented the prey from responding totally to the population of the first predator would detract from the cyclic behavior; and any alternate prey for the first predator would do the same. It is probably for this reason that the one ungulate–predator system that does show cyclic tendencies is the Isle Royale moose–wolf system (Peterson et al. 1984, Peterson 1988), which approaches a 1 predator–1 prey system.

In ungulate–vegetation systems, the herbivores feed on an array of plant species, with preference scales ordering the sequence of feeding pressures on the plant species. The process is more complex than merely feeding on, and eliciting dynamics in, a single plant species. Under pristine conditions there was also an array of predatory species, including humans, each with slightly different feeding niches and dependencies, that added a range of diverse constraints on the ungulates in addition to those imposed by the vegetation.

Finally, there is empirical evidence that casts doubt on the existence of this type of cyclic behavior in most ungulate populations. The time lags driving such behavior consist of actual rates of change r being functions of population size at some earlier time period. When the rate of change for the current point in time r_t is plotted as a function of current population size N_t, the function is a circular or elliptical one as McCullough (1992), and before him Royama (1977) and Berryman (1981), has shown (Fig. 6-3).

In fact, the observed r_t/N_t functions in ungulate populations are

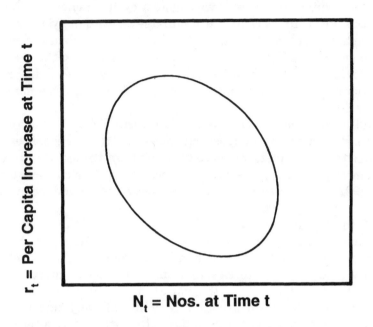

r_t = Per Capita Increase at Time t

N_t = Nos. at Time t

Figure 6-3. Relationship between the per capita rate of increase at time t (r_t) and the population size at time t (N_t) in a time-lagged, cycling population. Compare with Fig. 6-2c, the same relationship in a non-time-lagged, noncycling population. This figure is adapted from Fig. 3 in McCullough (1992).

commonly found to be linear in some form, whether straight-line (e.g., Fig. 6-2c) or curvilinear. Merrill and Boyce's (1991) conclusion that the Yellowstone northern herd elk population can be represented by a logistic model implies a linear r_t/N_t function, and Boyce's (1991:187) conclusion that the herd is globally stable would follow from a herd functioning in a logistic manner. And we have discussed above our own calculation of a linear r_t/N_t function in the herd. Elsewhere, straight linearity is not so clear, although we cited a number of examples of it above. Fowler (1981, 1987) and McCullough (1990, 1992) discuss the evidence and biological rationale for curvilinearity in ungulate r_t/N_t functions. But none of these suggest the ellipsoid functions characteristic of populations undergoing limit cycles (Fig. 6-3).

Hence there is little theoretical basis or empirical evidence indicating that ungulate–vegetation systems fluctuate in this Lotka-Volterra manner. As we noted previously, Caughley (1976a) concluded from his review of ungulate–vegetation dynamics that such cycles have not been observed. The one empirical exception appears to be the very simple Isle Royale system.

We do not suggest that ungulate populations do not fluctuate. Indeed, there are numerous examples of such variations associated with climatic variations. McCullough (1989) discussed fluctuations in desert bighorn populations associated with variations in precipitation and inferred oscillatory trends. A combination of severe drought in 1988, winter weather conditions, and food shortage induced winter mortality on the order of 20 percent of the Yellowstone northern elk herd in 1988–1989. But our conclusions address intrinsically driven, Lotka-Volterra-type, herbivore–vegetation limit cycles.

In closing this section, we turn to the value and policy implications. Even if such cycles did occur, any decision to accept them as desirable behavior in park ecosystems should in our opinion be explicitly provided for in the goals set for parks. McCullough (1989) raises this issue in contemplating bighorn sheep management directions in Death Valley: "realities of the time scale must be confronted. Most Americans will not be satisfied that a certain condition will recur again several generations in the future." The American public should be made fully aware of the temporal implications of any goals that rejected management and allowed park ecosystems to cycle over periods longer than human generations.

Process Management

One of the newer concepts in natural-area management, alluded to in some of the quotes above, is "process management" and variations on that term. Boyce (1991:190) rejected the term "natural-process management" because "so much semantic baggage is associated with the word natural," and suggested in its stead "ecological-process management."

The rationale that gave rise to this concept is the realization that ecosystems are in continuous change and cannot be frozen in their state at points in time. The latter, in the view of some observers, was implied by the Leopold Committee's injunction to preserve "vignettes of primitive America." The objective of process management is to:

> Maintain the elements of change and heterogeneity. Discard the notion of some idealized state for the ecosystem, and allow change to occur. In order to maintain ecosystem resilience, it is the ecological processes in

ecosystems which we need to conserve, not some particular state of the system. (Walker 1989)

[A]llow ecological processes of nutrient cycling, plant succession, fire, decomposition, competition, predation, symbiosis, birth, and death to operate unimpeded by human intervention. (Boyce 1991:190)

It is our impression that a further rationale for this concept is to account for some of the consequences of natural-regulation management. A result of the burgeoning ungulate populations could be, and in some cases has been, the suppression and even elimination of both plant and animal species. If management focused on processes rather than entities, there need be no concern for significant changes in the states of the systems, including loss of species from park ecosystems.

Our response is again based on both value and scientific considerations, and now in this order. Bonnicksen (1989b) protests that:

[P]rocess management, such as letting wildfire burn as a process, "is actually changing the meaning and purpose of our national parks." . . . I believe that national parks and wilderness areas were not set aside to preserve fire or abstractions such as "natural regulation" or natural processes, they were set aside for a host of values that fire may or may not have had a role in creating.

The implication here is that national parks were set aside for the public, which comes to them to see the entities not the processes that mostly can neither be seen nor experienced. The founding legislation, like the 1916 Organic Act, so indicates: "The fundamental purpose of said parks is to conserve the scenery and the natural and historic objects and the wildlife therein."

From a scientific perspective, one must ask what role humans should play in process management. Typical of related NPS policy issues, thought or mention of aboriginal effects, which certainly were processes, is usually missing from discussions of process management. Boyce (1991:196), after concluding that we can never fully comprehend what the aboriginal effects were, remarks that "Learning how ecological processes operate in Yellowstone with minimal human influence, and observing the changes that occur, seems more appropriate than arbitrary interference." And he states that the objective of ecological-process management "is to allow ecological processes . . . to operate unimpeded by human intervention" (p. 190).

But, he continues, "human intervention may occasionally be necessary to restore or protect the functioning of ecological processes, particularly where the system has been significantly disturbed." And later, "Ecological process management does not imply hands-off management, but rather carefully reasoned intervention with a directed goal." Restoring wolves, perpetuating grizzly bears, eliminating exotics, and mitigating modern human impacts "will require active management." In short, "we need all components of the ecosystem if we are to engage in ecological-process management" but apparently not aboriginal effects and compensation for other missing constraints on animals.

As always depending on park goals, we do not have the same concerns as Bonnicksen except for the Service's selective acceptance of human influence and its willingness to shrug off park species as a consequence of what could be ill-considered management. Instead, we find this another nonargument. To advocate preserving processes is tantamount to advocating the preservation of species. Species carry out processes. Any suggestion to concentrate on processes and ignore species is self-contradictory.

However, we do have the same reaction to this concept that we have discussed in connection with each of the above items: An extremely complex entity, the functioning (the collective processes) of ecosystems, is being given superficial consideration in park science and management, and cursory use in policy verbiage. There is no way that the concept of process management, in the casual ways in which it is commented on, can be translated into clear directions for park management. We do not believe that most references to the idea come from any significant thought about the bewildering complexity of what is being verbalized.

One must begin by asking: All processes? The organisms of each species—plants, animals, microorganisms—carry on and are involved in a myriad of processes: physiological, demographic, behavioral, genetic/evolutionary, community, and ecosystem. Every species engages in three, four, or perhaps more orders of magnitude of ecological processes. The total number of ecological processes in national parks is this number per species times the several thousand species occupying it. Can park managers realistically be asked to preserve all the processes in their areas? If so, they are also being asked to preserve all species.

Beyond this, what of the rates of the processes? Does process management include not only preservation of the processes themselves but also in some semblance of the rates at which they functioned under pre-Columbian conditions? If it does, it must not only preserve all of the species, but do so in approximately their pre-Columbian densities.

These are not facetious questions. They follow from any serious thought about the implications of a directive to engage in process management.

If the purpose of park management is to preserve whole ecosystems, that purpose cannot be served without preserving both components and processes. Both are inextricably part of the essence of what we call ecosystems. Preserving the species of an ecosystem, and in the approximate densities of what contemporary ecology considers to be reasonably intact ecosystems, is tantamount to process management. It is also conceptually and operationally more workable for park management.

"The Great Experiment"

Wright (1992a:43) avers that the decision to stop culling elk in Yellowstone in the late 1960s "rightfully could be called an experiment"; and Despain et al. (1986) call it "the great experiment." There was no mention of an experiment in the initial documents announcing the new policy (Anon. 1967a,b), nor in Cole's (1971) paper describing natural regulation. Houston (1971) did in 1971 speak of testing a hypothesis; but in his 1982 book, which summarized the first 10 years of research on what is now being called an experiment and where one would expect some reference to it, he said nothing about it being an experiment. Rather, in his introduction, he referred to the culling of the preceding era as "experimental perturbations." After searching the documentary and published record on the topic, Kay (1990a:19) concluded that the first reference to natural-regulation management as an experiment was by Meagher (1985), who was also coauthor of Despain et al. (1986), which appeared one year later and touted "the great experiment."

Our reason for raising the issue here is again a case of examining how science relates to policy in NPS. The first point to note, and one that we made in Chapter 2, is that the prevailing large-mammal-management policy in most of the NPS System is natural regulation. Does it then follow that the management program for the majority of the System is an experiment? If so, how well has "the experiment" been designed to follow standard scientific procedures for experimentation?

Proper experimentation includes a null hypothesis, replicated treatments, an experimental design, and an appropriate monitoring plan (Romesburg 1981, Macnab 1983, Diamond 1986b, Kay 1987, Boyce 1991:192). Macnab (1983), in discussing proper experimentation in wildlife management in general, presents essentially our view on the matter, much of it reiterating the above comments:

> There are prerequisites to achieving clear insight from management. . . . The rules of experimental design, controls, replication, and balance (where needed) must be followed strictly to allow unambiguous interpretation of the results. Secondly, the manager must identify the assumptions upon which the management action is based and state them as hypotheses. Thirdly, the effect of the manipulation must be measured and the results reported, particularly if the expected result is not achieved. The rejection of a hypothesis is not a disaster but an advancement of knowledge.

Macnab (1983) continues with a description of how experimentation is typically used in wildlife management, which we think describes "the great experiment" in NPS:

> The expected result, if it is announced at all, is stated in terms so general as to defy objective verification of achievement or lack thereof. Monitoring the effect of the treatment is often desultory and seldom rigorous. There is no replication, and the absence of controls or levels of treatment guarantees that the manager will be unable to determine whether the result was caused by his treatment, by some extraneous factor, or by interaction between the two.

Houston (1971) did articulate a set of falsification criteria for natural regulation in Yellowstone which included: (1) The northern herd would not irrupt beyond the 6,000–9,000 animals he considered to be the equilibrium level. Five years later (Houston 1976), after the herd had increased substantially, he revised the prediction to 12,000–15,000 animals. (2) The winter-range vegetation would not depart from "natural" conditions; any departure would not be due to ungulates. These are qualitative criteria, and it can be debated whether the herd increases to 20,000 or more in the winters of 1988–1989 and 1992–1993 constitute irruptions. Moreover, the research during the overgrazing studies of the latter 1980s concentrated on the herbaceous vegetation and found no suppression of primary production. Hence park officials argue that Houston's criteria have not been falsified.

But as discussed in Chapter 3, there is evidence of effects on composition of the herbaceous vegetation (cf. Kay 1990a, Frank and McNaughton 1992). And there is extensive evidence of effects on woody vegetation, which the overgrazing researchers did not address, and on associated fauna. On the basis of this evidence, Kay (1990a) and Boyce (1991) have both concluded that the events of the years since Houston's hypothesis have falsified it, general and qualitative as the criteria are. And Rocky Mountain regional chief scientist Dan Huff has conceded to us that in his view the Yellowstone northern elk herd is significantly impacting the ecosystem beyond what was originally hypothesized and currently acknowledged by park biologists. Yet the management policy continues, and we are not aware of any falsification criteria for any of the other parks.

While acknowledging the northern herd's effects on the ecosystem, Huff has commented to us, "Maybe it's OK to try this on one or two areas and see what happens." And Porter (1992:310) notes, "our best hope of learning about natural processes is to let some ecosystems follow an unrestrained course and observe closely."

Our response is that this approach does not pose any explicit and meaningful scientific question. There are dangers with this kind of unfocused, let's-see-what-happens-if approach. The first is that one cannot make enlightened decisions on what to measure in order to track the changes. Everything in an ecosystem cannot be measured by a typical research team. Without systematic manipulation of one or a few variables well supported by controls, a succinct hypothesis on what the manipulative influence may be, and quantitative falsification criteria defined on a discreet time frame, there is a distinct risk of not measuring important changes and failing to perceive critical effects. Some parks do not have any biologists, cannot make any measurements, and will be unable to document any effects.

By the same token, it is difficult if not impossible to select criteria by which to judge the experiment a success or failure and whether to end or continue it. Appraising the results of the great experiment in Yellowstone, Despain et al. (1986) conclude, "for now the northern range appears to be doing fine." We surely need an ecologically more meaningful assessment.

Perhaps most important, this open-ended approach subjects the ecosystem to such unknown risks as the loss of endangered species or ecological damages that cannot be repaired in a time frame relative to human lifetimes. The abrupt closing of the Yellowstone dumps, over the cautionary objections of biologists who had been studying the park grizzlies for 10 years (Craighead and Craighead 1967, Craighead 1979), ran a real risk of losing a threatened species from the park. Indeed, the population dropped significantly, as discussed in Chapter 3. As numerous critics have opined, the action was taken without sufficient safeguards and careful observation. The National Academy of Sciences review (Cowan et al. 1974) concluded, "The research program carried out by the National Park Service administration since 1970 has been inadequate to provide the data essential for devising sound management policies for the grizzly bears of the Yellowstone ecosystem."

Beyond these biological and management questions, there are in the great experiment approach what in our judgment are policy problems. For one, the action did not follow the provision in *Management Policies* (Anon. 1988a:1.4) that we cited in Chapter 2: "It is NPS policy to treat potential impairments in the same manner as known impairments. When there is thought to be resource impairment, actions shall be based on strategies that retain the resource in an unimpaired condition until such time as doubts are resolved."

And second, we return to the prospect: if natural regulation is the prevailing policy for the System, and it is an experiment, it must then follow that many parks in the System are being subjected to the risks of the great experiment. By what open procedure, with public participation, was this systemwide policy, with the risks it entails for the public resources, adopted? A major premise of this book is that policies in a public agency should be set by public process and not by agency fiat.

Concluding Remarks

This has been a long and detailed, largely critical discussion of science, primarily ecological, in NPS. Although it may appear that our major purpose has been to search out things in agency procedure to criticize, our motivation has been much more substantive and positive. It arises out of our concern for how well science has served resource management in NPS, and in turn how well resources are being managed in the parks.

National-park management has de facto been in the business of managing whole ecosystems for some time, and numerous authors in recent years have been calling attention to this reality (cf. Agee and Johnson 1988a, Bishop et al. 1989, Keiter and Boyce 1991). Ecosystems are arguably the most complex entities addressed by science. Although ecology is still a young science, it has already generated a mammoth literature that reports an immense amount of empirical evidence and an extensive framework of sophisticated theory. We have indulged in the level of detail on the above topics to give some sense of that complexity and the subtle nuance of the theoretical questions.

Management is the application of science, and the quality and effectiveness with which management is carried out are inevitably functions of the quality of its underlying science. Science does not advocate goal and policy directions. But the latter are properly and effectively served when high-quality science clearly and fully elucidates a priori the consequences of goal and policy alternatives, assists in the design of management programs established to achieve the goals, and follows through by analyzing the results once a decision is made. If scientific quality is wanting, the consequences of policy alternatives may not be fully, or even correctly, understood, management decisions may be inappropriate, management programs may not be effectively evaluated, and the resources are placed at risk.

Some very good science has been conducted in NPS. The avian ecology, marine biology, and hydrologic research and modeling investigations in Everglades have been excellent science and promise to provide the understanding needed to restore and manage that complex system. There has been high-quality research under way on fire ecology in the Sierra Nevada parks. Freemuth (1991) comments on the excellence of air-quality research in the System; and an excellent monitoring program in Channel Islands is keyed to a well-conceived model of that park's ecosystem. We know of other examples as well.

But the same cannot be said about some of the other very important parks in the System. We have found a disturbing number of cases of inadequate facility with the relevant literature, superficial grasp of ecological theory, and intellectual insularity. The superficial and ambiguous use of the ecological concepts discussed in this chapter, which end up leading policy and management, is one manifestation. When that superficiality is coupled with the organizational and policy constraints on objectivity discussed in the last chapter, there is real cause for concern that science in the System has not only failed to provide an effective service to resource management, but has worked to its disbenefit. In our view, these problems with the science underlie the long contention and lack of consensus on Yellowstone.

In fairness, park biologists have been spread thinly over an array of projects for which they may not have had the specialized training, have been pressed into service writing resource-management plans, and at times have been called on for public-relations functions. Too often they have been isolated in parks away from libraries and current literature, have attended professional conferences infrequently, have had limited interaction with other researchers, and in general have had insufficient contact with the scientific mainstream. Research budgets have been meager and whimsical.

All of this underscores the need voiced by the National Research Council study that we commented on in Chapter 5: If the agency is to have a quality research program, and science is to serve resource management effectively, it must be separated from park management into its own independent administrative structure, have a separate budget line, and be given strong leadership by a scientist with outstanding credentials. It is hoped that these conditions will be provided by formation of the National Biological Survey.

7

Future Directions

The National Park System is a treasure of inestimable worth to the American people. Valuable as it is today for recreation, education, and science, it will have even greater value in the future. Changes both in and outside the United States will produce a nation and culture in a century or two the characteristics of which we cannot possibly imagine. The national parks, historic and cultural sites, monuments, seashores, and wild and scenic rivers will provide a tangible link to and knowledge of the past in a way that no amount of written and photographic documentation can. The result will be better self-knowledge and understanding for the American public, and the wisdom and character which that brings. Former NPS director George B. Hartzog Jr. (1988) made this same point in beautiful prose: "Our parklands are the delicate strands of nature and culture that bond generation to generation. They are, moreover, the benchmarks of our heritage."

The preservation of this national treasure—the monuments and vestiges of the nation's prehistory, immense wealth of natural resources with which it was built, and highlights of its history along the way—is the central ethic of the National Park Service. The agency should feel a tremendous sense of pride and excitement over being entrusted with this important public service to the nation. That sense should be a wellspring of high morale, esprit, and commitment. We offer the following recommendations in the hope that they may help the Service satisfy the values that the American public attaches to the national parks and their natural resources.

The Need to Set Explicit Goals

As we have stated several times above, the parks are a public resource and exist to satisfy social values. Foresta (1984:261) comments, "In a democracy any public organization must ultimately base its goals on society's interests and values."

In Chapter 2 we generalized the values that the parks serve into four categories: recreational, educational, scientific, and environmental/preservational. In turn, goals are set to address those values, and policies and management plans are developed to achieve the goals. As Porter (1991) and Underwood and Porter (1991) discuss, the goals are the focal points which lead the program dynamics.

We now add that management goals should be focal points for, and guide research in, the parks. Where the purpose of management is to achieve the goals, the functions of research in the System should be to provide a knowledge base for management, assist in its design, and maintain continuous scrutiny on how well management is achieving the goals. Thus we will argue in this chapter that research should be a service to policy setting and management. Secretary of Interior Babbitt has recently commented that the other Department of Interior agencies are "clients" of the National Biological Survey. We contend that the NBS should be considered a *service organization* to the other agencies.

We inferred System goals from a sequence of documents dating back to the Yellowstone Act. Yet, there is currently a chorus of criticism over the ambiguity and inconsistency, if not absence, of Park Service natural-resources goals. In a 1987 symposium, Ecosystem Management for Parks and Wilderness, Johnson and Agee (1988) stated in their keynote address, "park and wilderness goals will have to be stated in more precise terms, depending on the values represented by the individual area." In a closing address, these same authors commented on the recurring theme expressed during the symposium that there is a "need to define precisely the management objectives for park and wilderness areas" (Agee and Johnson 1988a).

Bonnicksen (1989b) and Bonnicksen and Stone (1982b,c) stressed the same point. Porter (1991) and Underwood and Porter (1991) discussed the importance of clear goal setting to guide management programs at Saratoga National Historical Park, Gettysburg National Military Park, and more recently in the System as a whole (Porter et al. 1994). In March 1989 one veteran NPS biologist raised the same point, asking rhetorically, "What are we managing the parks for?" The Gordon Commission (Bishop et al. 1989) recommended that NPS "Install and refine the concepts of ecological management . . . [including] establishing preservation and visitor impact management goals." One member of the commission told us, "They've got to decide what it is they want."

In November 1991, the Renewable Natural Resources Foundation and Utah State University cosponsored a two-day workshop at Snowbird, Utah, on fire policy in the national parks. Participating were 53 individuals from NPS, as well as representatives from other federal and Canadian agencies and academia. After two days of deliberation, the group concluded on its final day that the Service's biggest policy need is a clear statement of goals. This need may also be responsible in part for what, in the view of observers whom Foresta (1984:1) cites, is a lack of direction in the agency. Foresta himself comments, "It is felt that as a result, the Park Service no longer knows what its purpose is nor that of the Park System it manages." And at a Jekyll Island, Georgia, meeting of NPS Southeast Region superintendents in May 1989, former director George B. Hartzog Jr. commented that NPS is "an agency in crisis" (Chase 1989).

Why the System is not better focused can only be speculated on. Causation is always difficult to demonstrate. One reason, as discussed in Chapter 2, may be the failure to perceive the importance of explicit goal formulation. Another possible reason could be the dual use and preservation mandate (Rockwood 1988) and the historical momentum of heavy emphasis on tourism (Sellars 1989, 1992). Any function that fares as poorly in the budget process as resource management cannot be brimming with self-assurance.

Another reason may be weak leadership at the top that fails to convey a strong sense of mission, commitment, and pride. A number of NPS personnel with whom we have spoken have commented on this weakness. This leadership vacuum may be exacerbated by having political appointees in the directorship who average less than four years in office. Still another reason—perhaps the flip side of the weak leadership problem—may be the extreme decentralization of power along with the political shackles at the park level. This tends to prevent any System view and accountability, according to Policy Director Carol Aten.

Despite all the criticism, we have found a sufficient thread in agency documents to where we could infer a set of reasonably concrete System goals. But the major NPS policy and management documents should, in our judgment, begin with explicit, forceful statements of the important social values that the System serves and the associated, broad goals set to satisfy those values. *Management Policies* (Anon. 1988a) and *NPS-77* (Anon. 1991a) both begin with dry discussions of law and policy and the history of the System's development.

Goal Setting at the Park Level

It is at the park level that the need for goal specificity is greatest. Park goals must be sufficiently detailed to provide clear guidance for policies and on-the-ground management. They will vary across this vast System just as the characteristics of the parks and associated management needs vary and as the authorizing legislations vary. Yet they must fall within the scope of the System goals or they exacerbate the balkanization we have described.

There is undoubtedly much of this in the authorizing bills and in the general management plans (GMPs) and resource-management plans (RMPs) for each park. *Management Policies* charges the parks with writing "statements for management" into the GMPs for each park (Anon. 1988a:2.5). *NPS-77* (Anon. 1991a:Ch. 4, p. 2) prescribes statements on "natural resource values and purposes" in the objectives sections of the RMPs.

We have examined a small sample of enabling acts, and in 1992 we requested of Director Ridenour a sample of the GMPs and RMPs. This request was never answered, so we cannot comment on the goal statements in these documents. What we can do is comment on the goal-setting *process* on the basis of information we have received and acquired. Coming from a group of individuals outside NPS, our perspective on the process is likely to be different from that of persons inside the agency. Following these comments, we will recommend a set of policy and management procedures contingent on adoption of goals.

Importance of Public Input. As a public process addressing a public resource, goal setting in NPS should be an open procedure involving all concerned interest groups. Our data are mixed on the extent to which this is true in the agency, and we do not have a good overall sense of it.

Numerous observers have told us that public involvement in NPS is often ad hoc, variably sought, and discretionary. Agency employees have reported that superintendents exercise discretion over whether to proceed with a full-fledged environmental impact statement (EIS) or settle for the less-demanding environmental assessment (EA), and often opt for the latter. Even when the full EIS procedure is followed, public input may at times be tightly controlled and orchestrated (Anunsen 1993).

Policy Office Chief Carol Aten has told us that policies are set "mostly internally." They may be sent out for public comment, but the public is not involved in the original formulation. The inter-agency team assigned to evaluate fire policy following the 1988 Yellowstone fires concluded that "There was little opportunity for citizen participation in the development of fire management plans" (Philpot et al. 1988). It also seems clear that the natural-regulation policy was adopted internally.

Yet NPS does seek public input. *Management Policies* (Anon. 1988a:2:6) states that formulation of GMPs for the parks should follow NEPA procedures. And *NPS-77* (Anon. 1991a:Ch.4, p. 5) specifies that it is not GMP development per se that is subject to an EIS, but rather the individual management activities specified in the RMPs. Indeed, Yellowstone has recently completed an EIS on wolf restoration in the park; Olympic is doing the same for mountain goat management; and preparation of the Yellowstone Vision for the Future document sought extensive public input.

In March 1993, the superintendent of Capitol Reef National Park sent letters to universities in the region inviting them to send to an April meeting interested individuals who could provide input into formulation of the next GMP for the park. We do not have a sense of how widespread this practice is, but we assume that it is carried out elsewhere.

In general, goal setting in NPS seems to us more internalized than in other federal land-management agencies. This is true at a time when other agencies are moving out of an era when the dominant goal- and policy-setting approach was by agency fiat and into a more open, participatory mode (Wagner 1994). It may well be that NPS needs a formal legislative mandate for planning similar to the one provided the Forest Service by the National Forest Management Act.

Goal Setting Not a Scientific Process (per se). As a corollary of the last point, we do not see goal setting as a scientific process in the sense of scientists setting goals purely on the basis of scientific implications of goal options. Rather, science in our view has two functions in goal setting. One is that parks have values for science. Science as an institution and subset of society has the right to advocate those values in the collective, social process of considering all values in goal setting. But science is only one of the voices, and goals should not be primarily "science driven" unless that is the societal preference.

The other function should involve scientific application and should be value neutral. This is the important function of elucidating the technical consequences of alternative goal options among which decisions can be made by broader, societal representation. Without this input, goal setting would not be enlightened and rational; it would simply become a power process.

Conflicting Values. Clearly, goal setting entails the problem of conflicting values. The dual, NPS legislative mandate is one case in point. Excess public use can damage the resources that parks are established to protect. The demands of concessionaires conflict with the values of the environmental community. National values attached to the System may conflict with local values attached to parks and with those of the local representatives and senators who consider the parks to be part of their districts/states. Local resistance to wolf restoration in Yellowstone and grandfathered grazing in new parks are examples of the latter.

Changing Public Values. Closely related to the dilemmas of conflicting values is the problem of change in public values. Obviously the values that the American public attaches to national parks today are quite different from what they were in the early years of the System. As Rockwood (1988) comments, "At the time Yellowstone was created and the National Park Service was established the concept of an 'ecosystem' did not exist." Goal setting not only must operate under the constraint of laws set early in the history of the System; it must also respond to newer social values, but somehow sense and avoid hasty response to ephemeral public tastes and preferences.

Integration of Park and System Goals

In our opinion, goal setting at national and at park levels needs better integration, the former serving as an umbrella for the latter. Park or unit natural-resources goals will clearly vary. Obviously the goals of parks committed to preserving intact ecosystems, those protecting T and E species, and those preserving cultural resources are different. But these need to be subsumed by broad, forcefully articulated System goals that logically tie together the disparate units of the organization. Such unity could promote the accountability and discipline that Carol Aten considers inadequate.

In sum, it is our impression that the Service needs to be more consistent, forceful, explicit, and open in goal setting. The process needs to involve, indeed seek the participation of, all concerned interest groups: other federal agencies, state agencies, and concerned private interests.

The need is especially great at the park level, where goal options are more real and specific than at the national level, and where local interest groups are most affected by goal decisions. Such localized goal and policy setting is increasingly being used in natural-resources situations and is acquiring its own lexicon: "a strategy of localism" (Chase 1988), "constituency-based multiresource management" (Behan 1990), "interest-group pluralism" (Wagner 1994), and more generally "community-based decision making" (Chase 1988). Bonnicksen (1989b) urges closer adherence to NEPA procedures.

The benefits to this greater emphasis on participatory, explicit goal setting could be at least three-fold: (1) It could provide stronger direction and coherence for the agency as a whole; (2) it would give more effective and precise guidance to park management; and (3) it could well be a means of deflecting whimsical, localized political pressures and ensuring more effective resource management.

In conclusion on goal setting in the parks, the process should precede development of the general management plans. We recommend that the superintendents convene meetings of all interest groups concerned with their units, including representation as appropriate from both local and national interests (cf. Wagner 1994 for examples elsewhere in resource management). There should be one to three scientists—from NPS, NBS, or nongovernment—present to portray for the participants the technical consequences of goal alternatives but not to advocate their personal values and goal preferences. The goals should clearly be in keeping with the units' enabling legislation and System policies. And they should be explicit enough to enable policymakers and managers to design clear management protocols that can achieve the goals.

Goal setting would not be an annual process. Once set, they should hold for three to five years, probably longer. But they might usefully be reviewed every three to five years to ascertain whether or not they were still appropriate and whether they were clear enough to guide management efforts.

Park-Level Policies and Management

Where goal setting is primarily a public process, formulating park management policies calls for more scientific input. It requires public participation but also prescribes the technical detail, scientifically based, of management programs.

Park-Specific, Ecologically Defined Policies

As discussed in Chapter 2, policies (or what Porter 1991 calls objectives) are statements or prescriptions of management protocols designed to achieve goals. As we have seen, both goals, as discussed above, and policies, as discussed in Chapter 2, are set at several governmental levels. Our concern here is with park-level policies and management for natural-resources issues.

Since goals determine policies and management procedures, it is useful here to review the general types of goals most often advocated:

1. *Parks as havens of unsullied nature that, in the absence of humans and their activities, provide spiritual renewal.* This is the Nash and Rolston goal discussed in Chapter 2. The associated management policy is no intervention, advocated on the value and ideological grounds that management intrusions would violate the biocentric purity implicit in the goal's values—the wildness that Carter (1994) advocates. We add the caveat that the decision not to manage is in fact a management decision, which has ecological implications. Those implications need to be assessed and made clear to anyone making the goal decisions (we will discuss the implications below). This goal need not be a monolith across the entire National Park System. It could be selected for only some of the units.

2. *The great experiment.* This is a scientific goal that addresses the question what happens if the ecosystems are left alone to seek their own ends? Advocates of this goal are somewhat equivocal on the need for management. Nonmanagement is argued pragmatically out of fear that we do not sufficiently understand the ecology of park ecosystems to be confident about the consequences of our intervention. Thus Boyce (1992b) concluded, "in most cases we will do best to allow ecological processes to function unhampered by human intervention." But elsewhere (1991:203) he endorses some kinds of management—restoring predators, removing exotics, mitigating tourist impacts—yet omits mention of animal population control. Presumably the first three are tolerated in order to

restore and maintain "naturalness," but the last is *contra naturam*.

It is fair to point out as we did above that this goal is advocated by some scientists and internally by the Park Service, addresses science values, but has not been adopted by the open, public, goal-setting process that we advocate. One can ask whether it is proper for a small group of scientists and Park Service employees to subject public parks to the risks of this use when the broader public has not acquiesced in the goal.

3. *Preservation of "intact" or "healthy" ecosystems.* This is the implicit goal advocated virtually throughout the System's history. We will argue below that its attainment entails a willingness to engage and participate in active management.

4. *Preservation of T and E species.* This goal is explicit in contemporary policy documents; depending on the circumstances, it can require a policy of active management.

5. *Maintenance of biodiversity.* This, too, is explicit in current policy documents and also can require a policy of management.

6. *Simulate historical scenes in cultural areas.* This is obviously a goal in current System policy and more often than not requires active management as stated above.

7. *Parks as drive-through game parks where large numbers of unharassed animals are standing about for easy observation by casual observers.* This is now the condition with large deer populations in many eastern parks, including cultural units, and western parks with large numbers of elk. This goal can be achieved in the short run with no management but in the long run could be lost because the animals would so degrade their ecosystems that the ecosystems would eventually become unfavorable for them.

Some of these goals are compatible with one another and could be addressed by the same or similar management policies, which could be the case with goals 1, 2, and 7 and perhaps goals 3, 4, and 5. In some cases goals 1, 2, 3, 4, 5, and 7 could be compatible but in most cases they would not. Current ad hoc NPS policies maintain that goals 1, 2, and 3 are compatible. They can be in some cases, but we will discuss below why they often, perhaps usually, are not.

Once goals are adopted, policies need to be succinct and specific in order to provide clear and concrete guidance for management.

Here again, this may be the case in the GMPs and RMPs. But because our request for them was never granted, we can only comment at this point on some aspects of the policy process.

We see the process as requiring a much more substantial scientific input than goal setting, which is more a public process. If the goals are those requiring advertent management, then the policies must prescribe measurable, quantitative characteristics of the ecosystems in each unit that management should seek to achieve. This approach has already been proposed by Bonnicksen (1989c, Bonnicksen and Stone 1982c, 1985) and was recommended by the Vail agenda (Briggle et al. 1992): "Identify measurable objectives for desired resource conditions."

Specifying these ecological parameters for all of the parks in the System with natural resources involves an aggregate of ecological knowledge beyond that held by ecologists formerly in NPS and now in NBS, or any other agency. It must draw on the experience and insights of the entire ecological community.

Accordingly, we recommend that the ecological parameters constituting the management objectives of each park be articulated for each unit by panels of ecologists, both outside and within NPS, who are most knowledgeable about the ecology of each park's region. This recommendation closely parallels that of the Gordon Commission, which urged that NPS establish "national, regional, and park Ecosystem Management Advisory Panels."

The professional ecological community has—through the efforts of The Wildlife Society in this review, adoption of the Ecological Society of America's Sustainable Biosphere Initiative (Lubchenco et al. 1991), formation of the Association of Ecosystem Research Centers, the Renewable Natural Resources Foundation, numerous actions of the American Institute of Biological Sciences, and willingness of other professional societies—volunteered assistance in the management of renewable natural resources. It could provide no better service in this regard than to collaborate with NPS in park management by serving on these panels. In fact, the community has already taken one step in this direction by participating in the Workshop for a National Park Service Ecological Research Program in Albuquerque in 1992 (Risser and Lubchenco 1992), from which one recommendation was "science cooperative groups" analogous to the panels recommended here. The functions of these panels would be to collaborate with NPS in

1. Specifying the detailed, quantitative ecological characteristics for which park ecosystems would be managed. These characteristics would be (a) the structure and function of whole

ecosystems in parks where preservation of such systems was the adopted goal; (b) the nature of the landscape in historic parks, as Porter (1991, Porter et al. 1994) discusses; (c) the character of the systems needed to maintain biodiversity in areas with this goal; and (d) the ecosystems needed to preserve T and E species in parks so designated.

2. Developing criteria for deciding the nature and degree of management protocols, including when management intercession is called for.

3. Developing a menu of parameters for the monitoring needed by each park and the procedures and designs for those measurements.

In some cases, it might be sufficient to have a single panel for a group of parks in a region of relatively uniform ecology (e.g., northeastern deciduous forest, Colorado Plateau, Sierra Nevadas). In other cases where parks are unique and/or isolated, or contain especially complex ecological situations, or are large flagship parks, it might be desirable to have panels for individual parks.

The Whys, Whens, and Hows of Management

If there is a professional chorus urging explicit goal statements, there are equally clarion exhortations to NPS to engage in active management. These calls go back 30 years. Active management was the dominant message of the Leopold Committee, although it has either been ignored or meanings have been imputed to the committee that it neither stated nor implied. The Gordon Commission (Bishop et al. 1989), firmly endorsing the Leopold Committee's charge, stated, "The concept of 'naturalness' is not a simple and comprehensive guide for management"; and commission member Jerry Franklin told us (March 21, 1990), "they've got to abandon icons like naturalness." Bonnicksen (1989a) has been one of the most vocal critics of natural-regulation management. Brussard (1991) remarked, "if Yellowstone, the largest national park in the lower 48 states, . . . is too small for natural regulation to succeed, such a management philosophy is surely doomed to fail in the smaller national parks as well."

In a paper presented at the 1992 Ecological Society of America annual meetings, Norman Christensen, who had chaired the Greater Yellowstone Coordinating Committee's review of fire policy after the 1988 fires, averred that "Naturalness is not a realistic or even desirable management goal." After reviewing Yellowstone fire policy, Christensen et al. (1989) urged active management. And we have in this review criticized the newer definitions of natural as being unknowable and unattainable as management objectives. Indeed, NPS policy documents (Anon. 1988a) firmly endorse management.

However, management is a means, not an end. Whether or not to manage, and if so where and how, are totally determined by park goals. Hence the whys of management are to achieve those ends. Our position is that whatever management it takes to achieve park goals is the appropriate action. Otherwise the goals are pointless, and park resources are asea without compass, rudder, or screw. Moreover, when to manage is determined by scientific assessments that judge intervention to be necessary for goal attainment.

Given these premises, and the proviso that goals 1 and 2 eschew advertent management, we turn now to some hows of management in those parks where goal 3 has been decided upon as it has been at the national level. Thus we are not recommending management on the basis of our own values but purely contingent upon publicly decided-upon goals.

In some parks—perhaps remote ones with intact ecosystems—nonintervention and reliance on natural processes may be sufficient for goal attainment. In these cases, the management policies for goals 1, 2, and 3 can be the same. But in most cases, the evidence indicates to us that nonintervention cannot be relied on to maintain healthy ecosystems. As Brussard (1991) commented:

> The major advantage of active management for biodiversity is simply that it will work better than the current policy of natural regulation. . . . While this degree of interference may sound to some like treating national parks like backcountry zoos, it is far preferable to just wishfully thinking that natural regulation will result in their retaining a full complement of species and communities a century from now.

The reasoning voiced repeatedly by Brussard and other authors who similarly urge intervention is that park ecosystems are not self-contained and intact and hence cannot continue functioning as healthy or intact systems, or in some reasonable semblance of pre-Columbian form. If the goals are to preserve some semblance of that form, management must mitigate impacts from the outside and substitute for the inadequacies for reasons we have explored in previous chapters:

1. We discussed in Chapter 4 the welter of external forces imping-
   ing upon park ecosystems. If the systems are to remain within
   the conditions specified by the advisory panels, management
   will need to mitigate the impacts to the extent possible. Some
   effects, like global warming and increased ultraviolet radia-
   tion, will be beyond mitigation. But park research and monitoring should measure such effects on the systems. Control or
   elimination of exotics, on the other hand, is one form of external impacts that in many cases is susceptible of mitigation.

2. Some parks are too small to encompass the home ranges of
   large, highly mobile species. In moving outside the parks to
   obtain their needs, they lose the protection that parks afford.
   Yellowstone grizzlies are, of course, the prototype of this problem. The same appears true of Denali caribou and wolves, and
   moose in exceptional winters. Mitigation could reduce the animals' mobility by supplying their needs through management.
   It is well established that grizzly bear mobility is an inverse
   function of food abundance.

3. Species have been lost from park ecosystems, both through ill-
   advised management action, as in the case of predator control,
   and through Newmark's (1986, 1987) island biogeographic
   effect. Transplant and restoration, as Boyce advocates for
   Yellowstone wolves and Peterson (1994) for Isle Royale wolves,
   can provide mitigation.

4. Original population-limiting factors have been removed. If
   parks are not literally fenced, as in the case of Kruger National
   Park in South Africa and our own Wind Cave, they are often de
   facto fenced by encroaching urbanization and other economic
   development, and/or by a fence of gun barrels. As a result, emigration is no longer available as a population release.
   Moreover, most parks no longer have a full complement of
   predators and aboriginal hunting. Those with large herbivorous mammals commonly experience population increases to
   the point of significantly impacting their ecosystems. If park
   ecosystems are to be maintained in order to achieve goal 3,
   artificial population limitation will often be the only means of
   achieving that objective.

If Not Vignettes or Carrying Capacities, Then What? If park management is to achieve a goal of managing to preserve healthy or intact ecosystems, it needs specific criteria that characterize such systems and toward which it can manage. Up to this point, we have either ourselves criticized, or reviewed other investigators' criticisms of, system states that have been advocated previously. This is particularly the case with parks that have large ungulate populations, which pose some of the most widespread and serious "problems." As a result we have left the topic in limbo up to this point and need now to try to dispel some of the ambiguity and make concrete suggestions.

We have criticized the idea of carrying capacity as an explicit guide for management action on the grounds that ungulate herbivory is too complex to lend itself to any easily derived, quantitative management criterion. Moreover, as a measure of animal numbers ("the number of animals that a given vegetation can support . . . " etc.), it is too limited to be a useful management criterion for an entire ecosystem. Yet we believe it essential that management actions in parks with large ungulates include a thorough understanding of the effects of different ungulate species and numbers on their systems, particularly the vegetation. Hence park personnel need this understanding, whether provided by research in the parks, the knowledge of outside consultants, the published literature, or some combination thereof.

We have also reviewed criticisms of preserving the conditions that prevailed at the time of European contact, the Leopold report's "vignettes of primitive America." These critiques are usually based on two grounds. One is that we can never know exactly what those conditions were (cf. Boyce 1991). The other, going all the way back to the Robbins report (Ackerman et al. 1963), is that ecosystems are continually changing. To preserve conditions that prevailed in 1492, even if we knew what they were and it were possible to do so, would be to freeze in time a transient state (preserve a snapshot). That would give undue emphasis to one out of a range of states and, in preventing natural change, would create a highly unnatural situation.

Yet ecology and resource management cling to a general notion or assumption that North American ecosystems at the time of European contact were healthy and intact and a desirable state for which management should strive. Hence the Park Service goal of the natural, or what would prevail if Europeans had not altered them; Anderson's (1991) criterion of the degree of "naturalness,"

mentioned in Chapter 6, as the complement of native species currently in an area compared with the suite of species in the area
prior to European settlement; and the current efforts of the Bureau
of Land Management, in developing criteria of livestock-grazing
effects, to allude frequently to presettlement conditions as reference points. Even critics of striving for these conditions (e.g., Boyce
1991) implicitly advocate doing so when they recommend eliminating exotics and reintroducing extirpated species. This is tantamount to restoring some desirable, previous state.

Thus there is a lingering and pervasive assumption that the pre-
Columbian condition, imperfectly as it is known, was a desirable
one that land management, including that of national parks,
should try to emulate in some degree. That condition is commonly
presumed to have been in some significant degree what today we
call healthy or intact. We have in previous chapters implied that
same synonymy.

The question then arises as to what that condition was, especially when there were large ungulates, which are the most visible,
and often the most influential, animals affecting North American
ecosystems. Another widespread assumption, probably formed in
part by analogy with the large bison herds of the central continental grasslands, is that the continent, in pre-Columbian times, was
teeming with ungulate herds.

At least for the Intermountain West, this assumption is now
being called into question by three lines of evidence discussed in
Chapters 3, 5, and 6. One is archaeological, with Frison (1971,
1978) and Wright (1983, 1984) concluding that ungulates in general, and elk and moose in particular, were scarce in Jackson Hole,
Wyoming, in pre-Columbian times. Kay (1990a,b, 1994b), examining the entire archaeological record, has generalized this conclusion to the whole Intermountain region. The second line is historical accounts (Rush 1932, Kay 1990a), which has its detractors
(cf. Anon. 1992). But this evidence consists not only of early
remarks on ungulate numbers, but comments on vegetation and
other fauna as well, and agrees with the other two sources. The
third line of evidence is early photographs of Yellowstone, which
portray a very different vegetation that could not have persisted in
the presence of contemporary ungulate numbers. Conditions in the
photographs appear more like today's inside park exclosures, and
outside the park where elk numbers are suppressed by hunting.

There are similar though less substantial indications for Rocky
Mountain and other western parks. And all of this marches with
the mounting worldwide evidence, discussed in the last chapter,

from archaeologists and anthropologists of substantial landscape effects by subsistence cultures; and from predation studies in Canada and Alaska that show significant limitation on ungulate numbers by intact, large-carnivore communities. Kay (1990a,b, 1994b) hypothesizes that ungulate numbers in the Intermountain West in pre-Columbian times were held at low densities by a combination of mammalian carnivores and aboriginal hunting.

Park policies, at least in western parks, maintain that high ungulate populations and severely impacted ecosystems, such as occur in them today, are what prevailed in prehistory. But this view must in part be a legacy of the historical stereotype of pre-Columbian ungulate abundance, a view from which the burden of evidence is now shifting away. And the current reality is that parks do provide refuge for megafaunal species that cannot persist in numbers, or at all, on the outside in the face of hunting and other human disturbances. But in more fundamental ecological aspects—e.g., vegetation, associated microfauna, hydrology—many outside ecosystems, when judged by the emerging criteria (cf. Woodley et al. 1993, Grumbine 1994), exist in greater health, are more intact, or have greater integrity than do systems inside many parks.

If, then, a policy emerges (or the NPS ones in place in its policy documents are in fact addressed) that park management should preserve healthy ecosystems that are as nearly as possible like those of pre-Columbian times, what are the specific characteristics of such systems that management can emulate? Is it possible to compile a firm list of quantitative system parameters that managers can strive to attain? Or are these, as the critics claim, unknowable and therefore unattainable?

There is no simple, easy, or unequivocal answer—it must lie somewhere in between. Obviously we will never know exactly what conditions prevailed. The ecosystems of western North America (unlike those in much of Europe, Asia, and North Africa) have been impacted by settlement recently enough, and have sufficient recuperative power and remnants of earlier times, that they can recover some semblance of the preindustrial state if given relief from herbivourous pressures. This is contingent upon suppression of ungulate numbers to some level approximating those of prehistory.

This statement is somewhat at odds with the new multiple-equilibrium paradigm discussed in Chapters 2 and 6. It is not yet clear how widely this hypothesis applies, even in arid and semiarid regions for which it has been inferred. We cited the Big Bend

National Park situation in Chapter 2 as an apparent exception, and there is evidence for Clementsian recovery in the North American Great Basin Desert following release from grazing. And in more mesic situations, the return of deciduous forest to abandoned cropland is one of the most pronounced ecological changes in eastern North America in the past century.

Judging when the desirable state has been reached is purely a judgment call and can only be made by persons with intimate knowledge of ecosystem structure in the areas involved. The knowledge will come from long-standing personal research on the vegetation, which will include understanding the sensitivity of different plant species to grazing or browsing, or familiarity with the findings of others who have developed that understanding. It will come from exhaustive review of historical sources and photographic archives. And it will come from familiarity with vegetation in relatively undisturbed areas. Given this knowledge, and that of current ecological theory and literature, it should be possible for park management to achieve and preserve intact ecosystems that bear some semblance of presettlement conditions.

Up to this point the discussion has largely focused on western parks. Given that the eastern states have been settled and impacted by Europeans for up to two centuries longer than the Intermountain West, establishing any sense of pre-Columbian conditions and ungulate numbers may present special problems. But recourse to the archaeological record and exhaustive review of historical sources should provide an even greater understanding. The region has a more extensive historical record of early conditions (cf. McDonnell and Pickett 1993). And eastern North American archaeologists are challenging the wildlife ecologists' stereotypes, assumptions, and "myths" about pre-Columbian wildlife numbers with eye-widening inferences (cf. Neumann 1984, 1985, 1989, 1994) about those numbers. They are chiding the wildlifers for ignoring the archaeological record.

If early conditions still remain unclear, the region is fortunate to have large numbers of eminent ecologists with in-depth knowledge of the characteristics of healthy or intact ecosystems who could judge the state of park conditions affected by high deer densities, and who could judge when those conditions had reverted to a healthy and intact state following relief from heavy deer pressures. Assistance from this intellectual resource should be sought if NPS pursues goal 3 of establishing and preserving healthy and intact ecosystems in eastern parks.

Employ the Least Management Possible. We recommend the minimum management necessary to achieve park goals. Because knowledge will always be imperfect, we recommend that management interventions be the minimum needed to maintain or restore park ecosystems within the parameters defined by the advisory panels. Management is not an end in itself, and it should only be used with that viewpoint.

Base Management on Quality Research. We agree with the current NPS policy that management measures should be based on research. But having said that, we recognize that the reality of that attractive, abstract idea is immensely more complex than the simple words convey. Porter et al. (1994) argue that NPS management goals are too vague to provide clear guidance for decisions on controlling white-tailed deer populations even though there is adequate System policy structure to carry it out. And they contend further that progress in ecological research is so slow that "we are not likely . . . soon" to have the scientific understanding ("a litmus test") on which such decisions can be made. Ludwig et al. (1993) and Hilborn and Ludwig (1993) pose much the same argument, challenging the assumption that more ecological research will guide national decisions on sustainable resource use. Rather, optimum levels of exploitation must be determined by trial and error.

Holling (1993) counters with the argument that these pessimistic prospects for ecological advance are based on a research philosophy of reductionism and experimental science. He argues instead for "a science of the integration of parts" that acknowledges uncertainty, unpredictability, and "an inherent unknowability." Management must move forward, expecting the unexpected and judgment errors, but always prepared to learn from these and correct.

The bottom line for all of this is that we will never have perfect knowledge, and to delay management decisions until we do is a path to inaction. Interestingly, while posing the deterrents to deer population control in the parks, Porter et al. (1994) comment, "Clearly, many parks now have deer populations that are too large in the context of cultural and natural-resources management goals." Apparently the evidence is sufficient to convince these three professionals that control is justified.

Schullery (1992) quotes Norman Christensen as saying that "ignorance will not provide a reprieve from managing." And Boyce (1991) quotes Forest Service chief Jack Ward Thomas as commenting, "To say we don't know enough is to take refuge behind a half truth and ignore the fact that decisions will be made regardless of the amount of information available."

To emphasize what we do not know is to ignore what we do know. We now have an immense store of scientific information and brilliant ecologists with deep understanding of every part of the United States. All of that needs to be brought together to provide the context for management decisions. This should be done in collaboration with the park advisory panels, who should have full access to all relevant research information. Management actions should then be taken with careful observation of the results and a readiness to modify the course if observation so indicates.

Consider Management As Tests of Hypotheses. Again because of knowledge inadequacies, we agree with Christensen's comment at the 1992 Ecological Society meetings that management measures should be considered hypotheses, or what Walters (1986) terms "adaptive management." They should be monitored closely, and if their effects change ecosystem components and/or processes beyond the limits specified by the advisory panels, they should be changed.

Monitoring Is Essential. Monitoring ecosystem variables is an indispensable part of the whole process, especially as a part of adaptive management. Numerous reviews—the Gordon Commission, Vail agenda, National Research Council—have stressed the importance of monitoring. Yet Wright (1992a:185), when completing his manuscript in 1991, concluded that on average 14 major parks had only developed about one-fifth of the needed monitoring effort and only two-fifths of the needed baseline inventories.

Monitoring is no less essential to measure the status of systems not under active management to determine if and when management is needed to maintain ecosystems within prescribed parameter values, or to restore them to those values. The Vail agenda recommends: "Use measurable parameters or indicators sensitive enough to provide an early warning of change. Work with other agencies involved in developing monitoring protocols. Give monitoring priority to resources that are at risk" (Briggle et al. 1992:125). As we proposed above, one function of the advisory panels would be to assist in selecting the appropriate parameters and indicators.

In conclusion, we recommend active, carefully studied management programs in the parks where they are needed to achieve park goals. This is not something new for the System; it is advocated now in *Management Policies,* as we quoted in Chapter 2. And in fact a considerable amount is already under way.

Animal population limitation is already being practiced. Bison, elk, and prairie dogs are being culled in Wind Cave National Park. In Big Bend in 1990, 3,639 brown-headed cowbirds were removed from the Panther Junction area to provide some relief for a struggling population of black-capped vireos (Fleming 1990). Exotics are being controlled or eliminated in numerous parks.

Great Smoky Mountains National Park may be approaching subtle ecosystem management to stem the loss of conifers, discussed in Chapter 4. Experimental addition of calcium and magnesium to the soil in red spruce stands by Oak Ridge National Laboratory ecologists (Samuel B. McLaughlin, personal communication, April 26, 1993) is already showing improved tree physiology and enhancement of tree condition. The next research phase will test the hypothesis that calcium and magnesium amendment will stem the wooly adelgid attacks on Fraser fir by improving that species' physiology and thereby strengthening its defensive action against the insect. If successful, population control of an exotic herbivore that is severely altering the composition of the ecosystem will be achieved by restoring tree physiology through soil amendment designed to mitigate environmental insults from the outside. That amendment could become routine park-management practice.

Other efforts are being made to restore or assist struggling species populations. Wolf restoration to Yellowstone appears imminent. Again in Big Bend Park, seeds of Indian paintbrush (*Castilleja elongata*) were removed and planted in the Desert Botanical Garden in Phoenix in order to increase the number of individuals of the species (Ecker and Hodgson 1990). And 10 plants of Chisos Mountains hedgehog cactus were transplanted to the Chihuahuan Desert Visitor Center in Alpine, Texas, and mechanically pollinated, again to build up the population for replanting in the park (Miller 1990). McCullough (1989) recommends maintenance of viable desert bighorn sheep populations in each of the mountain ranges of Death Valley National Monument through judicious waterhole development and transplantation of animals into ranges that lose their populations. Rocky Mountain National Park has had an active program to restore peregrine falcons. More and more it is becoming obvious that preserving remnant populations of T and E species requires specialized management attention (Belovsky et al. 1994).

Thus active management is being practiced in numerous parks to achieve goal 3, the restoration and maintenance of healthy ecosystems. It will also be needed in many cases for goals 4, 5, and 6. Preservation of T and E species may require substantial ecosystem alteration in order to provide the conditions needed by the species in question. Maintenance of biodiversity in some parks is likely to require genetic mixing, habitat manipulation, and species reestablishment. Maintaining historical scenes already involves cultivation and manipulation of ornamental plant species and agricultural crops.

In sum, active management has been recommended repeatedly by professional reviews and contemporary scientists, is prescribed in current NPS policy statements, and is being practiced in numerous parks. We recommend that the Service adopt it openly, confidently, and unapologetically as the System norm, but only where it is needed to achieve clearly articulated park goals. We do not recommend management as a goal or in the abstract. It is a means, not an end. And we add the proviso that it be done minimally, competently, well buttressed by the best available science, free of ideological biases that blind its practitioners to what is actually occurring, and supported by monitoring to check its progress.

The Service is ambivalent and hesitant over the prospect of management in many quarters of the agency. In part this is out of the fear, mentioned above, that we do not understand ecosystems sufficiently well to be able to anticipate the consequences of our actions. This is the psychology that dwells on the emptiness of the glass.

Ecology has made great progress in the past 50 years. But its effective application depends on thorough familiarity with its knowledge base, a familiarity that we have found wanting in a disturbing number of places in NPS in the course of this review. That lack of familiarity is a likely source of the fear that we do not know enough to manage ecosystems.

We reiterate the point we made above: No management is in fact a management strategy that has its own ecological implications. To be consistent, anyone fearing advertent management actions because of the consequences must also fear nonmanagement for the same reason. Moreover, on the question of ungulate populations, control is the *conservative* management strategy. Reduced ungulate populations will rapidly rebuild if the controls are removed—the Yellowstone northern elk herd rebounded after the controls of the 1960s. But a distorted vegetation will take decades or centuries to restore itself, longer if there has been significant soil loss or disturbance. If plant or animal species are lost from an area, they may never be recovered. A stream, geomorphically altered when riparian vegetation is removed, is not likely to rebuild its structure and biota in human lifetimes.

Finally, hesitancy over management may arise from the view that no management is the path of least resistance and is thought to carry the fewest personal risks. This is a default on the public trust to protect this invaluable national treasure that we call the National Park System.

Park Service Queries of the Committee

During the fall of 1989, slightly over a year after this review began, officials of the NPS Natural Resources Office in Washington met with representatives of The Wildlife Society twice (October 2 and November 6) to discuss aspects of this review. In both cases, NPS officials asked a number of questions, which they hoped this review would address. It is appropriate at this point in our review to respond to these, and provide the comments asked of us.

- *Should NPS manage parks to preserve endangered species? Is it within the intent of their legislation? Is it acceptable if, in so doing, the management works to the disfavor of some components of the biota? Where should they be restored?* There are four questions here, the first two being goal questions. We are not advocating goals in this review and hence we decline to answer the first. However, the fact that this question should be asked reflects the hesitancy that we encounter in the agency. The answer is contained in the Service's own policy documents. The mandates of the Endangered Species Act cover the parks, as *Management Policies* (Anon. 1988a:4:11) comments. Moreover, that document states, "the National Park Service will identify and promote the conservation of all federally listed, threatened, endangered, or candidate species within park boundaries and their critical habitats. . . . Active management programs will be conducted as necessary." In short, the goal is in place and the question is answered.

  Whether or not preserving T and E species is within the intent of NPS legislation can be answered better by NPS officials than by us. The national-level legislation appears to us to be sufficiently broad to accommodate it, and it is clearly within the intent of the Endangered Species Act. We have only seen the park-specific enabling legislation for a few of the early parks, and these too appear broad enough. But obviously we have not seen the background documentation on most of the 361 units in the System.

Given that the goal is already established for the System, we refer back to our recommendation that the agency engage in whatever management is needed in those parks assigned the T and E goal. Our general thesis in this review is that NPS should abandon narrow, doctrinaire commitments to ideologies like "natural"; assume a more flexible, ecologically enlightened posture; and embrace whatever active management is needed to reach its goals. Given a more flexible management philosophy, and in parks where protection of T and E species is stated in their goals, we see no problem with management designed to protect endangered species, even if it disfavors other ecosystem components.

Where NPS should focus on endangered species obviously depends first and foremost on which parks have them. A decision to manage for preservation of saltwater crocodiles could only be made for Everglades. Beyond this, such a decision would have to be in keeping with the enabling legislation forming the parks in question, and once again the adoption of T and E preservation in their goals.

- *Same questions for managing to maximize biodiversity.* Our responses here are the same as for the last questions. This is again a goal question that we decline to answer, but again the goal is already in place, as *Management Policies* sets forth. The agency should not be hesitant in moving forward to achieve it. We add two caveats. Climax ecosystems may be less diverse than seral ones. Maximizing diversity may entail active management, a fact the Leopold Committee firmly pointed out 30 years ago. But we have no problems with that management if goal attainment depends on it.

Moreover, in our view there are some of the same ambiguities in the concept of diversity that reside in the concepts we analyzed in the last chapter. There probably are several value components: aesthetics; the population viability value of genetic diversity; the potential future values, as yet unknown, of plant and animal species; and the environmental values of natural ecosystems. As a public-relations effort, NPS should publicize the fact that it is contributing to these values.

We recommend that NPS review Forest Service rationale and provision for biodiversity in their forest plans in response to the mandate of the National Forest Management Act. This would provide some sense of that agency's thinking and practices in managing for biodiversity in the national forests.

• *A number of eastern parks have burgeoning deer populations. What should NPS do about them?* This question is handled nicely by Porter (1991), and we have little to add. The answer hinges once again on park goals. If the actions of the deer populations are inimical to attainment of clearly defined goals, the deer herds should be reduced. Reduction by native predators would be preferable. But if that is not possible, we believe that NPS should openly and unapologetically proceed with artificial reduction. We discussed the more recent reticence of Porter et al. (1994) earlier.

• *Should NPS adopt an ecosystem or community perspective in park management, or should it focus on individual species?* Again a goal question. In parks where preserving endangered species is a goal, the focus will need to be on the species, and the ecosystem will need to be manipulated to favor them. This will involve a detailed understanding of the ecological needs of the species. Expert advice should be sought from specialists. In parks where the primary goal is to preserve reasonably intact ecosystems, the perspective is obviously different. Here the management objectives will need to be articulated by the advisory panels comprised of ecologists knowledgeable about the different ecosystem components in the region.

• *Can ungulates self-regulate in an area the size of the Yellowstone ecosystem? Are there differences between large parks and small ones like Wind Cave?* We basically answered this question in the last chapter. To begin with, we assume that the query is about self-limitation rather than self-regulation. And we assume further that the question is whether the animals' density-dependent interaction with their food supply, perhaps coupled with other constraints such as weather, will halt population growth at some density.

The answer to this part of the question is unequivocally yes. There are limits to the resources of any area beyond which further population growth is not possible. Natality and/or survival rates fall until the growth rate declines to zero. This appears to have occurred with Yellowstone elk and perhaps Olympic elk.

If the reference to self-regulation contains the further implied question as to whether population growth will be limited largely by resource competition at densities below which there are significant impacts on other components of the ecosystem, we believe not. Prehistorically, diverse predator communities, aboriginal hunting, and free dispersal all acted with inclement weather, interspecific competition, and density-dependent intraspecific competition for food to impose a heavy limiting weight on ungulate populations. When much of that weight is removed, populations simply rise to higher levels at which they significantly impact their systems. We believe this is occurring in a considerable number of parks.

The same principles hold in both small and large parks. It may simply take longer for populations to reach limiting densities in large ones than in small ones. Increasing park size by adding new land, as with the efforts to increase winter range in Yellowstone, does not change the basic pattern. It only postpones the time at which limitation and extreme ecosystem impacts occur.

The pattern is somewhat more complex in populations subsisting in highly variable environments, such as desert bighorn sheep in Death Valley (McCullough 1989). Here the populations fluctuate markedly with year-to-year variations in precipitation. There is much more stochastic noise in the system, and populations may spend a considerable amount of time simply recovering from unfavorable periods. But eventually such a population will increase to densities where resources limit. Modeling studies have repeatedly shown that a random-walk time series will eventually rise to very high numbers. The Merrill and Boyce (1991) findings that Yellowstone elk rates of increase are in part influenced by warm-season precipitation affecting summer range production suggests that the behavior of this herd may only vary quantitatively from Death Valley bighorns.

- *Park management has blundered in the past with such ill-advised intrusive management as predator control and artificial feeding of ungulates. Can NPS be at all confident that if it henceforth engages in more management, it will not make similar mistakes?* We appreciate the agency's caution in this regard, but those actions were begun three-fourths of a century ago, when there were no park scientists, ecology was in its early infancy, and wildlife management had not emerged as a discipline. The concern dwells in the past. The glass has been substantially filled.

  Although there are still extensive unknowns in our understanding of ecological systems, we now have a vast store of knowledge about them that could be used in park management if researchers and managers will exert the effort to become conversant with that store. A blind, unconfident refusal to apply that knowledge is as unenlightened as the early, ill-fated management actions.

  But our firm proviso is that any management decisions be illuminated by quality science. We are less concerned about the adequacy of science to provide that illumination than whether in some quarters of the organization it will be used effectively. And once again, it needs to be approached as adaptive management.

- *Are the policies on exotics appropriate?* As a general principle, we concur with those policies as they facilitate attainment of park goals. Although it will never be possible to re-create the ecosystems that prevailed before European contact, or those that would occur today had there been no European immigration, the goal and policy history of the System holds that there is educational, recreational, environmental, and scientific value in developing and maintaining facsimiles of those systems to the extent that our knowledge allows, and studying them. Hence, parks with such goals should appropriately operate under policies that call for systems free of exotics.

  But we have some concerns that overtones of the naturalness ideology have made the policies on exotics too rigid and ill-considered. As a result they potentially place NPS in awkward positions while at the same time obscuring important scientific questions that could be addressed in national parks.

To begin with, the NPS distinction between invasion by feral domestics and wild species from outside the Western Hemisphere—and the addition of species native to the hemisphere, especially those of the same continents in which the parks occur—is to us a useful one. There would seem to be no equivocation on the question of getting burros out of Grand Canyon and Death Valley; goats, pigs, and domestic rabbits out of Haleakala and Hawaii Volcanoes; and wild boars out of Great Smoky.

But some awkward consistency problems arise over the policy of eliminating native species that spread into the parks as a result of human action but not those that extend their ranges on their own accord. It is only a matter of time before the opponents of mountain goat extermination in Olympic ask why NPS is not doing the same with elk in Mount Rainier and bighorn sheep in Grand Canyon. Archaeological studies indicate that sheep have been absent from the canyon for the past 1,000 years. Recent arrivals have come from populations established by Arizona Department of Fish and Game transplants near the park.

Research on the invasion of new species into the parks could provide useful insights on two important ecological questions. One is the effects of immigration of previously absent native species into ecosystems. Recent paleoecological work by Davis (1986) and others in the eastern United States and the packrat midden work in the West (Betancourt et al. 1990) is showing that what we today call communities in specific locations are merely the pro tem assemblages of species whose distributions are in constant flux. On a time scale of centuries and millennia, both plant and animal community composition are in constant change.

The question of interest on a shorter time scale (cf. Pimm 1991) is: how do community and ecosystem processes for a given combination of species absorb, and adjust to, the entry of a new species? A corollary question is: what is the role of species diversity in community and ecosystem function? The arrival of goats in Yellowstone, regardless of their source, bighorns in Grand Canyon, and moose in Rocky Mountain could provide interesting research opportunities for addressing these questions in the few somewhat-intact North American ecosystems provided by the parks. We add the proviso that the new species should be maintained at natural densities through management if the pre-Columbian population checks are not present to do so.

A further question relates to the general tendency for exotics to succeed in disturbance situations, and to be denied entrance into relatively intact systems. Is the expansion of timothy in the Yellowstone grasslands a function of the heavy elk grazing pressures, and might this be stemmed with relief from those pressures? Perhaps of greater interest, does the exclusion pattern hold in undisturbed island ecosystems, as in Hawaii Volcanoes and Haleakala? And having evolved with low herbivore diversity, might they be more sensitive to herbivory than continental biotas and hence more prone to invasion of exotics if subjected to increased herbivory?

These seem to us worthwhile considerations in setting and carrying out policies on exotics.

- *What should be the policies on reintroduction and restoration?* Newmark's (1986, 1987) findings give every reason to believe that the parks will continue to lose species as they have in the past. Soulé et al. (1979) had earlier documented a similar pattern in Southeast Asian islands of the Sunda Shelf and predicted it for East African game parks. Again, where it contributes to goal attainment, we consider it perfectly appropriate for NPS to restore these through reintroduction from other areas or from captive-bred populations. Soulé et al. comment:

> East Africa contains the greatest concentration of large mammals in the world. The loss of this living heritage would be a tragedy and a human disgrace. Our results suggest that intensive scientific management practices will have to be instituted if such losses are to be prevented. . . . A laissez-faire approach to management is obviously indefensible. . . . The transport of large numbers of animals between reserves in order to replenish diminishing stocks will have to be routine if species diversity and genetic variation are to be conserved.

The same views surely apply to the American parks.

Certain conditions need to hold, which NPS has undoubtedly considered already: transplants should come from genetic stocks as near as possible to those that had been in the parks, come from bioclimatic areas similar to those of the parks, and be released in sufficient numbers to confer a high probability of population viability. Moreover, they should only be released in parks in which the environmental conditions are favorable for the animals. If a species' disappearance was occasioned by deterioration in its environment, it should not be reintroduced unless and until the environmental inadequacies have been mitigated.

- *What should be done with park animal populations that are reservoir hosts and/or vectors of diseases communicable to humans and/or domestic animals (Lyme disease, brucellosis, rabies, etc.)?* Obviously the influences bearing on management decisions addressing these problems go beyond the welfare of park resources alone, and we cannot offer any suggestions for general policies. This, like all management decisions, turns on values, and it seems evident that the external risks must be weighed against the effects on the resources. The decisions are broader societal ones than those purely for park resources and beyond the scope of this review. We note with interest the decision of the Canadian government to eliminate the brucellosis-prone bison herd in Wood Buffalo National Park and reintroduce disease-free animals (Fuller 1991).

- *Is research a valid use of parks? Should park research play a role in studying global climate change?* At this point, we will only answer yes to both questions and address the subject of research at greater length below.

- *What should be the National Park Service's role in the twenty-first century?* The National Park System is a public resource, established for the welfare of the American people. The National Park Service's role has been since 1916, and will continue to be, to serve as steward of the System, managing it so that its values are available to the nation's citizenry today and in the future. The pressures on the System will grow as the U.S. population, and its demands on the land for more goods and amenities, increase. As a result, the agency's task will become more difficult while the value of its services to the American people will become greater.

It seems clear to us that the value of the System rests first and foremost on the state of its resources, both natural and cultural. The System's recreation, tourism, scientific, and educational values will decline if the quality of the resources declines. Parks that lose their resources will no longer have any unique value and will no longer be distinguishable from the rest of the altered landscapes across the country. For these reasons the first responsibility of the Park Service is, in our opinion, to protect the resources and, to the extent possible in the face of the pressures applied to the System, work for the sustainability of the resources into the future.

As pressures grow on the System, resource protection will require increasingly knowledgeable, competent, and resolute management. Achieving that level of management, we believe, will require at least four fundamental changes in the agency, largely covered in the last chapter but perhaps meriting some amplification here.

The first change is greater emphasis on resource management within the System. We are not alone in calling for this change. The Vail agenda recommended, "Revise the National Park Service management planning process to emphasize resource protection" (p. 127). The imbalance of the dual mission must be changed.

That greater emphasis, and other changes recommended below, will cost more money, something hard to come by in an era with large federal budget deficits and a massive national debt. Some avenues that should be explored are to shift allocation within the budget process. If necessary, expenditure on tourist services should be reduced by curtailing tourist flow. This is a recommendation not only for reallocating funds but protecting resources. Parks should not be allowed to go the way of Yosemite, which has become a virtual Coney Island to the detriment of its resources. Elsewhere, tourist resource damage is occurring in Rocky Mountain, Olympic, and Glacier. The Park Service would do well to study the smooth procedures by which Kruger National Park manages its visitor flow.

We believe the Service should resist addition of new, low-quality, pork-barreled parks, which spread its funds more thinly. Foresta (1984, 1987), Sudia (1985), Freemuth (1989), NPS historian Sellars (1989, 1992), and policy chief Aten (personal communication) have all commented on the reduction in System standards by these kinds of additions. Foresta (1987) has contrasted the American political procedure with the more measured, professional, executive process in Canada for adding units. Moreover, we believe NPS should critically scrutinize each unit in the System and determine whether funds could be saved by phasing out some low-standard and perhaps lightly used units.

The second change discussed above, also advocated by numerous other reviews and underscored by many of the NPS personnel with whom we have consulted, is increased professionalism in the agency's personnel. Agency personnel themselves include this among their recommendations in the Vail agenda, as discussed in Chapter 4.

As we have mentioned, we have heard this concern for increased professionalism repeatedly during discussions with agency personnel. Regional chief scientist Dan Huff's comment to this effect includes the development of a professional ethic: advocating decisions on what is in the best interests of the resources rather than on "political pressures or pleasing your boss . . . situational ethics." And the admonitions come from outside the agency, Alston Chase (1986, 1989) being a strong advocate for increased ecological training of Park Service personnel.

Yet despite the Vail agenda's recognition of the complexity of the management issues facing NPS, and the inability of "resource-management generalists" to cope with these, the report goes on to advocate, "Continue the current series of the 18-month resource-management training course and evaluate its effectiveness." As persons both inside NPS and extramural university researchers working in the parks have pointed out to us, this course takes personnel with no prior natural-resources training, often maintenance and clerical personnel, and puts them through an 18-month series of short courses in which they are given a smattering of information from a variety of subjects.

We applaud the Service's attempts to enhance the professionalism of its personnel. But at the risk of a committee made up largely of academicians appearing to be self-serving, we must say that these efforts are far short of what is needed to address the demanding tasks well portrayed by the Vail agenda. At the least, a full four-year baccalaureate degree is needed to provide the minimum understanding of statistics, natural sciences, humanities, mathematics, social sciences, and resource management, which would confer some reasonable measure of professional credentials and competence. In fact there is debate currently under way in professional circles on whether or not the bachelor's degree should be considered a professional degree in this day and time, and for many resource-management agencies the master's degree is the entry-level degree. The Park Service's intent to upgrade the professional level is laudable, but the standards fall short of the need. The organization is demanding too little of itself and not taking seriously enough its responsibility to protect the resources.

The third needed change, discussed at length in the last chapter, is to improve the quality, status, and influence of science. We will add some comments below on administrative aspects.

The fourth needed change, which we touched on in Chapter 4, goes beyond the Park Service itself to shifting the balance of political forces in which it operates. Freemuth (1989) explores this issue in connection with NPS in lucid detail.

As with so many public-land issues, most of the political problems surrounding the Service stem from a tension between local and national values and politics. Public-land policy decisions are always compromises between these, but in our opinion the balance in the National Park System is tilted far too strongly toward the local, as we have seen. Resource-degrading decisions are made at the behest of the concessionaires, gateway communities, local interest groups, and local Congressional delegations. Provincial political forces limit the freedom of the superintendents to make decisions that are in the best interests of the resources, while at the same time empowering them to avoid or ignore national-level efforts to set firm policies and promote coherence in the organization.

We are not alone in this view. There is a welter of calls to depoliticize the organization, and an equal number of proposals for changing its organizational structure. One of the most common, recommended by former NPS director Hartzog (1988), was introduced as a bill into Congress in 1988 by Representative Bruce Vento (D., Minn.). It passed the House but never was voted on in the Senate. The proposal would take NPS out of the Department of Interior and establish it as an independent agency like the Smithsonian or NASA. The director would be appointed by the president for a five-year term (Hartzog would like to see it longer), subject to confirmation by the Senate. This plan would insulate NPS from the secretary of Interior, raise the stature of the director, and give him/her at least five years' security to make politically unpopular decisions. The proposal is endorsed by the National Parks and Conservation Association and by Frome (1992), but recommended against by Soden and Freemuth (1991).

Baden (1988) advocates placing the parks in the hands of such conservation organizations as The Wilderness Society, Sierra Club, National Wildlife Federation, or The Nature Conservancy. One of our committee members proposes placing NPS administration under a national commission. Hess (1993) recommends that Congress remove Rocky Mountain National Park from the System and designate it as an independent and irrevocable conservation trust. Its board of directors would be composed of five park employees and two faculty members each from the University of Colorado and Colorado State University.

Evaluation of these alternatives is beyond the scope of this report and will have to be left for other studies. But the fact that they are being proposed by so many individuals knowledgeable about, and concerned over the welfare of, the national parks is strong testimony to the existence of fundamental problems in the System.

Culling and Animal-Welfare Issues

Needless to say, the issue of management intervention to control large-mammal populations (or for that matter any animal population—we commented above on brown-headed cowbird control in

Big Bend National Park and prairie dog control in Wind Cave) has been debated for decades. There are two major aspects to this debate: the purely scientific and methodological, and the ethical questions, which we will now address in that order.

The ecological rationale for culling in the early part of this century was to insert human population limitation on large herbivore populations as a substitute for preindustrial constraints removed by technological societies. Biologists observed ecological effects from high densities of herbivores in protected natural areas, which they believed were not characteristic of preindustrial conditions, and concluded that population reductions were necessary to prevent untoward effects on the ecosystems.

Some sources (cf. Houston 1982, Despain et al. 1986, Caughley and Sinclair 1994) have attributed this rationale to a strong influence of range-management thinking that contained stereotypes on how a landscape, maximally productive of animal commodities, should appear. In our judgment this has been something of a strawman argument. The first text in range management, Sampson's, was published in 1923. But this was substantially pasture and animal-husbandry oriented. The first text with a strong ecological orientation was Stoddart and Smith's, appearing in the first edition in 1943.

The first concerns for the Yellowstone elk situation appeared in U.S. Bureau of Biological Survey reports between 1910 and 1920. Skinner wrote of "the elk situation" in 1928 in the *Journal of Mammalogy*. Wright and his two coworkers, who had received their university education at the University of California at Berkeley and had had no range-management training, endorsed ungulate control in *Fauna 1*, published in 1933.

The entire wildlife field, including in the eastern United States, where range management was a virtually unknown discipline, was in the first half of this century becoming increasingly aware of the reality and effects of rising ungulate populations. A significant milestone in that awareness was undoubtedly the Aldo Leopold et al. (1947) paper on overpopulated deer ranges, written when Leopold was department head at the University of Wisconsin. That paper appeared 14 years after his pioneering text, *Game Management* (1933), in which his term "Game Range" (Chapter 5) implied the geographic distribution of a species and what we today call habitat.

The advent of natural-regulation management in the late 1960s challenged the above rationale. Its position was based on (1) inference from the evidence that the condition of ecosystems in parks today does not differ significantly from what it was in preindustrial times, (2) the assumption that ungulate populations limit their densities below where they exert "unnatural" impacts on their ecosystems, and (3) the assertion that predators did not play a significant role in limiting ungulate densities.

As discussed in Chapter 2, NPS generally adopted natural regulation for the entire System, although not totally (e.g., Wind Cave). East African parks also adopted the philosophy, but even there some biologists left the door open for culling, depending on park goals (Laws 1981, Parker 1983). And more recently, Botkin (1990) considers the rise and crash of the Tsavo National Park elephant population, along with its deforestation, as "breakdown in the management of living resources." In the southern African countries, park management has unswervingly retained culling among its practices (cf. Younghusband and Myers 1986).

In our view, (1) the evidence now indicates that numerous large ungulate populations in American parks have significantly altered their ecosystems from the conditions that prevailed in earlier times; (2) there is no substantial evidence that these populations will limit their own densities below where they materially impact their systems, although there are some ungulate populations that do exist for yet undetermined reasons at low densities; and (3) intact predator communities do now, where present, and in all probability did in pre-Columbian times, significantly limit many ungulate populations. Their densities probably were further limited by aboriginal hunting and ungulate dispersal.

This now presents an ecological rationale for culling, which is in fact a return to the original paradigm and supported by stronger scientific underpinnings. But the *decision* to cull remains, like all management decisions, a goal matter. If park goals are to let animal populations build up to high densities so that they are easily seen by tourists, or if parks are to be maintained for totally natural experiences, absent any human intervention, in both cases without concern for the long-term impacts on park ecosystems, then culling is not appropriate. But if park goals are to preserve reasonably intact ecosystems in some semblance of pre-Columbian conditions and prehistoric checks are gone, then we see no alternative to the selective use of culling in situations where ungulate numbers rise to levels that are inimical to these goals.

There is a diverse methodology for culling. Trapping and immobilization techniques abound for catching and transporting animals. The major problem is finding areas to release them. In the West, there is little potential for release of wild ungulates on other public lands where agency managers are working to limit livestock numbers in the interests of range improvement. There may be some potential for release before hunting seasons, or on Indian reservations for subsistence, sport, or fee hunting if their administrators were favorably disposed to this approach. We have spoken to several Native Americans who, as individuals, have expressed interest in this idea.

Fertility control is another emerging technique that shows promise in an array of species ranging from feral horses (Wagner et al. 1991) and African lions (Seal et al. 1976) to white-tailed deer (Matsche 1977) and grey squirrels (Johnson and Tait 1983).

And finally there is lethal control. Although it would be the least expensive, we do not favor public hunting in national parks and monuments because it might set a precedent that could not be controlled and because of the risk it might pose for species not intended for control. But it could be useful and economical in other units of the System like recreation areas, national seashores, and definitely in national preserves, a category that was established to permit public hunting. Where control is needed, our preference for the national parks and monuments is for it to be carried out by NPS employees. There are alternative methods for doing this. Winter shooting by park rangers during the 1960s to reduce the Yellowstone elk herd is well known. In Kruger National Park, employees immobilize animals with drug-containing darts fired from helicopters, and formerly dispatched the animals humanely on the ground. More recently, the animals are removed alive and given or sold to game ranches.

Whatever the ecological rationale and methodology available, the freedom of park managers to engage in culling can be constrained by public responses motivated by ethical considerations and emotional reactions. The interactions between the wildlife profession and animal-welfare organizations have been rather defensive, confrontational, and uncommunicative. It is not clear whether the two sides will ever arrive at an accommodation on the issues, but it would seem that a first step is to promote understanding of each other's positions by openly elaborating underlying assumptions and reasoning. The wildlife rationale for culling is basically the ecological argument made above. The animal-welfare views are posed from an ethical basis. Abstracting from Wagner's (1988, 1995) analyses, we now explore the premises, both stated and implicit, and implications of the ethical positions held.

Ethical codes are prescriptions of human behavior, the thou-shalts and thou-shalt-nots of human action. Those who espouse animal-welfare positions advocate certain codes of behavior toward nonhuman animals and enjoin others to behave according to those codes. Most people in American society advocate some measure of restraint in interactions with animals, and hence most individuals follow some form of animal-welfare ethics. But, needless to say, the positions vary profoundly between individuals.

When anyone asserts that others should behave in certain ways, it is reasonable to ask who or what authority so enjoins us? Why should we behave in such a manner? These are nothing less than the age-old questions debated by moral philosophers throughout the history of philosophy.

Historically there have been only two general answers to these questions. One is an appeal to religious authority accepted on faith, in which case the injunctions are absolutes. The problem with this in the case of animal-welfare ethics is that different religions hold contradictory views on many animal issues. One or more of the world's major religions (1) prohibits consumption of the meat of noncloven-hoofed mammals, but not other meats; (2) prohibits consumption of beef, but not other meats; (3) prohibits consumption of all meats; or (4) does not prohibit the consumption of any meat. The Koran, revealed word of God for devout Muslims, prescribes the *zebh* slaughter of food animals, which involves draining their blood before their death, something that must clearly be abhorrent to faithful Hindus. Some religions engage in animal sacrifice.

Each religion considers its codes to be "true," and the natural human inclinations are to accept as ideal or valid the moral codes of the religious–cultural backgrounds in which individuals have lived. But if we take a detached, global view, there is no way of choosing from among these authorities to ascertain what is ideal moral judgment short of our natural, ethnocentric tendencies.

The other view among moral philosophers is that ethical codes are secular constructs of the human mind. Rightness and wrongness are what people say they are. But the obvious problem here is that different people in a society hold different convictions on what is proper human behavior. This prompted Russow (1990) to comment in connection with animal-welfare issues that there is no "adequate and generally accepted moral theory that will generate unassailable, defensible solutions. For every ethical theory advanced in philosophical discussion, several oppose it, and consensus among moral philosophers is not to be found."

What develops out of this ethical relativism in a democratic system is that different subsets of society adopt different ethical codes to which their members subscribe and which they often attempt to persuade other subsets to adopt. If they succeed in convincing a majority of people of their views, theirs becomes the normative ethic for the society. It may subsequently become codified into law, at which point compliance is enforced by government, which is to say by society. But until this codification, no component of society has the right to force its views on others.

Precise details of moral positions, strength and passion of conviction, and personal ethics vary among individuals within an ethical subset. Consequently, patterns of persuasion range from gentle exchange of views and a live-and-let-live approach through others across a spectrum of behaviors to coercion and violence. The latter end of the spectrum encroaches on the rights of others and itself becomes unethical to the point of criminality in the context of society as a whole.

Much of this perspective applies to the animal-welfare sentiments of American society. It is clear that there is widespread emotional attachment to animals and concern for their welfare, as Kellert's (1980) surveys have shown. And Congress has passed animal-care legislation. But the details of these sentiments vary across a wide range, and include, at one end, the formal, animal-welfare organizations. Even the latter are not a monolith, ranging from moderate groups to extremist, violence-prone ones.

The animal-welfare groups mostly oppose culling in national parks. But although there is surely concern within the general public on the matter, it is not certain that there would be majority opposition if the case for it were clearly explained, or that the sentiments would be as hardened as those of the welfare organizations. Patently, the majority of American society does not espouse as strong views as the animal-welfare groups: there is no mass movement to stop eating meat, eggs, and dairy products, or discontinue wearing wool and leather, or stop using lab animals in biomedical research.

Moreover, there are two sides to the question of humaneness in connection with culling populations to restrict densities. It would be hard to fathom the logic of an argument claiming it to be more humane to let an animal population increase to the point of protracted starvation deaths than to end the lives of healthy animals quickly with well-placed rifle shots. In the winter of 1988–1989, some 4,000 elk in Yellowstone's northern range died of malnutrition and winter weather. In the spring the landscape was so littered with dead elk that park rangers dragged carcasses away from the roads to reduce the visual impact. That such winter elk mortality in Yellowstone is density dependent (Houston 1982) indicates that both the total amount of suffering and intensity experienced by each animal are functions of population size.

Another consequence of letting ungulate populations build to extreme densities is the effects they have on other animals in the system. Browsing out woody vegetation—and herbaceous for that matter—destroys habitat of many animals. Other mammals, birds, and individuals of other taxa are placed at risk by being forced to use suboptimal conditions or having to disperse to unfamiliar terrain.

In the final analysis, having parks with intact ecosystems is a value to the American people. The animal-welfare groups have no right to prevent management measures that perpetuate that value for the public as long as the majority of society accepts such management.

The Park Service should mount an aggressive public-information effort to explain the values and goals of the national parks, and the rationale for its management efforts, working particularly with the media. In the process, the public would learn a great deal about ecology and environmental problems. NPS has a valuable educational program now with its interpretive efforts in the parks. But it should be expanded to a broader public by going to the media. This would be preferable to, and should supplant, its present media efforts to promote increased tourism. At the same time it would be favorable public relations for the Service. Gerard et al. (1993) outline detailed strategies for interacting with animal-welfare organizations in the course of proceeding with animal-control programs.

There is increasing willingness within the animal-welfare community to acknowledge these complexities of conservation issues. John Grandy of the Humane Society of the United States commented at the March 1990 NPS symposium in Denver on large-mammal management in the parks: "We don't mind killing things if we have to. We don't mind manipulating things if we have to. But we believe in as little of it as possible."

The Defenders of Wildlife organized originally in 1959 to oppose predator control, mostly in the western United States by the federal government, and was known for some time as a primarily animal-welfare organization. But it has vastly broadened its mission in recent years, with its major focus now on preserving biodiversity. Its executive director, Rupert Cutler, stated at the same 1990

Denver symposium that NPS should explore a variety of measures to reduce excessive deer populations in parks: drive deer out of park boundaries to public hunters, change the status of units to allow public hunting, and other means. Parks should be managed on an ecosystem basis that includes the protection of rare plants from high deer densities, according to Cutler.

Roger Anunsen, attorney for Fund for Animals in Salem, Oregon, and husband of the Fund's northwest regional coordinator, Cathy Sue Anunsen, while not speaking for the Fund or Mrs. Anunsen, remarked to us (December 10, 1992), "We have to preserve the ecosystem." He would be willing to agree to culling if a clear case could be made for it. We do not know how widespread these views are among members of the Fund. But the fact that the organization spent a half million dollars to helicopter 565 burros out of Grand Canyon in 1980 (Erickson et al. 1981) clearly indicates an acknowledgment of ecosystem-management needs and a willingness to contribute its resources to those needs. Mr. Anunsen also told of his belief that organizations demanding the more expensive control measures should be prepared to share in the cost.

Finally, some of the most zealous individuals in the animal-welfare movement concede the merit of alternative viewpoints. Tom Regan (1983), intellectual leader of the animal-rights subset of the animal-welfare movement, states that the "rights view" does favor species and ecosystem preservation. And Ingrid Newkirk (1992), national director of the militant People for the Ethical Treatment of Animals, concedes on another matter the practical necessity of euthanizing animals for which a place cannot be found.

The basic reality is that animals unremittingly continue to reproduce each year. In preindustrial times, nonhuman population checks plus use by subsistence cultures caused as many deaths as the number of animals born, populations occurred at rough equilibria, and ecosystems functioned in diverse and sustainable form. Removal of the mortality causes without checks on reproduction now allows populations to increase to levels detrimental to themselves and their ecosystems.

Restoration and maintenance of healthy systems require human intervention to limit artificially where the prehistoric checks have been removed. There is no other way to achieve such systems if their maintenance is adopted as a park goal. Anyone preventing such limitation must bear the onus of being a party to the destruction of an invaluable American asset.

Research Role in the National Park System

We have contended that a strong research effort is essential to achieving national-park goals. We now suggest what we believe should be its functions, aspects of administrative organization, and directions.

The Functions of Science in the System

There is currently under way a considerable amount of debate on the role of science in environmental and natural-resources policy. Some of this addresses the matter in the Park Service (cf. Chase 1986, 1987, Rolston 1990, Hess 1993), particularly the question of how much leadership and influence science should have in the System.

In our view, the argument is misplaced. Science cannot lead or set directions for the Service's management of the parks. As discussed above, those directions must be set by societal values and the park goals designed to satisfy them. Science is only a service to attainment of its goals. It is neither a goal nor an end in itself. Any recommendation here to strengthen the role of science in the organization is not intended in any way to give science some sort of power to decide Park Service management directions, but rather to enhance the clarity with which the goals are articulated and the effectiveness with which they are attained. An increase in the use of science for the parks is not a threat to, but rather increased support for, management.

And we do recommend that increase for the reason that the Park Service is in the business of managing ecosystems, probably the most complex entities addressed by science. As we discussed in Chapter 5, reviews dating all the way back to the Leopold and Robbins studies, and more recently the Gordon Commission and NRC studies, have all pointed out that ecosystem management is too complex to be carried out effectively without strong scientific support. Indeed, the agency's own personnel in the Vail agenda opined, "Never in the history of the National Park Service has it been more important for science and scholarship to play an integral role in park management" (p. 128).

We see four general functions for science in the System:

1. Elucidation in goal setting. As we commented above, goal setting is not a scientific process, nor is it done by scientists per se.

But there is a need for one or more scientists to portray the technical consequences of proposed goal options during the deliberations so that those consequences are well understood when the goal decisions are made.

2. There is a need for scientific input into park policy setting, management planning, and execution. This should include participation in decisions on the ecosystem characteristics to be managed for, what management practices to employ, when they should be changed, what monitoring procedures to install, and articulating park research priorities, all in the context of the resource-management plans. And we agree with Boyce (1991) that each park should operate with one or more ecosystem models, and with Norman Christensen that management actions should be considered hypotheses. The latter could be framed in the context of the model(s), which would then pose hypotheses on what effects would be predicted on what parts of the system, what parts to monitor to test the hypotheses, and what research is needed to permit hypothetical predictions.

3. There needs to be an effective research program aimed at understanding park ecosystems, in order to support management planning and execution, and monitoring. This does not mean that the science should be short term, superficial, and highly applied. To the contrary, it should be long-term basic research designed to provide a deep understanding of park ecosystem structure and function, which will then thoroughly enlighten management.

4. The parks should be areas in which research is carried out that contributes to the broader, national ecological-research need (cf. Risser and Lubchenco 1992). As relatively intact ecosystems, parks provide research opportunities at one end of the land-modification spectrum, all of which needs to be investigated to develop a thorough understanding of ecosystem structure and function. As the earth's environments change in the future under such influences as global warming, ozone depletion, and declining biodiversity, the effects will need to be studied at all points along the spectrum, including the relatively undisturbed, national-park end. Again, this is goal dependent, and follows from goal 3, the preservation of intact and healthy ecosystems.

Organizational and Staffing Considerations

We believe that parks, at least the major ones, need small staffs of scientists to participate in functions (1) and (2) above. These should be knowledgeable people with Ph.D.-level backgrounds and probably attached to resource management in the parks.

Function (3) now becomes the service responsibility of the National Biological Survey; but it incurs the proximity dilemma discussed in Chapter 5:

1. Research and management must interact to promote a mutual understanding of the management needs.

2. Management must have a voice in articulating research priorities that help solve the management problems.

3. The relationship must be close enough that researchers have a clear sense of the management problems, and it must create a sufficient atmosphere of trust to induce management to be open to research results.

It may be that building a bridge between NPS and NBS should be a major responsibility of the NPS regional chief scientists. Their responsibility would be to maintain rapport between research and park management, and particularly the relevance of research to those problems. This would be primarily a coordinating function that would include (1) facilitating interaction with the advisory panels, (2) bringing together park and NBS personnel to develop research plans and priorities, and (3) reviewing management implications of research with the superintendents. Park superintendents should have a strong voice in deciding research priorities, but they should not have veto power over projects. Final decisions should be made by the NBS with due consideration for park needs. The chief scientists would serve as advocates for those needs in the decision process.

All of this would make the chief scientists' positions delicate ones since they will have no administrative line authority and will operate largely in a mode of coordination and persuasion. Hence their personal traits will be crucial to their success. And the support of the NPS and NBS directors, and that of the secretary of Interior's office, will be essential.

Since the management–research relationship will now become

an interagency one, new administrative responsibilities will shift to the secretary's office. These will include the charges that research be relevant to management needs, and that management changes implied by research results are made whether or not there is bureaucratic resistance to such changes on the part of park management.

How park research should be organized at the field level is subject to several considerations. In general, the researchers need closer contact with the mainstream of science, including full access to libraries, the literature flow, other scientists, computer facilities, and laboratories. This would tend to argue against basing them in the parks, where many are too isolated. One possibility, suggested to us by some biologists formerly in NPS, would be to develop regional research centers analogous to the Forest Service's experiment stations. These might be placed on university campuses to provide access to facilities and academics, or in towns central to a group of parks. There appears to be movement in this direction in NBS with formation of the Fort Collins, Colorado, center. However, still other biologists have commented to us that it is best for them to remain in the parks, where they retain familiarity with park ecologies and management problems.

Scientists conducting research for the parks should have the best available training and stiff standards of employment. This means doctoral-level people and preferably those who have some research maturity. The NBS will probably never have the resources to retain enough researchers to address every park's needs, so limited personnel should be assigned to the highest priority natural-resources problems in the System. But it should also contract with academic and private researchers to help solve its research problems, always with the proviso that they address subjects relevant to park-management needs.

All research should be initiated with proposals by both NBS and extramural investigators, submitted competitively, and subjected to firm, anonymous, national peer review. Reviewers should be rigidly screened for conflict of interest using procedures like those of the National Science Foundation. This would generally exclude as reviewers personnel from the parks or regions in which the proposed research would occur, academic researchers currently holding Park Service funding, and current or prior personal or academic relationships.

Research Directions

New emphasis should be placed on archaeological, paleoecological, and ethnohistoric research to reconstruct as much as possible the character of pre-Columbian ecosystems in the park regions. Whether this will be done under the aegis of the National Biological Survey remains to be seen. We accord it high priority.

Park ecological research should in many, perhaps most, cases adopt an ecosystem format. This could be designed in the context of the ecosystem models that Boyce (1991) recommends. Even those parks with the largest research programs that claim to do ecosystem research generally lack such models. In reality, their research is often not truly ecosystem research. They tend to field an array of research projects that concentrate on individual species, species groups (e.g., grassland vegetation), and two-component interactions (e.g., ungulate–vegetation relations), which collectively do not constitute ecosystem research. As has been pointed out repeatedly in the past by other authors, too many of the projects concentrate on the "charismatic megafauna."

While we recommended earlier that the parks be used for research contributing to the greater, national ecological-research need, we are somewhat uncertain as to who all of the players should be in this effort. Clearly, such research should be carried out by extramural investigators funded by sources other than the parks and NBS. And to the extent that such research facilitates park management by contributing necessary understanding of their ecosystems, then in our view NBS-funded basic research is appropriate in the parks. For example, it may be necessary to understand the effects of acid precipitation or global warming on national-park ecosystems in order to prescribe appropriate mitigation measures. At the same time, such research would contribute knowledge of these problems that would be applicable to a broader range of national concerns.

Our hesitancy is in cases of park research funded by that agency which contributes to its new, enormous mission of determining status, trend, and causation in the American biota, but may not be directly relevant to park management. We believe that there is a need for more management-oriented research in the park than has taken place in the past. We are concerned that the priority of the new NBS mission will compete with the priority for enhanced park-management research.

In total, the national parks are an immense, potential research resource. Their unique ecosystems provide research opportunities not available over most of the area of the nation. They have a huge management task in preserving those systems, and that task requires a strong scientific base to make it effective. NBS funds should be used to support research that provides that base, but in the process the research will contribute to the total accumulation of scientific understanding. At the same time, the parks are invaluable laboratories for broader research that may not have immediate relevance to park management and should be supported by such sources as the National Science Foundation. That research, too, will contribute to the total accumulation of scientific understanding and in many cases will ultimately assist park management.

This research potential is only one of the numerous values that the National Park System holds for the American people, values that combine to form a national treasure unparalleled anywhere else in the world.

Literature Cited

Ackerman, E.A., M. Bates, S.A. Cain, F.F. Darling, J.M. Fogg, Jr., T. Gill, J.M. Gillson, E.R. Hall, C.L. Hubbs, W.J. Robbins, Chairman. 1963. A report by the Advisory Committee to the National Park Service on Research. Washington, D.C.: Nat. Acad. Sci.—Nat. Res. Council.

Agee, J.K., and D.R. Johnson. 1988a. A direction for ecosystem management. Pp. 226–232 *in* Agee and Johnson (eds.) 1988b.

Agee, J.K., and D.R. Johnson (eds.). 1988b. *Ecosystem Management for Parks and Wilderness*. Seattle: Univ. Washington Press.

Aldous, S.E., and L.W. Krefting. 1946. The present status of Isle Royale moose. *Trans. No. Amer. Wildl. Conf.* 11:296–308.

Allen, D.L., and A.S. Leopold. 1977. Memorandum to the Director of the National Park Service Re: A review and recommendations relative to the NPS Natural Science Program.

Amato, D., and D. Whittemore. 1989. Status report on Yellowstone grizzly bear. Greater Yellowstone Coalition.

Anderson, J.E. 1991. A conceptual framework for evaluating and quantifying naturalness. *Cons. Biol.* 5:347–352.

Andrewartha, H.G., and L.C. Birch. 1954. *The Distribution and Abundance of Animals*. Chicago: Univ. Chicago Press.

Anon. n.d. Endangered species in the national parks. U.S. Dept. Int. Nat. Park Serv. color brochure.

———. 1962a. Statement regarding control of excess wildlife populations within national parks.

———. 1962b. Long-range management plan for northern Yellowstone wildlife and range. Yellowstone Nat. Park, Yellowstone Nat. Park., WY: mimeo.

———. 1967a. Natural control of elk. U.S. Dept. Int. Nat. Park Serv., Yellowstone Nat. Park: mimeo.

———. 1967b. Administrative policy for the management of ungulates. U.S. Dept. Int. Nat. Park Serv., Yellowstone Nat. Park: mimeo.

———. 1968. Compilation of the administrative policies for the national parks and national monuments of scientific significance (Natural Area Category)/(Revised August 1963). U.S. Dept. Int. Nat. Park Serv.

———. 1975. Park managers blamed for dying elk. *Bozeman* [Mont.] *Daily Chronicle* 64 (June 2, 1975).

———. [1977a]. *Elk Island National Park Master Plan: Public Participation Program Stage 2: Plan Proposals*. Calgary: Parks Canada West Region.

———. 1977b. Management objectives for northern Yellowstone elk.

U.S. Dept. Int. Nat. Park Serv., Yellowstone Nat. Park Info. Paper No. 10: mimeo.

———. 1978. Chapter IV Natural Resource Management. Pp. ii + IV–1 to IV–23 *in* Management Policies. U.S. Dept. Int. Nat. Park Serv., Washington, D.C. [Entire report not seen.]

———. 1988a. *Management Policies*. Washington, D.C.: U.S. Dept. Int. Nat. Park Serv.

———. 1988b. *Natural Resources Assessment and Action Program*. U.S. Nat. Park Serv., Washington, D.C.: Off. of Nat. Res.

———. 1991a. *Natural Resources Management Guideline: NPS-77*. Washington, D.C.: U.S. Dept. Int. Nat. Park Serv.

———. 1991b. Bear viewing platform built at Katmai/NPS subverts key park plan. *Sierra Club Alaska Rept.* 17:3.

———. 1992. Introduction. Pp. 1–29 *in* Anon. [ed.] 1992.

———. [ed.] 1992. *Interim Report: Yellowstone National Park Northern Range Research*. Yellowstone Nat. Park Res. Div.

———. [1993]. Multi-park proposal . . . Management of ungulate populations in two Rocky Mountain National Parks. U.S. Nat. Park Serv. Proj. No. RMRO-N-411.011.

Anunsen, C.S. 1993. Deception in the Olympics. *Animals' Agenda*, Jan.–Feb. 1993:25–27, 42.

Anunsen, C.S., and R. Anunsen. 1993. Response to Scheffer. *Cons. Biol.* 7:954–957.

Armentano, T.V., and O.L. Loucks. 1983. Air pollution threats to U.S. national parks of the Great Lakes region. *Environ. Cons.* 10:303–313.

Baden, J. 1988. Let nature groups bid for control. *Wall Street Journal*, November 23, 1988.

Barmore, W.J. 1968. Memorandum to supervisory research biologist. Yellowstone Nat. Park, WY, March 13, 1968.

Bartmann, R.M., G.C. White, and L.H. Carpenter. 1992. Compensatory mortality in a Colorado mule deer population. *Wildl. Monog.* 121:1–39.

Bear, G.D., G.C. White, L.H. Carpenter, R.B. Gill, and O.J. Essex. 1989. Evaluations of aerial mark-resighting estimates of elk populations. *J. Wildl. Mgt.* 53:908–915.

Beetle, A.A. 1974a. The zootic disclimax concept. *J. Range Mgt.* 27:30–32.

———. 1974b. Range survey in Teton County, Wyoming. Part IV—quaking aspen. Univ. Wyo. Agr. Exp. Sta. Bull.

———. 1979. Jackson Hole elk herd: A summary after 25 years of study. Pp. 259–262 *in* Boyce and Hayden-Wing 1979.

Begon, M., and M. Mortimer. 1981. *Population Ecology: A Unified Study of Animals and Plants*. Sunderland, MA: Sinauer.

————, J.L. Harper, and C.R. Townsend. 1986. *Ecology: Individuals, Populations, and Communities.* Sunderland, MA: Sinauer.

Behan, R.W. 1990. The RPA/NFMA: Solution to a nonexistent problem. *West. Wildlands Winter* 1990:32–36.

Bella, D.A. 1985. The university: Eisenhower's warning reconsidered. *J. Prof. Issues in Engineering* 111:12–21.

————. 1987. Organizations and systematic distortion of information. *J. Prof. Issues in Engineering* 113:360–370.

————. 1992. Ethics and the credibility of applied science. *U.S.D.A. Forest Serv. Pacific NW Res. Sta. Gen. Tech. Rept. PNW GTR* 299:19–32.

Belovsky, G.E., J.A. Bissonette, R.D. Dueser, T.C. Edwards, Jr., C.M. Luecke, M.E. Ritchie, J.B. Slade, and F.H. Wagner. 1994. Management of small populations: Concepts affecting the recovery of endangered species. *Wildl. Soc. Bull.* 22:307–316.

Belsky, A.J., W.P. Carson, C.L. Jensen, and G.A. Fox. 1993. Overcompensation by plants: Herbivore optimization or red herring? *Evol. Ecol.* 7:109–121.

Bergerud, A.T. 1992. Rareness as an antipredator strategy to reduce predation risk for moose and caribou. Pp. 1008–1021 *in* McCullough and Boyce 1992.

————, W. Wyett, and B. Snider. 1983. The role of wolf predation in limiting a moose population. *J. Wildl. Mgt.* 47:977–988.

Berryman, A.A. 1981. *Population Systems: A General Introduction.* New York: Plenum Press.

Betancourt, J.L., T.R. Van Devender, and P.S. Martin. 1990. *Packrat Middens: The Last 40,000 Years of Biotic Change.* Tucson: Univ. Arizona Press.

Birkedal, T. 1993. Ancient hunters in the Alaskan wilderness: Human predators and their role and effect on wildlife populations and the implications for resource management. *Proc. Conf. Research and Resource Mgt. in Parks and Publ. Lands* 7:228–233.

Bishop, S., W. Burch, R. Cahn, R. Cahill, T. Clark, R. Dean, J. Franklin, J.C. Gordon, G. Gumerman, B.J. Howe, B. Howell, R.W.E. Jones, D. Latimer, S.P. Leatherman, H. Mooney, V. Wyatt, and E. Zube. 1989. National parks: From vignettes to a global view. Nat. Parks and Cons. Assoc., Washington.

Bloom, H. 1989. Final audit report on natural resource research activities. National Park Serv. (No. 90–19). U.S. Dept. Int. Off. Inspect. Gen., Washington, D.C.

————. 1992. Audit report/Protection of natural resources, National Park Service U.S. Dept. Int. Off. Inspect. Gen. Rept. No. 92–I–1422, September 1992.

Bonnicksen, T.M. 1989a. Fire management in Yellowstone: Theology or science? Pres. Symp. on the Greater Yellowstone Ecosystem, April 14, 1989, Laramie, WY.

————. 1989b. Statement of Dr. Thomas M. Bonnicksen before the Committee on Interior and Insular Affairs Subcommittee on National Parks and Public Lands and the Committee on Agriculture Subcommittee on Forests, Family Farms and Energy, United States House of Representatives, concerning the joint oversight hearing on the 1988 western forest fire season, January 31, 1989.

————. 1989c. Standards of authenticity for restoring forest communities. Pres. 1st Ann. Conf. Soc. for Ecol. Restoration, Oakland, CA, January 16–20, 1989.

Bonnicksen, T.M., and E.C. Stone. 1981. The giant sequoia-mixed conifer forest community characterized through pattern analysis as a mosaic of aggregations. *Forest Ecol. and Mgt.* 3:307–328.

————. 1982a. Reconstruction of a presettlement giant sequoia-mixed conifer forest community using the aggregation approach. *Ecol.* 63:1134–1148.

————. 1982b. Managing vegetation within U.S. national parks: A policy analysis. *Environ. Mgt.* 6:101–102.

————. 1982c. Managing vegetation within U.S. national parks: A policy analysis. *Environ. Mgt.* 6:109–122.

————. 1985. Restoring naturalness to national parks. *Environ. Mgt.* 9:479–486.

Botkin, D.B. 1990. *Discordant Harmonies: A New Ecology for the Twenty-First Century.* New York: Oxford Univ. Press.

Boyce, M.S. 1989. *The Jackson Elk Herd: Intensive Wildlife Management in North America.* Cambridge: Cambridge Univ. Press.

————. 1991. Natural regulation or the control of nature? Pp. 183–208 *in* Keiter and Boyce 1992.

————. 1992a. Wolf recovery for Yellowstone National Park: A simulation model. Pp. 123–138 *in* McCullough and Barrett 1992.

————. 1992b. Intervention versus natural regulation philosophies for managing wildlife in national parks. *Oecol. Montana* 1:49–50.

————, and L.D. Hayden-Wing. 1979. *North American Elk: Ecology, Behavior and Management.* Laramie: Univ. of Wyoming.

Bradley, W.P. 1982. History, ecology, and management of an introduced wapiti population in Mount Rainier National Park, Washington. Univ. Washington Ph.D. Dissert.

Bratton, S.P. 1979. Impacts of white-tailed deer on the vegetation of Cade's Cove, Great Smoky Mountains National Parks. *Proc. Southeast Assoc. Fish and Wildl. Agencies* 33:305–312.

Braun, C.E., D.R. Stevens, K.M. Giesen, and C.P. Melcher. 1991. Elk, white-tailed ptarmigan and willow relationships: A management dilemma in Rocky Mountain National Park. *Trans. No. Amer. Wildl. and Nat. Res. Conf.* 56:74–85.

Briggle, W.J., H.L. Diamond, D.J. Evans, C.R. Jordan, J. Kalt, L.W. Lane, Jr., H.A. Robinson, R.C. Cunningham, J.C. Sawhill, P. Odeen, J. Leape, A.A. Rubin, N. Nelson, and A. O'Neill. [1992]. National parks for the 21st century/The Vail agenda/Report and recommendations to the Director of the National Park Service. U.S. Nat. Park Serv. Document No. D–726.

Brussard, P.F. 1991. The role of ecology in biological conservation. *Ecol. Appl.* 1:6–12.

Carbyn, L. 1983. Wolf predation on elk in Riding Mountain National Park, Manitoba. *J. Wildl. Mgt.* 47:963–976.

Carter, D. 1994. The problem and the solution. *High Country News* 26, Aug. 8, 1994:13.

Cassirer, E.F., D.J. Freddy, and E.D. Ables. 1992. Elk responses to disturbances by cross-country skiers in Yellowstone National Park. *Wildl. Soc. Bull.* 20:375–381.

Caughley, G. 1976a. Wildlife management and the dynamics of ungulate populations. Pp. 183–246 *in* T.H. Coaker (ed.). *Applied Biology Vol. I.* New York: Academic Press.

———. 1976b. The elephant problem—an alternative hypothesis. *E. Afr. Wildl. J.* 14:265–283.

———. 1981a. Overpopulation. Pp. 7–19 *in* P.A. Jewel and S. Holt (eds.). *Problems in Management of Locally Abundant Wild Mammals.* New York: Academic Press.

———. 1981b. Comments on natural regulation of ungulates (what constitutes a real wilderness?). *Wildl. Soc. Bull.* 9:232–234.

———, and J.H. Lawton. 1981. Plant–herbivore systems. Pp. 132–166 *in* R.M. May (ed.). *Theoretical Ecology: Principles and Applications,* 2nd ed. Sunderland, MA: Sinauer.

———, and A.R.E. Sinclair. 1994. *Wildlife Ecology and Management.* Boston: Blackwell.

Chadde, S., and C. Kay. 1988. Willows and moose: A study of grazing pressure, Slough Creek Exclosure, Montana, 1961–1986. Mont. Forest and Cons. Exp. Sta. Res. Note No. 24.

———, and C.E. Kay. 1991. Tall-willow communities on Yellowstone's northern range: A test of the "natural-regulation" paradigm. Pp. 231–262 *in* Keiter and Boyce 1991.

Chase, A. 1986. *Playing God in Yellowstone: The Destruction of America's First National Park.* Boston: Atlantic Monthly Press.

———. 1987. How to save our national parks. *The Atlantic Monthly,* July 1987:34–44.

———. 1988. Are national parks endangered species? *Courier,* Sept. 1988: 36–38.

————. 1989. National Park Serv. needs leadership but isn't getting it. Universal Press Syndicate in *Salt Lake Tribune,* May 28, 1989.

————. 1992. Mintzmyer getting what she dished out as activist. *Jackson Hole Guide,* August 12, 1992, D 16.

Cheatum, E.L. 1962. [Letter to John Craighead], from Office of the President, no address, March 2, 1962.

Christensen, N.L., J.K. Agee, P.F. Brussard, J. Hughes, D.H. Knight, G.W. Minshall, J.M. Peek, S.J. Pyne, F.J. Swanson, J.W. Thomas, S. Wells, S.E. Williams, and H.A. Wright. 1989. Interpreting the Yellowstone fires of 1988: Ecosystem responses and management implications. *BioScience* 39:678-685.

Clark, T.W., E.D. Amato, D.G. Whittemore, and A.H. Hoovey. 1991. Policy and programs for ecosystem management in the Greater Yellowstone Ecosystem: An analysis. *Cons. Biol.* 5:412–422.

————, and S.C. Minta. 1994. *Greater Yellowstone's Future: Prospects for Ecosystem Science, Management, and Policy.* Moose, WY: Homestead Publ.

Clements, F.E. 1928. *Plant Succession and Indicators: A Definitive Edition of Plant Succession and Plant Indicators.* New York: The H. W. Wilson Co.

Clifford, F. 1993. Scientists fight over who's faithful to Yellowstone. *Los Angeles Times,* November 22, 1993:1, 20, 21.

Clutton-Brock, T.H., F.E. Guiness, and S.D. Albon. 1982. *Red Deer: Behavior and Ecology of Two Sexes.* Chicago: Univ. Chicago Press.

Coggins, G.C. 1987. Protecting the wildlife resources of national parks from external threats. *Land and Water Law Rev.* 22:1–27.

Cole, G.F. 1971. An ecological rationale for the natural or artificial regulation of native ungulates in parks. *Trans. No. Amer. Wildl. and Nat. Res. Conf.* 36:417–425.

————. 1974. Population regulation in relation to *K.* Pres. Ann. Meeting Montana Chapter of The Wildl. Soc., Feb. 22, 1974, Bozeman, MT.

————. 1983. A naturally regulated ungulate population. Proc. Symp. on Nat. Reg. of Wildl. Pop., Northwest Sec. of The Wildl. Soc., March 10, 1978, Vancouver, B.C.: 62–81.

Colombe, L. 1994. Isle Royale not seen as key to recovery. *Daily Mining Gazette,* Houghton, MI: March 26, 1994.

Connolly, G.E. 1978. Predators and predator control. Pp. 369–394 in J.L. Schmidt and D.L. Gilbert (eds.). *Big Game of North America: Ecology and Management.* Harrisburg, PA: Stackpole Books.

Consolo, S.L. 1989. Letter to James Teer, President, The Wildlife Society, dated January 18, 1989, Yellowstone National Park, WY.

Coughenour, M.B. 1991. Biomass and nitrogen responses to grazing of upland steppe on Yellowstone's northern winter range. *J. Appl. Ecol.* 28:71–82.

————. 1992. The Parker transects revisited: Long-term herbaceous vegetation trends on the northern winter range, 1954–1989. Abstract *in* Anon. [ed.] 1992.

———, and F.J. Singer. 1991. The concept of overgrazing and its application to Yellowstone's northern range. Pp. 209–230 *in* Keiter and Boyce 1992.

Cowan, I. McT., D.G. Chapman, R.S. Hoffman, D.R. McCullough, G.A. Swanson, and R.B. Weeden. 1974. [Report of the National Academy of Sciences] Committee on the Yellowstone Grizzlies. Mimeo.

Craighead, F.C., Jr. 1979. *Track of the Grizzly*. San Francisco: Sierra Club Books.

Craighead, J.J. 1991. Yellowstone in transition. Pp. 27–39 *in* Keiter and Boyce 1991.

———, and F.C. Craighead. 1967. Management of bears in Yellowstone National Park. Special. Unpub. Rept. to Nat. Park Serv.

Crawley, M.J. 1983. *Herbivory: The Dynamics of Animal–Plant Interactions*. Berkeley: Univ. California Press.

Davis, G.E., W.L. Halvorson, and W.H. Ehorn. 1987. Science and management in U.S. national parks. *Bull. Ecol. Soc. Amer.* 69:111–114.

Davis, M.B. 1986. Climatic instability, time lags, and community disequilibrium. Pp. 269–284 *in* J. Diamond and T.J. Case (eds.). *Community Ecology*. New York: Harper & Row.

Davis, S.M., and J.C. Ogden (eds.). 1994. *Everglades: The Ecosystem and Its Restoration*. Delray Beach, FL: St. Lucie Press.

Decker, D.J., R.E. Shanks, L.A. Nielsen, and G.R. Parsons. 1991. Ethical and scientific judgements in management: Beware of blurred distinctions. *Wildl. Soc. Bull.* 19:523–527.

Despain, D.G., D. Houston, M. Meagher, and P. Schullery. 1986. *Wildlife in Transition: Man and Nature on Yellowstone's Northern Range*. Boulder, CO: Roberts Rhinehart.

DeWitt, C. 1989. Let it be. *Rest. & Mgt. Notes* 7:80–81.

Diamond, J.M. 1986a. The environmentalist myth. *Nature* 324:19–21.

———. 1986b. Overview: Laboratory experiments, field experiments, and natural experiments. Pp. 3–22 *in* J. Diamond and T.J. Case (eds.). *Community Ecology*. New York: Harper & Row.

———. 1988. The golden age that never was. *Discover*, December 1988:71–79.

———. 1992. Must we shoot deer to save nature? *Nat. Hist.* 8:2–8.

Dobyns, H.F. 1983. *Their Numbers Become Thinned: Native American Population Dynamics in Eastern North America*. Knoxville: Univ. Tennessee Press.

Dottavio, F.D., P.F. Brussard, and J.D. McCrone. 1990. Protecting biological diversity in the national parks: Workshop recommendations. Washington: U.S. Dept. Int. Nat. Park Serv.

Downs, A. 1966. *Inside Bureaucracy*. Boston: Little, Brown & Co.

Dyksterhuis, E.J. 1946. The vegetation of the Fort Worth prairie. *Ecol. Monog.* 16:1–29.

———. 1949. Condition and management of range land based on quantitative ecology. *J. Range Mgt.* 2:104–115.

Eberhardt, L.L., R.R. Knight, and B.M. Blanchard. 1986. Monitoring grizzly bear population trends. *J. Wildl. Mgt.* 50:613–618.

Ecker, L., and W. Hodgson. 1990. Propagation of *Castilleja elongata* and *Festuca ligulata* from Chisos Mountains, Big Bend National Park, Texas. *Big Bend Nat. Park 1990 Research Newsletter:* 11–12.

Ehrlich, P.R., and J. Roughgarden. 1987. *The Science of Ecology.* New York: Macmillan.

Elfring, C. 1985. Wildlife and the National Park Service. Pp. 281–304 *in* A.S. Eno and R.L. Di Silvestro (eds.). *Audubon Wildlife Report 1985.* New York: The Nat. Audubon Soc.

Ellis, J.E., and D.M. Swift. 1988. Stability of African pastoral ecosystems: Alternate paradigms and implications for development. *J. Range Mgt.* 41:450–459.

Engstrom, D.R., C. Whitlock, S.C. Fritz, and H.E. Wright. 1991. Recent environmental changes inferred from the sediments of small lakes in Yellowstone's northern range. *J. Paleolimnol.* 5:139–174.

———. 1994. Reinventing erosion in Yellowstone's northern range. *J. Paleolimnol.* 10:159–161.

Erickson, G.L. 1981. The northern Yellowstone elk herd—A conflict of policies. Pres. *Western Proc. Ann. Conf. Western Assoc. of Fish and Wildl. Agencies* 61:92–108.

Erickson, L., E.R. Hall, W.M. Schirra, and D.L. Allen. 1981. Report to Secretary of Interior James G. Watt: mimeo.

Errington, P.L. 1946. Predation and vertebrate populations. *Quart. Rev. Biol.* 21:144–177, 221–245.

Finley, R.B., Jr. 1983. Letter to the editor. *The Wildlifer* 199:34.

Fleming, C.M. 1990. Black-capped vireo headstart program. *Big Bend Nat. Park 1990 Research Newsletter:* 37.

Foresta, R.A. 1984. *America's National Parks and Their Keepers.* Washington, D.C.: Resources for the Future, Inc.

———. 1987. New national parks: Lessons from the United States and Canada. *Forum for Appl. Res. and Pub. Policy,* Summer 1987: 95–108.

Fowler, C.W. 1981. Density dependence as related to life history strategy. *Ecol.* 62:602–610.

———. 1987. A review of density dependence in populations of large mammals. *Current Mammal.* 1:401–441.

Fox, L., and J. Coffey (eds.). [1993]. Planning for the future: A strategic plan for improving the natural resource program of the National Park Service. Washington, D.C.: U.S. Dept. Int. Nat. Park Serv.

Frank, D.A. 1990. Interactive ecology of plants, large mammalian herbivores, and drought in Yellowstone National Park. Syracuse Univ. Ph.D. Dissert.

——, and S.J. McNaughton. 1992. The ecology of plants, large mammalian herbivores, and drought in Yellowstone National Park. *Ecol.* 73:2043–2058.

——, and S.J. McNaughton. 1993. Evidence for the promotion of aboveground grassland production by native large herbivores in Yellowstone National Park. *Oecologia* 96:157–161.

Franz, J.M. 1962. Definitions in biological control. *Proc. Intern. Cong. Entom.* 11:670–674.

Freemuth, J.C. 1989. The national parks: Political versus professional determinants of policy. *Publ. Adm. Rev.*, May/June 1989: 278–286.

——. 1991. *Islands Under Siege: National Parks and the Politics of External Threats.* Lawrence: Univ. Press of Kansas.

Friedel, M.N. 1991. Range condition assessment and the concept of thresholds: A viewpoint. *J. Range Mgt.* 44:422–426.

Frison, G.C. 1971. Prehistoric occupations of the Grand Teton National Park. *Naturalist* 21:34–37.

——. 1978. *Prehistoric Hunters of the High Plains.* New York: Academic Press.

Frome, M. 1992. *Regreening the National Parks.* Tucson: Univ. Arizona Press.

Fryxell, J.M., J. Greever, and A.R.E. Sinclair. 1988. Why are migratory ungulates so abundant? *Amer. Nat.* 131:781–798.

Fuller, W.A. 1991. Disease management in Wood Buffalo National Park, Canada: Public attitudes and management implications. *Trans. No. Amer. Wildl. and Nat. Res. Conf.* 56:50–55.

Gaillard, D., and L. Wilcox. 1993. Memo to: GYC Members Re: GYC's position on grizzly bears. Greater Yellowstone Coalition, Bozeman, MT.

Gardner, J.L. 1951. Vegetation of the creosote-bush area of the Rio Grande Valley in New Mexico. *Ecol. Monog.* 21:379–403.

Gassaway, W.C., R.D. Boertje, D.V. Grangaard, D.G. Kellyhouse, R.O. Stephenson, and D.G. Larsen. 1992. The role of predation in limiting moose at low densities in Alaska and Yukon and implications for conservation. *Wildl. Monog.* 120:1–59.

George, J.C. 1987. Everglades wildlife. U.S. Dept. Int., Nat. Park Serv. Dir. of Publ. Handbook 143.

Gerard, G.T., B.D. Anderson, and T.A. De Laney. 1993. Managing conflicts with animal activists: White-tailed deer and Illinois Nature Preserves. *Nat. Areas J.* 13:10–17.

Goldstein, B. 1992. The struggle over ecosystem management at Yellowstone. *BioScience* 42:183–187.

Gómez-Pompa, A., and A. Kaus. 1992. Taming the wilderness myth. *BioScience* 42:271–279.

Grimm, R.L. 1939. Northern Yellowstone winter range studies. *J. Wildl. Mgt.* 3:295–306.

Grumbine, R.E. 1994. What is ecosystem management? *Conserv. Biol.* 8:27–38.

Gysel, C.W. 1960. An ecological study of the winter range of elk and mule deer in the Rocky Mountain National Park. *J. Forestry* 58:696–703.

Hadley, E.A. 1990. Late Holocene mammalian fauna of Lamar Cave and its implications for ecosystem dynamics in Yellowstone National Park, Wyoming. No. Ariz. Univ. M.S. Thesis.

Hadwen, S. 1922. Reindeer in Alaska. U.S. Dept. Agr. Bull. No. 1089: 1–74.

Hamilton, W.L. 1994. Recent environmental changes inferred from the sediments of small lakes in Yellowstone's northern range (Engstrom et al., 1991). *J. Paleolimnol.* 10:153–157.

Harrison, P.D., and M.I. Dyer. 1984. Lead in mule deer forage in Rocky Mountain National Park, Colorado. *J. Wildl. Mgt.* 48:510–517.

Hart, J.H. 1986. Relationship among aspen, fungi, and ungulate browsing in Colorado and Wyoming. Unpub. report.

Hartzog, G.B., Jr. 1988. Raze eyesores and insulate director. *Wall Street Journal,* November 23, 1988.

Haskell, D.A. 1993. Is the U.S. National Park Serv. ready for science? *George Wright Forum* 10:99–104.

Hassell, M.P., and R.M. May. 1990. Population regulation and dynamics. Proceedings of a Royal Society discussion meeting held on May 23–24, 1990. London: The Royal Soc.

Heady, H.F. 1975. *Rangeland Management.* New York: McGraw-Hill.

Hess, K., Jr. 1993. *Rocky Times in Rocky Mountain National Park: An Unnatural History.* Boulder: Univ. Press of Colorado.

Hilborn, R., and D. Ludwig. 1993. The limits of applied ecological research. *Ecol. Appl.* 3:550–552.

Hobbs, N.T., D.L. Baker, J.E. Ellis, D.M. Swift, and R.A. Green. 1982. Energy- and nitrogen-based estimates of elk winter-range carrying capacity. *J. Wildl. Mgt.* 46:12–20.

Holling, C.S. 1993. Investing in research for sustainability. *Ecol. Appl.* 3:552–555.

Horn, H.S. 1968. Regulation of animal numbers: A model counter example. *Ecol.* 49:776–778.

Houston, D.B. 1971. The status of research on ungulates in northern Yellowstone National Park. Pres. Amer. Assoc. Adv. Sci. Symp. on Research in National Parks, December 28, 1971.

———. 1973. Wildfires in northern Yellowstone National Park. *Ecol.* 54:1111–1117.

———. 1974. The northern Yellowstone elk, Parts I and II: History and demography. Yellowstone National Park, WY (Progress Rept.).

————. 1975. A comment on the history of the northern Yellowstone elk. *BioScience* 25:578–579.

————. 1976. The northern Yellowstone elk, Parts III and IV: Vegetation and habitat relations. Yellowstone National Park, WY (Progress Rept.).

————. 1982. *The Northern Yellowstone Elk: Ecology and Management.* New York: Macmillan.

————, B.B. Moorhead, and R.W. Olsen. 1986. An aerial census of mountain goats in the Olympic Mountain Range. *Northwest Sci.* 60:131–136.

————, E.G. Schreiner, B.B. Moorhead, and K.A. Krueger. 1990. Elk in Olympic National Park: Will they persist over time? *Natural Areas J.* 10:6–11.

Jackson, S.G. 1992. Relationships between birds, willows, and native ungulates in and around northern Yellowstone National Park. Utah State Univ. M.S. Thesis.

————. 1993. The effect of browsing on bird communities. *Utah Birds* 9:53–62.

Jardine, J.T. 1917. Increased cattle production on southwestern ranges. U.S. Dept. Agr. Bull. No. 588:1–32.

————. 1919. Range management on the national forests. U.S. Dept. Agr. Bull. No. 790:1–96.

Johnson, D.R., and J.K. Agee. 1988. Introduction to ecosystem management. Pp. 3–14 *in* Agee and Johnson 1988b.

Johnson, E., and A.J. Tait. 1983. Prospects for the chemical control of reproduction in the grey squirrel. *Mammal Rev.* 13:167–172.

Joslin, J.D., J.M. Kelly, and H. Van Miegroet. 1992. Soil chemistry and nutrition of North American spruce-fir stands: Evidence for recent change. *J. Environ. Qual.* 21:12–30.

Judd, R. 1993a. Vaccine may spare goats/But birth-control dart concept falling on deaf ears. *Seattle Times,* Thursday, April 8, 1993.

————. 1993b. Trail mix/Vaccine option to be explored. *Seattle Times,* Thursday, April 15, 1993.

Karr, J.R. 1993. Measuring biological integrity: Lessons from streams. Pp. 83–104 *in* Woodley et al. 1993.

Kay, C.E. 1987. Too many elk in Yellowstone? [Review of] *Wildlife in Transition: Man and Nature on Yellowstone's Northern Range* (1986. Don Despain, Douglas Houston, Mary Meagher, and Paul Schullery. Boulder, CO: Roberts Rhinehart). *Western Wildlands* 13:39–41,44.

————. 1988. The Conservation of Ungulate Populations by Native Americans in the Intermountain West: An Evaluation of Available Evidence. Unpub. ms.

————. 1989. Trends in Yellowstone's grizzly population: An alternative hypothesis. Pres. Symp. on The Greater Yellowstone Ecosystem, April 1989, Laramie, WY.

———. 1990a. Yellowstone's northern elk herd: A critical evaluation of the "Natural Regulation" paradigm. Utah State Univ. Ph.D. Dissert.

———. 1990b. The role of Native American predation in structuring large mammal communities. Pres. 6th Intern. Conf. of the Intern. Council of Archaeozoology. Smithsonian Inst., Washington, D.C., May 21–25.

———. 1992a. Observations on the historical distribution and abundance of wolves in the Yellowstone ecosystem. Second No. Amer. Symp. on Wolves and Their Status, Biology and Management/ Abstracts: 30.

———. 1992b. [Review of] *The Jackson Elk Herd: Intensive Wildlife Management in North America* (1989. Mark S. Boyce. Cambridge: Cambridge Univ. Press). *J. Range Mgt.* 45:315–316.

———. 1994a. The impact of native ungulates and beaver on riparian communities in the Intermountain West. *Nat. Res. and Env. Issues* 1:23–44.

———. 1994b. Aboriginal overkill: The role of Native Americans in structuring western ecosystems. *Human Nature* 5:359–398.

———, and S. Chadde. 1992. Reproduction of willow seed production by ungulate browsing in Yellowstone National Park. Pp. 92–99 *in* Proc. Symp. sponsored by U.S.D.A. Forest Serv. Intermount. U.S. Forest Serv. Gen. Tech. Rept. INT-289.

———, and F.H. Wagner. 1992. Historical condition of woody vegetation on Yellowstone's northern range: A critical evaluation of the "natural regulation" paradigm. Abstract *in* Anon. [ed.] 1992.

Keddy, P.A., H.T. Lee, and I.C. Wisheu. 1993. Choosing indicators of ecosystem integrity: Wetlands as a model. Pp. 61–79 *in* Woodley et al. 1993.

Keigley, R.B. 1995. Cottonwood architecture as an index of browsing history in Yellowstone. Ms. submitted.

Keiter, R.B. 1989. Taking account of the ecosystem on the public domain: Law and ecology in the Greater Yellowstone Region. *Univ. Colorado Law Rev.* 60:923–1007.

———, and M.S. Boyce. 1991. Greater Yellowstone's future: Ecosystem management in a wilderness environment. Pp. 379–413 *in* Keiter and Boyce (eds.) 1991.

———, and M.S. Boyce (eds.). 1991. *The Greater Yellowstone Ecosystem: Redefining America's Wilderness Heritage.* New Haven: Yale Univ. Press.

Keith, L.B. 1974. Some features of population dynamics in mammals. *Trans. Int. Congr. Game Biol.* 11:17–58.

Kellert, S.R. 1980. American's attitudes and knowledge of animals. *Trans. No. Amer. Wildl. and Nat. Res. Conf.* 45:111–124.

King, A.W. 1993. Considerations of scale and hierarchy. Pp. 19–45 *in* Woodley et al. 1993.

Kittams, W.H. 1959. Future of Yellowstone wapiti. *Naturalist* 19:30–39.

Klomp, H. 1966. The dynamics of a field population of the pine looper, *Bupalus piniarius* L. (Lep., Geom.). *Adv. Ecol. Res.* 3:207–305.

Knight, R.R., and L.L. Eberhardt. 1985. Population dynamics of Yellowstone grizzly bears. *Ecol.* 66:323–334.

———, and L.L. Eberhardt. 1987. Prospects for Yellowstone grizzly bears. *Int. Conf. Bear Res. and Mgt.* 7:45–50.

[———, J. Beecham, F. Bunnell, C. Serveen, and J. Swenson.] 1983a. January 19, 1983, Memorandum to: Chairman, Interagency Grizzly Bear Steering Committee. From: Chairman, ad hoc Committee for Population Analysis. Subject: Committee findings.

[———, J. Beecham, F. Bunnell, C. Serveen, and J. Swenson.] 1983b. Errata sheet.

Krefting, L.W. 1951. What is the future of the Isle Royale moose herd? *Trans. No. Amer. Wildl. Conf.* 16:461–470.

Laws, R.M. 1981. Large mammal feeding strategies and related over-abundance problems. Pp. 217–232 *in* P.A. Jewell, S. Holt, and D. Hart (eds.). *Problems in Management of Locally Abundant Wild Mammals.* New York: Academic Press.

Laycock, W.A. 1991. Stable states and thresholds of range conditions on North American rangelands: A viewpoint. *J. Range Mgt.* 44:427–433.

Leopold, A. 1933. *Game Management.* New York: Charles Scribner's Sons.

———. 1941. Wilderness as a land laboratory. *The Living Wilderness,* 6:3.

———. 1949. *A Sand County Almanac and Sketches Here and There.* New York: Oxford Univ. Press.

———, L.K. Sowls, and D.L. Spencer. 1947. A survey of overpopulated deer ranges in the United States. *J. Wildl. Mgt.* 11:162–177.

Leopold, A.S., S.A. Cain, C.M. Cottam, I.N. Gabrielson, and T.L. Kimball. 1963. Wildlife management in the national parks. *Trans. No. Amer. Wildl. and Nat. Res. Conf.* 28:29–44.

Longino, H.E. 1990. *Science as Social Value: Values and Objectivity in Scientific Inquiry.* Princeton, NJ: Princeton Univ. Press.

Lubchenco, J., A.M. Olson, L.B. Brubaker, S.R. Carpenter, M.M. Holland, S.P. Hubbell, S.A. Levin, J.A. MacMahon, P.A. Matson, J.M. Melillo, H.A. Mooney, C.H. Peterson, H.R. Pulliam, L.A. Real, P.J. Regal, and P.G. Risser. 1991. The sustainable biosphere initiative: An ecological research agenda/A report from the Ecological Society of America. *Ecol.* 72:371–412.

Ludwig, D., R. Hilborn, and C. Walters. 1993. Uncertainty, resource exploitation, and conservation: Lessons from history. *Science* 260:17, 36.

Lyon, L.J., and A.G. Christensen. 1992. A partial glossary of elk management terms. U.S.D.A. Forest Serv., Intermount. Res. Sta. Gen. Tech. Rept. INT-288.

McCullough, D.R. 1979. *The George Reserve Deer Herd: Population Ecology of a K-Selected Species.* Ann Arbor: Univ. Michigan Press.

———. 1981. Population dynamics of the Yellowstone grizzly bear. Pp. 173–196 *in* C.W. Fowler and T.D. Smith (eds.). *Dynamics of Large Mammal Populations.* New York: John Wiley & Sons.

———. 1986. The Craigheads' data on Yellowstone grizzly bear populations: Relevance to current research and management. *Int. Conf. Bear Res. and Mgt.* 6:21–32.

———. 1989. Report on a Review of Management of Bighorn Sheep in Death Valley National Monument. Unpub. ms.

———. 1990. Detecting density dependence: Filtering the baby from the bathwater. *Trans. No. Amer. Wildl. and Nat. Res. Conf.* 55:534–543.

———. 1992. Concepts of large herbivore population dynamics. Pp. 967–984 *in* McCullough and Barrett 1992.

———, and R.H. Barrett (eds.). 1992. *Wildlife 2001: Populations.* London: Elsevier.

McCutchen, H.E. 1993. Ecology of high mountain black bear population in relation to land use at Rocky Mountain NP. *Park Sci.* 13:25–27.

McDonnell, M.J., and S.T.A. Pickett (eds.). 1993. *Humans As Components of Ecosystems: The Ecology of Subtle Human Effects and Populated Areas.* New York: Springer-Verlag.

Macfarlane, G. 1994. Nothing yet beats leaving things alone. *High Country News* 26, June 27, 1994:12.

McInnes, P.F., R.J. Naiman, J. Pastor, and Y. Cohen. 1992. Effects of moose browsing on vegetation and litter of the Boreal Forest, Isle Royale, Michigan, USA. *Ecol.* 73:2059–2075.

Mackintosh, B. 1991. The national parks: Shaping the system. Div. of Publ. and Employees Dev. Dir., Nat. Park Serv., U.S. Dept. Int., Washington, D.C.

Macnab, J. 1983. Wildlife management as scientific experimentation. *Wildl. Soc. Bull.* 11:397–401.

———. 1985. Carrying capacity and related shibboleths. *Wildl. Soc. Bull.* 13:403–410.

McNaughton, S.J. 1979. Grazing as an optimization process: Grass-ungulate relationships in the Serengeti. *Amer. Nat.* 113:691–703.

————. 1983. Compensatory plant growth as a response to herbivory. *Oikos* 40:329–336.

Mangis, D., J. Baron, and K. Stolte. 1988. Acid rain and air pollution in desert park areas. U.S. Dept. Int. Nat. Park Serv. Tech. Rept. NPS/NRAQO/NRTR–91/02.

Matsche, G.H. 1977. Fertility control in white-tailed deer by steroid implants. *J. Wildl. Mgt.* 41:731.

Mattson, D.J., R.R. Knight, and B.M. Blanchard. 1992. Cannibalism and predation on black bears by grizzly bears in the Yellowstone ecosystem, 1975–1990. *J. Mammal.* 73:422–425.

————, and J.J. Craighead. 1994. The Yellowstone grizzly bear recovery program: Uncertain information, uncertain policy. Pp. 101–129 *in* T.W. Clark, R.P Reading, and A.L. Clarke (eds.). *Endangered Species Recovery: Finding the Lessons, Improving the Process*. Washington, D.C.: Island Press.

May, R.M. 1973. *Stability and Complexity in Model Ecosystems*. Princeton, NJ: Princeton Univ. Press.

————. 1981. Models of single populations. Pp. 5–29 *in* R.M. May (ed.). *Theoretical Ecology: Principles and Applications*, 2nd ed. Sunderland, MA: Sinauer.

Meagher, M. 1971. Winter weather as a population regulating influence on free-ranging bison in Yellowstone National Park. Pres. Amer. Assoc. Adv. Sci. Symp. on Research in National Parks, December 28, 1971.

————. 1974. Yellowstone's bison a unique wild heritage. *Nat. Parks and Cons. Mag.* 48:9–14.

————. 1985. Yellowstone's free-ranging bison. *Naturalist* 36:20–27.

Merrill, E.H., and M.S. Boyce. 1991. Summer range and elk population dynamics in Yellowstone National Park. Pp. 263–273 *in* Keiter and Boyce 1991.

Messier, F. 1991. The significance of limiting and regulating factors on the demography of moose and white-tailed deer. *J. Anim. Ecol.* 60:377–393.

————, and M. Crete. 1985. Moose–wolf dynamics and the natural regulation of moose populations. *Oecologia* 65:691–698.

Miller, D. 1990. Rescue and propagation of the Chisos Mountains hedgehog cactus. *Big Bend Nat. Park 1990 Research Newsletter:* 16.

Mintzmyer, L. 1990. The bear facts: Grizzly's future tied to public support. *Grizzly Tracks/1990 Interagency Grizzly Bear Committee Report:* 1, 6.

Mlot, C. 1991. The trouble with deer. *BioScience* 41:754–755.

Nash, R. 1973. *Wilderness and the American Mind*. Revised edition. New Haven: Yale Univ. Press.

Neumann, T.W. 1984. The opossum problem: Implications for

human–wildlife competition over plant foods. *No. Amer. Archaeol.* 4:287–313.

———. 1985. Human–wildlife competition and the passenger pigeon: Population growth from system destabilization. *Human Ecol.* 13:389–410.

———. 1989. Human–wildlife competition and prehistoric subsistence: The case of the eastern United States. *J. Mid. Atlantic Archaeol.* 5:29–57.

———. 1994. The structure and dynamics of the prehistoric ecological systems in the eastern woodlands: Ecological reality versus cultural myths. Pres. Symp. on Late Woodland Archaeological Research in the Middle Atlantic: Models to Investigate, Mid. Atlantic Archaeol. Conf., Ocean City, MD.

Newkirk, I. 1992. Total victory, like checkmate, cannot be achieved in one move. *The Animals' Agenda* 12:43–45.

Newmark, W.D. 1986. Mammalian richness, colonization, and extinction in western North American national parks. Univ. Michigan Ph.D. Dissert.

———. 1987. A land-bridge island perspective on mammalian extinctions in western North American parks. *Nature* 325:430–432.

Nicholson, A.J. 1933. The balance of animal populations. *J. Anim. Ecol.* 2:132–178.

Noy-Meir, I. 1975. Stability in grazing systems: An application of predator–prey graphs. *J. Ecol.* 63:459–481.

Olmstead, C.E. 1979. The ecology of aspen with reference to utilization by large herbivores in Rocky Mountain National Park. Pp. 89–97 *in* Boyce and Hayden-Wing 1979.

Olson, T.L., B.K. Gilbert, and R.C. Squib. 1995. The effects of increasing human activity on brown bear use of an Alaskan river. Ms. in review.

Parker, I.S.C. 1983. The Tsavo story: An ecological case history. Pp. 37–49 *in* R.N. Owen-Smith (ed.). *Management of Large Mammals in African Conservation Areas.* Pretoria, RSA: Haum Educ. Publ.

Pastor, J., and R.J. Naiman. 1992. Selective foraging and ecosystem processes in boreal forests. *Amer. Nat.* 139:690–705.

———, B. Dewey, R.J. Naiman, P.F. McInnes, and Y. Cohen. 1993. Moose browsing and soil fertility in the boreal forests of Isle Royale National Park. *Ecol.* 74:467–480.

Patten, D.T. 1968. Dynamics of the shrub continuum along the Gallatin River in Yellowstone National Park. *Ecol.* 49:1107–1112.

———. 1993. Herbivore optimization and overcompensation: Does native herbivory on western rangelands support these theories? *Ecol. Appl.* 3:35–36.

Peek, J.M. 1980. Natural regulation of ungulates (what constitutes a real wilderness?). *Wildl. Soc. Bull.* 8:217–227.

Pengelly, W.L., J.J. Craighead, C.M. Senger, P.L. Wright, R.D. Taber, R. Hoffman, W.R. Woodgerd, and G.F. Weisel. n.d. [1961 or 1962]. Statement regarding the management of the northern Yellowstone elk herd. Missoula, MT.

Peterson, R.O. 1988. The pit or the pendulum: Issues in large carnivore management in natural ecosystems. Pp. 105–117 *in* Agee and Johnson 1988b.

———. 1994. Study of wolf decline: Isle Royale National Park. Unpub. Final Rept. to U.S. Nat. Park Serv.

———, R.E. Page, and K.M. Dodge. 1984. Wolves, moose, and the allometry of population cycles. *Science* 224:1350–1352.

Philpot, C., B. Leonard, C.E. Cargill, B.L. Cornell, B. Evison, T.F. Folbrath, D.E. Stepanek, C.W. Tandy, B.M. Kilgore, and H.F. Layman. 1988. Report on fire management policy. Washington, D.C.: U.S. Dept. Agr. and U.S. Dept. Int.

Pimm, S.L. 1991. *The Balance of Nature? Ecological Issues in the Conservation of Species and Communities.* Chicago: Univ. Chicago Press.

Porter, W.F. 1991. White-tailed deer in eastern ecosystems: Implications for management and research in national parks. U.S. Dept. Int. Nat. Park Serv. Nat. Res. Rept. NPS/NRSUNY/ NRR–91/05.

———. 1992. Burgeoning ungulate populations in national parks: Is intervention warranted? Pp. 304–312 *in* McCullough and Barrett 1992.

Porter, W.F., M.A. Coffey, and J. Hadidian. 1994. In search of a litmus test: Wildlife management in U.S. national parks. *Wildl. Soc. Bull.* 22:301–306.

Primm, S.A., and T.W. Clark. n.d. The Greater Yellowstone policy debate: What is the policy problem? Jackson, WY: Northern Rockies Conservation Cooperative.

Pring, G.W. 1987. Resource protection and the national parks: Meeting the challenge of the future. Pp. 9–19 in R. Herman and T. Bostedt-Craig (eds.). *Proceedings of the Conference on Science in the National Parks 1986, Volume 1, The Plenary Sessions.* Washington, D.C.: The George Wright Soc. and the Nat. Park Serv.

Pyne, S.J. 1989. The summer we let wildfire loose. *Nat. Hist.* 8:45–49.

Ramenofsky, A.F. 1987. *Vectors of Death: The Archaeology of European Contact.* Albuquerque: Univ. New Mexico Press.

Ratcliffe, H.M. 1941. Winter range conditions in Rocky Mountain National Park. *Trans. No. Amer. Wildl. Conf.* 6:132–139.

———, and L. Sumner. 1945. National park wildlife ranges. *Trans. No. Amer. Wildl. Conf.* 10:246–250.

Redford, K.H. 1990. The ecologically noble savage. *Orion Nature Quart.* 9:25–29.

Regan, T. 1983. *The Case for Animal Rights.* Berkeley: Univ. California Press.

Reinhardt, R. 1989. Careless love: The pitfalls of affection in the incomparable valley of Yosemite. *Wilderness* 52:17–26.

Risenhoover, K.L., and S.A. Maass. 1987. The influence of moose on the composition and structure of Isle Royale forests. *Canad. J. Forest Res.* 17:357–364.

Risser, P.G., and J. Lubchenco (eds.). 1992. Report of a workshop for a National Park Service ecological research program. Albuquerque: [U.S. Dept. Int. Nat. Park Serv.]

———, A.M. Bartuska, J.W. Bright, R.J. Contor, J.F. Franklin, T.A. Heberlein, J.C. Hendee, I.L. McHarg, D.T. Patten, R.O. Peterson, R.H. Wauer, and P.S. White. 1992. *Science and the National Parks.* Washington, D.C.: National Acad. Press.

Rockwood, T.H. 1988. Organizational responses to a conflicting mandate: Legitimacy and structural adaptations in the National Park Service. Washington State Univ. M.A. Thesis.

Rolston, H., III. 1990. Biology and philosophy in Yellowstone. *Biol. and Philos.* 5:241–258.

Romesburg, H.C. 1981. Wildlife science: Gaining reliable knowledge. *J. Wildl. Mgt.* 45:293–313.

Rose, D.A. 1992. Implementing endangered species policy. Pp. 94–116 *in* W.R. Mangun (ed.). *American Fish and Wildlife Policy: The Human Dimension.* Carbondale: So. Illinois Univ. Press.

Rosenzweig, M.L., and R.H. MacArthur. 1963. Graphic representation and stability conditions of predator–prey interactions. *Amer. Nat.* 97:209–223.

Rosgen, D.L. 1993. Stream classification, streambank erosion, and fluvial interpretations for the Lamar River and main tributaries for USDI National Park Serv./Yellowstone National Park. Pagosa Springs, CO: Unpub. Rept.

Ross, R.L. 1990. Park Serv. remiss in management of Yellowstone. *Mont. Farmer Sportsman,* Sept. 1990.

Royama, T. 1977. Population persistence and density dependence. *Ecol. Monog.* 47:1–35.

Rush, W.M. [1932.] Northern Yellowstone elk study. Helena, MT: Montana Fish and Game Comm.

Russow, L.M. 1990. Section 1. Ethical theory and the moral status of animals. Hastings Center Rept., A Special Suppl., May/June 1990, Briarcliff Manor, NY.

Salwasser, H. 1988. Managing ecosystems for viable populations of vertebrates: A focus for biodiversity. Pp. 87–104 *in* Agee and Johnson 1988b.

Sampson, A.W. 1913. Range improvement by deferred and rotation grazing. *U.S. Dept. Agr. Bull.* No. 34:1–16.

———. 1919. Plant succession in relation to range management. U.S. Dept. Agr. Bull. No. 791:1–76.

———. 1923. *Range and Pasture Management.* New York: John Wiley & Sons.

Sax, J.L. 1979. Fashioning a recreation policy for our national parklands: The philosophy of choice and the choice of philosophy. *Creighton Law Rev.*12:973–985.

———. 1980. *Mountains Without Handrails: Reflections on the National* Parks. Ann Arbor: Univ. Michigan Press.

———, and R.B. Keiter. 1987. Glacier National Park and its neighbors: A study of federal interagency relations. *Ecol. Law Quart.* 14:207–263.

Schiff, A.L. 1962. *Fire and Water: Scientific Heresy in the Forest.* Cambridge: Harvard Univ. Press.

Schlesinger, W.H., J.F. Reynolds, G.L. Cunningham, L.F. Huenneke, W.M. Jarrell, R.A. Virginia, and W.G. Whitford. 1990. Biological feedbacks in global desertification. *Science* 247:1043–1048.

Schneebeck, R. 1986. State participation in federal policy making for the Yellowstone Ecosystem: A meaningful solution or business as usual? *Land and Water Law Rev.* 21:397–416.

Schullery, P. 1980. *The Bears of Yellowstone.* Yellowstone Nat. Park, WY: Yellowstone Library and Museum Assoc.

[———]. 1992. A new level of sophistication: Biennial scientific conference series begins well. *Yellowstone Sci.* 1:18.

Seal, U.S., R. Barton, L. Mather, K. Olberding, B.D. Plotka, and C.W. Gray. 1976. Hormonal contraception in captive lions (*Panthera leo*). *J. Zoo Anim. Medicine* 7:12–20.

Seip, D.R. 1992. Wolf predation, wolf control and the management of ungulate populations. Pp. 331–340 *in* McCullough and Barrett 1992.

Sellars, R.W. 1989. Science or scenery? A conflict of values in the national parks. *Wilderness* 52:29–38.

———. 1992. The roots of national park management: Evolving perceptions of the Park Serv.'s mandate. *J. Forestry* 90:16–19.

———. 1993a. Manipulating nature's paradise: National park management under Stephen T. Mather, 1916–1929. *Montana* 43:3–13.

———. 1993b. The rise and decline of ecological attitudes in national park management, 1929–1940: Part I. *George Wright Forum* 10(1):55–78.

———. 1993c. The rise and decline of ecological attitudes in national park management, 1929–1940: Part III (Conclusion): Growth and diversification of the National Park Service *George Wright Forum* 10(3):38–54.

Simms, S.R. 1992. Wilderness as a human landscape. Pp. 183–202 *in* S.I. Zeveloff, M.L. Vause, and W.H. McVaugh (eds.). *Wilderness Tapestry: An Eclectic Approach to Preservation.* Reno: Univ. Nevada Press.

Sinclair, A.R.E. 1977. *The African Buffalo: A Study of Resource Limitation of Populations.* Chicago: Univ. Chicago Press.

———, and M. Norton-Griffiths (eds.). 1979. *Serengeti: Dynamics of an Ecosystem.* Chicago: Univ. Chicago Press.

———. 1991. Science and the practice of wildlife management. *J. Wildl. Mgt.* 55:767–773.

Singer, F.J. 1989. Yellowstone's northern range revisited. *Park Science* 9:18–19.

———. 1990. Grazing responses of grasslands to ungulates on Yellowstone's northern elk winter range. Pp. 38–42 *in* F.J. Singer (ed.). *Grazing Influences on Yellowstone's Northern Range II: Range Summaries August 15, 1990.* Yellowstone National Park: U.S. Dept. Int. Nat. Park Serv.

———. 1992. Effects of long-term protection from elk grazing on bunchgrass and big sagebrush communities on Yellowstone's northern range. Abstract *in* Anon. [ed.] 1992.

Skinner, M.P. 1928. The elk situation. *J. Mammal.* 9:309–317.

Smith, N.S. 1988. Predictable results and peer review. *Wildl. Soc. Bull.* 16:225–226.

Snyder, J.D., and R.A. Janke. 1976. Impact of moose browsing on boreal-type forests of Isle Royale National Park. *Amer. Midl. Nat.* 95:79–92.

Soden, D.L., and J. Freemuth. 1991. The National Park Serv.: DOI or independent status. *Environ. Mgt.* 15:15–25.

Solomon, M.E. 1949. The natural control of animal populations. *J. Anim. Ecol.* 18:1–35.

———. 1964. Analysis of processes involved in the natural control of insects. *Adv. Ecol. Res.* 2:1–58.

Soulé, M.E., B.A. Wilcox, and C. Holtby. 1979. Benign neglect: A model of faunal collapse in the game reserves of East Africa. *Biol. Conserv.* 15:259–272.

Spalinger, D.E., T.A. Hanley, and C.T. Robbins. 1988. Analysis of the functional response in foraging in the Sitka black-tailed deer. *Ecol.* 69:1166–1175.

———, and N.T. Hobbs. 1992. Mechanisms of foraging in mammalian herbivores: New models of functional response. *Amer. Nat.* 140:325–348.

Stoddart, L.A., and A.D. Smith. 1943. *Range Management.* New York: McGraw-Hill.

———, A.D. Smith, and T.W. Box. 1975. *Range Management.* 3rd ed. New York: McGraw-Hill.

Sudia, T.W. 1985. National parks and domestic affairs. Unpub. ms.

————. 1989. Science and politics in the National Park Service. Pres. Conf. on Business and the Environment: Applying Science to Environmental Policy in Canada and the United States, June 3–6, 1989, Big Sky, MT.

Teer, J.G. 1988. [Letter to Frederic H. Wagner], Sinton, TX, June 6, 1988.

Tyers, D.B. 1981. The condition of the northern winter range in Yellowstone National Park—A discussion of the controversy. Montana State Univ. M.S. Thesis.

Underwood, H.B., and W.F. Porter. 1991. Values and science: White-tailed deer management in eastern national parks. *Trans. No. Amer. Wildl. and Nat. Res. Conf.* 56:67–73.

Underwood, R.J. 1989. Setting objectives for management of national parks and nature conservation reserves. Pp. 27–38 *in* N. Burrows, L. McCaw, and G. Friend (eds.). *Fire Management on Nature Conservation Lands*. West. Austr. Dept. Cons. and Land Mgt., Busselton, W. Australia.

U.S. Senate. 1967. Hearings before a Subcommittee of the Committee on Appropriations, United States Senate, Nineteenth Congress First Session, on Elk Population, Yellowstone National Park. Washington, D.C.: U.S. Gov't. Printing Off.

Van Miegroet, H., D.W. Johnson, and D.E. Todd. 1993. Foliar response of red spruce saplings to fertilization with Ca and Mg in the Great Smoky Mountains National Park. *Canad. J. For. Res.* 23:89–95.

Varley, G.C., G.R. Gradwell, and M.P. Hassell. 1973. *Insect Population Ecology: An Analytical Approach*. Oxford: Blackwell.

Varley, J.D. 1988. Managing Yellowstone National Park into the twenty-first century: The park as an aquarium. Pp. 216–225 *in* Agee and Johnson 1988b.

Vore, J.M. 1990. Movements and distribution of some northern Yellowstone elk. Montana State Univ. M.S. Thesis.

Wagner, F.H. 1969. Ecosystem concepts in fish and game management. Pp. 259–307 in G.M. Van Dyne (ed.). *The Ecosystem Concept in Natural Resource Management*. New York: Academic Press.

————. 1981a. Population dynamics. Pp. 125–168 *in* D.W. Goodall, R.A. Perry, and K.M.W. Howes (eds.). *Arid-Land Ecosystems: Structure, Functioning and Management*. Cambridge: Cambridge Univ. Press.

————. 1981b. Role of lagomorphs in ecosystems. Pp. 668–694 *in* K. Myers and C.D. MacInnes (eds.). *Proceedings of the World Lagomorph Conference Held in Guelph, Ontario, August 1979*. Univ. of Guelph.

————. 1987. North American terrestrial grazing. *Revista Chilena Historia Natural* 60:245–263.

————. 1988. *Predator Control and the Sheep Industry: The Role of Science in Policy Formation.* Claremont, CA: Regina Books.

————. 1989a. American wildlife management at the crossroads. *Wildl. Soc. Bull.* 17:354–360.

————. 1989b. Theory of science's role in natural resources and environmental policy—National parks a case study. Pres. Conf. on Business and the Environment: Applying Science to Environmental Policy in Canada and the United States, June 3–6, 1989, Big Sky, MT.

————. 1994. Changing institutional arrangements for setting natural-resources policy. Pp. 281–288 *in* M. Vavra, W. Laycock, and R. Pieper. *Ecological Implications of Livestock Herbivory in the West.* Denver: Soc. for Range Mgt.

————. 1995. Counterpoint: The should or should not of captive breeding, whose ethic? *In* M. Hutchins, T. Maple, B. Norton, and E. Stevens (eds.). *Ethics in the Ark: Zoos, Animal Welfare, and Wildlife Conservation.* Washington, D.C.: Smithsonian Inst. Press. In press.

————, and C.E. Kay. 1993. "Natural" or "healthy" ecosystems? Are U.S. national parks providing them? Pp. 251–264 *in* M.J. McDonnell and S.T.A. Pickett (eds.). *Humans As Components of Ecosystems: The Ecology of Subtle Human Effects and Populated Areas.* New York: Springer-Verlag.

————, C.D. Besadny, and C. Kabat. 1965. Population ecology and management of Wisconsin pheasants. *Wisc. Cons. Dept. Tech. Bull.* No. 34.

————, D.R. McCullough, J.W. Menke, E.S. Murray, B.W. Pickett, U.S. Seal, and M. Sharpe. 1991. *Wild Horse Populations: Field Studies in Genetics and Fertility.* Washington, D.C.: Nat. Acad. Press.

Walker, B. 1989. Diversity and stability in ecosystem conservation. Pp. 121–130 in D. Western and M.C. Pearl. *Conservation for the Twenty-first Century.* Oxford: Oxford Univ. Press.

Wallace, L.L. 1990. Forage species response to grazing. Pp. 62–63 in F.J. Singer (ed.). *Grazing Influences on Yellowstone's Northern Range II: Research Summaries August 15, 1990.* Yellowstone National Park: U.S. Dept. Int. Nat. Park Serv.

————, and S.A. Macko. 1993. Nutrient acquisition by clipped plants as a measure of competitive success: The effects of compensation. *Func. Ecol.* 7:326–331.

Walters, C. 1986. *Adaptive Management of Renewable Resources.* New York: Macmillan.

Warren, R.J. 1991. Ecological justification for controlling deer populations in eastern national parks. *Trans. No. Amer. Wildl. and Nat. Res. Conf.* 56:56–66.

Welch, C. 1993. Park to scientists: Shut up! *High Country News* 26, December 27, 1993:11.

Westoby, M. 1979/80. Elements of a theory of vegetation dynamics in arid rangeland. *Israel J. Bot.* 28:169–194.

———, B. Walker, and I. Noy-Meir. 1989. Opportunistic management for rangelands not at equilibrium. *J. Range Mgt.* 42:266–274.

Whitlock, C., S.C. Fritz, and D.R. Engstrom. 1991. A prehistoric perspective on the northern range. Pp. 289–305 *in* R.B. Keiter and M.S. Boyce (eds.). *The Greater Yellowstone Ecosystem: Redefining America's Wilderness Heritage.* New Haven: Yale Univ. Press.

Wilkinson, T. 1990. Goats test notions of "native" and "exotic" species. *High Country News* 23, October 22, 1990:5.

Willers, B. 1992. Toward a science of letting things be. *Conserv. Biol.* 6:605, 607.

Wood, C.A. 1994. Ecosystem management: Achieving the new land ethic. *Renewable Res. J.* 12:6–12.

Woodley, S., J. Kay, and G. Francis (eds.). 1993. *Ecological Integrity and the Management of Ecosystems.* Delray Beach, FL: St. Lucie Press.

Woodward, A., D.B. Houston, E.G. Schreiner, and B.B. Moorhead. 1992. Ungulate/forest relationships in Olympic National Park: Retrospective exclosure studies. *Northwest Sci.* 66:123.

Wooten, E.O. 1916. Carrying capacity of grazing ranges in southern Arizona. U.S. Dept. Agr. Bull. No. 367:1–40.

Wright, G.A. 1983. A report on Jerry Lake (48TE576): A posthorse Shoshone site in Grand Teton National Park. *Wyoming Archaeol.* 26:2–19.

———. 1984. *People of the High Country: Jackson Hole Before the Settlers.* New York: Peter Lang.

Wright, G.M., J.S. Dixon, and B.H. Thompson. 1933. *Fauna of the National Parks of the United States: A Preliminary Survey of Faunal Relations in National Parks.* Washington, D.C.: U.S. Gov't. Printing Off.

Wright, R.G. 1988. Wildlife issues in national parks. Pp. 169–196 *in* W.J. Chandler and L. Labate (eds.). *Audubon Wildlife Report,* 1988/1989. San Diego: Academic Press.

———. 1992a. *Wildlife Research and Management in the National Parks.* Urbana: Univ. Illinois Press.

[———]. 1992b. Case study: Removal of exotic mountain goats from Olympic National Park. Problem statement presented at Strategic Ecological Research Workshop, National Park Service, Feb. 24–26, 1992, Univ. New Mexico, Albuquerque.

Wuerthner, G. 1994a. Yellowstone: The great elk controversy. *Wild Forest Rev.* 1:57–59.

————. 1994b. Elk and playing God. *High Country News* 26, June 27, 1994:13.

Yaffee, S.L. 1982. *Prohibitive Policy: Implementing the Federal Endangered Species Act.* Cambridge: MIT Press.

York, J.C., and W.A. Dick-Peddie. 1968. Vegetation changes in southern New Mexico during the past hundred years. Pp. 157–166 *in* W.G. McGinnies and B.J. Goldman (eds.). *Arid Lands in Perspective.* Washington, D.C. Amer. Assoc. Adv. Sci.; Tucson: Arizona Press.

Younghusband, P., and N. Myers. 1986. Playing God with nature. *Internat. Wildl.* 16:4–13.

Zeide, B. 1994. Ecological research and environmental problems: Reflections on the National Biological Survey. *Bull. Ecol. Soc. Amer.* 75:53–54.

About the Authors

Ronald Foresta is professor in the Department of Geography, University of Tennessee, Knoxville. His studies of national park policies in both the Canadian and American park systems culminated in his 1984 book, *America's National Parks and Their Keepers.* More recently his research has focused on conservation policy in Brazilian Amazonia, which resulted in the book *Amazon Conservation in the Age of Development.*

R. Bruce Gill is wildlife research leader in the Division of Wildlife, State of Colorado Department of Natural Resources, where he is in charge of mammal research, and has developed census in methods for mule deer and worked on fertility-control methodology. His recent work has been focused on human dimensions in solving policy problems and with ethical issues in wildlife management.

Dale R. McCullough is professor in the Department of Environmental Science, Policy, and Management, University of California, Berkeley. A protégé of A. Starker Leopold's, he served for more than thirteen years on the faculty of the University of Michigan. His research has concentrated on the biology of large mammals including Michigan white-tailed deer, Australian kangaroos, and muntjacs in Taiwan, and resulted in his 1979 book, *The George Reserve Deer Herd: Population Ecology of a K-Selected Species,* and his 1992 edited book, with R. H. Barrett, *Wildlife 2001: Populations.*

Michael R. Pelton is professor in the Department of Forestry, Wildlife, and Fisheries, University of Tennessee, Knoxville. He has been conducting research on the mammalian fauna of Great Smoky Mountains National Park since 1968, with emphasis on black bears. His bear research has extended to Spain, Norway, and Russia, and he has served as president of the International Association of Bear Research and Management. He also served on the red wolf recovery team.

William F. Porter is professor of wildlife biology in the Department of Environmental and Forest Biology, State University of New York, Syracuse. His research has emphasized population biology and behavior of large vertebrates. He has been working for ten years with the National Park Service on wildlife issues, and has studied a number of Park Service units in the northeastern United States.

Hal Salwasser is Boone and Crockett Professor of Wildlife Conservation in the School of Forestry, University of Montana, Missoula. Also a former student of A. Starker Leopold's, he spent much of his professional career with the Forest Service before moving to Montana. He rose to the position of deputy director for wildlife and fisheries, was director of the Service's national parks programs, and was architect of its New Perspectives initiative. He served as president of The Wildlife Society during the latter stages of the present national parks study.

Joseph L. Sax is professor in the School of Law, University of California, Berkeley. Prior to this appointment he practiced law in Washington, D.C., and was professor of law at the University of Michigan. He has studied a number of public policy issues including western water law, federal public lands, and national parks, the latter resulting in his book, *Mountains Without Handrails: Reflections on the National Parks*. On leave from the university, he is currently serving as counselor to the secretary of Interior.

Frederic H. Wagner is professor of fisheries and wildlife, director of the Ecology Center, and associate dean of the College of Natural Resources, at Utah State University, Logan. Before moving to Utah he served as wildlife research biologist for the Wisconsin Conservation Department. Since relocating, his research has focused on ecology of animal populations and of arid lands. He has served as director of the U.S. International Biological Program's Desert Biome Project, and has been involved with a number of western public policy issues, particularly with the role of science in policy formation.

Index

Island Press Board of Directors

CHAIR
Susan E. Sechler
Executive Director, Pew Global Stewardship Initiative

VICE-CHAIR
Henry Reath
President, Collector's Reprints, Inc.

SECRETARY
Drummond Pike
President, The Tides Foundation

TREASURER
Robert E. Baensch
Senior Consultant, Baensch International Group Ltd.

Peter R. Borelli
President, Geographic Solutions

Catherine M. Conover

Lindy Hess
Director, Radcliffe Publishing Program

Gene E. Likens
Director, The Institute of Ecosystem Studies

Jean Richardson
Director, Environmental Programs in Communities (EPIC),
University of Vermont

Charles C. Savitt
President, Center for Resource Economics/Island Press

Peter R. Stein
Managing Partner, Lyme Timber Company

Richard Trudell
Executive Director, American Indian Resources Institute